CRITICAL METHODS IN POLITICAL AND CULTURAL ECONOMY

Critical Methods in Political and Cultural Economy offers students and scholars the first methods book for the critical school of International Political Economy (IPE). What does it mean to 'do' critical research? How do we write about the evidence we present? This volume explores our shared critical ethic to demonstrate how methods are transformative and reimagines research strategies as both an embodied practice and a social process.

By presenting methodologically informed ways of researching, enriched by real-life accounts from academics doing empirical research, the volume seeks to forge a new collaborative path that builds a critical ethic and modes of inquiry within International Political Economy. Substantive chapters advance the pluralism of the critical school of cultural political economy and seek to articulate its nascent research ethic. Short autobiographical vignettes articulate the professional journeys of contributors who 'do' critical political economy. There is practical advice on how to develop evidence from an iterative reflexive research strategy. Using this innovative format offers a guide to methods in critical political economy by engaging directly with the people doing research, not only as technical practice but also as lived experience.

The combination of research and practice presented throughout the book offers an extensive and authoritative framework for evaluating how methods are part of critical research and will be essential reading for all students and scholars of IPE.

Johnna Montgomerie is a Senior Lecturer and Deputy Director of the Political Economy Research Centre at Goldsmiths, University of London, UK.

RIPE SERIES IN GLOBAL POLITICAL ECONOMY

Series editors: James Brassett (*University of Warwick, UK*), Eleni Tsingou (*Copenhagen Business School, Denmark*), Susanne Soederberg (*Queen's University, Canada*) and Jacqueline Best (*University of Ottawa, Canada*)

The RIPE Series published by Routledge is an essential forum for cutting-edge scholarship in International Political Economy. The series brings together new and established scholars working in critical, cultural and constructivist political economy. Books in the RIPE Series typically combine an innovative contribution to theoretical debates with rigorous empirical analysis.

The RIPE Series seeks to cultivate:

- Field-defining theoretical advances in International Political Economy
- Novel treatments of key issue areas, both historical and contemporary, such as global finance, trade and production
- Analyses that explore the political economic dimensions of relatively neglected topics, such as the environment, gender relations and migration
- Accessible work that will inspire advanced undergraduates and graduate students in International Political Economy.

The *RIPE Series in Global Political Economy* aims to address the needs of students and teachers.

For a full list of titles in this series, please visit www.routledge.com/RIPE-Series-in-Global-Political-Economy/book-series/RIPE

Corporate Human Rights Violations
Global prospects for legal action
Stéfanie Khoury and David Whyte

The Global Political Economy of Raúl Prebisch
Edited by Matias E. Margulis

Critical Methods in Political and Cultural Economy
Edited by Johnna Montgomerie

CRITICAL METHODS IN POLITICAL AND CULTURAL ECONOMY

Edited by Johnna Montgomerie

Routledge
Taylor & Francis Group

LONDON AND NEW YORK

First published 2017
by Routledge
2 Park Square, Milton Park, Abingdon, Oxon OX14 4RN

and by Routledge
711 Third Avenue, New York, NY 10017

Routledge is an imprint of the Taylor & Francis Group, an informa business

© 2017 selection and editorial matter, Johnna Montgomerie; individual chapters, the contributors

The right of Johnna Montgomerie to be identified as the author of the editorial material and of the authors for their individual chapters, has been asserted in accordance with sections 77 and 78 of the Copyright, Designs and Patents Act 1988.

All rights reserved. No part of this book may be reprinted or reproduced or utilised in any form or by any electronic, mechanical, or other means, now known or hereafter invented, including photocopying and recording, or in any information storage or retrieval system, without permission in writing from the publishers.

Trademark notice: Product or corporate names may be trademarks or registered trademarks and are used only for identification and explanation without intent to infringe.

British Library Cataloguing-in-Publication Data
A catalogue record for this book is available from the British Library

Library of Congress Cataloguing-in-Publication Data
Names: Montgomerie, Johnna, editor.
Title: Critical methods in political and cultural economy/
edited by Johnna Montgomerie.
Description: Abingdon, Oxon ; New York, NY: Routledge, 2017. |
Series: RIPE series in global political economy |
Includes bibliographical references and index.
Identifiers: LCCN 2016042625 | ISBN 9781138934269 (hbk) |
ISBN 9781138934276 (pbk) | ISBN 9781315677811 (e-book)
Subjects: LCSH: International relations–Research–Methodology. |
Political science–Research–Methodology.
Classification: LCC JZ1234 . C73 2017 | DDC 337–dc23
LC record available at https://lccn.loc.gov/2016042625

ISBN: 978-1-1389-3426-9 (hbk)
ISBN: 978-1-1389-3427-6 (pbk)
ISBN: 978-1-3156-7781-1 (ebk)

Typeset in Bembo
by Out of House Publishing

For my dearest mother, *Alana Hardy Montgomerie*,
Thank you for everything you did to make me the person I am

CONTENTS

List of illustrations ix
Notes on the contributors x
Acknowledgements xiv

1 Reimagining critical methods 1
  Johnna Montgomerie

  Autobiographical vignettes:

  Self-reflections on 'the methods question' in feminist IR/IPE 16
  Anne Sisson Runyan

  Tea and text: cultivated intuition as methodological process 23
  Naeem Inayatullah and David Blaney

  Norms, political economy and serendipity: thinking
  pragmatically about IPE 28
  Christopher May

2 Forging new paths in the critical school 33
  Johnna Montgomerie

  Autobiographical vignettes:

  Redemptive political economy 51
  Robbie Shilliam

  Investigating those you love: labor and global governance 58
  Dimitris Stevis

Discourse, nature and critical political economy: American environmentalists debate immigration 64
John Hultgren

3 Developing a language of methods within the critical school 70
Johnna Montgomerie

Autobiographical vignettes:

Agility, intersectionality and deliberation: my path to an adaptive and transformative research process 83
Kia M. Q. Hall

(Dis)embodied methodology in International Political Economy 89
Nicola Smith

Critical methodology and the problem of history 94
Samuel Knafo

4 Iterative reflexive research strategy 100
Johnna Montgomerie

Autobiographical vignettes:

Doing research in the shadows of the global political economy 115
Nicola Phillips

Reflections on the archive as a critical resource 121
Chris Rogers

Qualitative research practices and critical political economy 125
Ian Bruff

5 On evidence and corroboration 129
Johnna Montgomerie

Autobiographical vignettes:

Everyday economic narratives 141
Liam Stanley

Social network analysis and critical political economy 146
Matthew Paterson

Conclusion 154
Johnna Montgomerie

Index *160*

ILLUSTRATIONS

Figures

4.1 Iterative reflexive research strategy   104
5.1 Emissions trading trans-national networks   149

Table

4.1 Methods for social research   108

CONTRIBUTORS

Editor biography

Johnna Montgomerie is a Senior Lecturer and Deputy Director of the Political Economy Research Centre (perc.org.uk) at Goldsmiths, University of London, UK. She has published widely in the area of financialisation, debt and the household. Her latest publications include 'Austerity and the Household: The Politics of Economic Storytelling' forthcoming in *British Politics* and 'Caring for Debts: How the Household Economy Exposes the Limits of Financialisation' with Daniela Tepe-Belfrage in *Critical Sociology*. She is committed to advancing an interdisciplinary research agenda that innovates political economy as a methodology not just a discipline. She lives in South London with her husband, two children and a bulldog.

About the contributors

David Blaney is Theodore Mitau Professor of Political Science, Ithaca College, New York. He works on the social and political theory of international relations/global political economy. With Naeem Inayatullah, he has co-authored *International Relations and the Problem of Difference* (Routledge 2004) and *Savage Economics: Wealth, Poverty and the Temporal Walls of Capitalism* (Routledge 2010). He recently co-edited two books (with Arlene Tickner) that explore the state of international relations as a global discipline: *Thinking International Relations Differently* (Routledge 2012) and *Claiming the International* (Routledge 2013).

Ian Bruff is Lecturer in European Politics at the University of Manchester, UK. He has published widely on capitalist diversity, neoliberalism and social theory. He recently completed a large cross-country project on the diversity of contemporary capitalism(s) with Matthias Ebenau, Christian May and Andreas

Nölke, which produced two German-language collections in 2013 (with Westfälisches Dampfboot and the journal *Periphere*) plus an English language special issue in 2014 (the journal *Capital & Class*) and an English-language volume in 2015 (with Palgrave Macmillan). He is currently researching the political economy of authoritarian neoliberalism in Europe and is the Managing Editor of the Transforming Capitalism book series published by Rowman & Littlefield International.

Kia M. Q. Hall earned a PhD in International Relations from the American University, where she conducted international development research about women who bake cassava bread, or ereba, in the Afro-indigenous Garifuna villages of Iriona, Honduras. Currently, she is a visiting research associate at Brandeis University's Women's Studies Research Centre. She is also a high school maths teacher.

John Hultgren teaches courses in environmental politics at Bennington College in rural Vermont. His research explores the theoretical and ideological foundations of environmental struggles. He is the author of *Border Walls Gone Green: Nature and Anti-immigrant Politics in America* (University of Minnesota Press 2015).

Naeem Inayatullah is Professor of Politics at Ithaca College. His work locates the Third World in international relations and global political economy. With David Blaney, he has co-authored *Savage Economics* (Routledge 2010) and *International Relations and the Problem of Difference* (Taylor & Francis 2004). He edited *Autobiographical International Relations* (Routledge 2011) and co-edited *Interrogating Imperialism* (Palgrave Macmillan 2006) and *The Global Economy as Political Space* (Lynne Rienner 1994). Recent work includes: 'Gigging on the World Stage: Bossa Nova and Afrobeat after De-Reification' (2016); 'A Problem with Levels: Engaging a Diverse IPE' (2015), both in *Contexto Internacional*; and *Narrative Global Politics* (Routledge 2016), co-edited with Elizabeth Dauphinee.

Samuel Knafo is a Senior Lecturer in the Department of International Relations at the University of Sussex. He is the author of *The Making of Modern Finance: Liberal Governance and the Gold Standard* (Routledge 2013), which was awarded the 2014 IPEG book prize. He has also published various articles on critical methodology, financial speculation and British financial governance.

Christopher May is Professor of Political Economy at Lancaster University, UK. After many years working on intellectual property rights, his recent work has turned to a wider focus on the rule of law and a renewed interest in the political economy of global corporations. He recently stepped down from senior university management and is enjoying getting back to life as a 'normal' academic.

Matthew Paterson is Professor of International Politics at the University of Manchester. His research focuses on the political economy of global environmental change. His publications include *Global Warming and Global Politics* (Routledge

1996), *Understanding Global Environmental Politics* (Palgrave Macmillan 2000), *Automobile Politics* (Cambridge University Press 2007), *Climate Capitalism: Global Warming and the Transformation of the Global Economy* (with Peter Newell, Cambridge University Press 2010) and most recently *Transnational Climate Change Governance* (with Harriet Bulkeley and eight others, Cambridge University Press 2014). He is currently focused on the political economy and cultural politics of climate change.

Nicola Phillips is Professor of Political Economy and the Head of the Department of Politics at the University of Sheffield, UK. She is the Chair of the British International Studies Association (BISA), a past Editor-in-Chief of the journal *New Political Economy* and one of the current editors of the *Review of International Political Economy*. Her research and teaching interests focus on global economic governance, labour in global production networks, and migration and development. Between 2010 and 2013, she held a prestigious Major Research Fellowship from The Leverhulme Trust, for research on forced labour and human trafficking for labour exploitation in the global economy. Her work on these topics has also been supported by grants from the Economic and Social Research Council and the Chronic Poverty Research Centre, and has involved field research across several regions of the world.

Chris Rogers is Associate Professor of Political Economy and Public Policy in the Department of Politics and International Studies (PAIS) at the University of Warwick. His research interests are in the politics of economic policy-making, Marxist political economy and Marxist state theory, and the co-operative movement. His most recent book, *Capitalism and Its Alternatives* (Zed Books) was published in 2014.

Anne Sisson Runyan is Professor of Political Science and Women's, Gender, and Sexuality Studies at the University of Cincinnati. Her most recent books include *Global Gender Issues in the New Millennium*, 4th edition (Westview Press 2014; 5th edition in progress), *Feminist (Im)Mobiliities in Fortress(ing) North America* (Ashgate 2013; lead editor), and *Gender and Global Restructuring*, 2nd edition (Routledge 2011; co-editor). She is an Associate Editor of the *International Feminist Journal of Politics*, the organiser of its fifth annual conference on 'Decolonizing Knowledges in Feminist World Politics' and the guest editor of the special issues arising from it. Her current project as the 2016 Fulbright Visiting Research Chair in North American Integration at York University, Canada is a book on gendered nuclear colonialism in North America.

Robbie Shilliam is a Professor in International Relations at Queen Mary University of London. He is author of multiple academic articles and monographs and, more recently, has curated an art installation. His efforts are to retrieve the archives and traditions of thought of enslaved Africans and their descendants in the Americas in order to re-assess the various European canons of thought that have predominantly framed understandings of enlightenment, modernity and capitalist development. He is co-convener of the British International Studies Association's Colonial/Postcolonial/Decolonial working group and a member of the International Advisory Board of the Transnational Decolonial Institute.

Nicola Smith is Senior Lecturer in Political Science at the University of Birmingham, UK. Her research explores the intersections between feminist political economy and queer theory, and recent publications include *Queer Sex Work* (Routledge 2015, edited with Mary Laing and Katy Pilcher), *Global Social Justice* (Routledge 2014/2011, edited with Heather Widdows) and *Body/State* (Ashgate 2013, edited with Angus Cameron and Jen Dickinson).

Liam Stanley is Lecturer in the Department of Politics at the University of Sheffield and an Associate Fellow at the Sheffield Political Economy Research Institute (SPERI). His research focuses on international and comparative political economy, the politics of fiscal consolidation and tax, and everyday narratives of politics and the economy. He has recently published in *New Political Economy*, *Political Studies*, *British Journal of Politics and International Relations* and *Politics*.

Dimitris Stevis is Professor of International Politics at Colorado State University. In broad terms his research explores the social governance of the world political economy in the areas of labour and the environment with particular attention to social and ecological justice and just transitions. He is currently working on collaborative projects about labour union environmentalism and environmental unionism and on the role of labour unions in greening the political economy, both in the USA and transnationally.

ACKNOWLEDGEMENTS

This volume was initially inspired by a conversation with Jacquie Best, acting as a RIPE Routledge series editor, which then became a research project in its own right that lasted many more years than originally anticipated. I must acknowledge the International Studies Association (ISA) workshop fund for their seed funding and the ESRC-funded Centre for Research on Socio-Cultural Change (CRESC) at the University of Manchester for its financial and scholastic support of this project. Especially the SLOM:lab network that continues to flourish and support multi-disciplinary work on social research methods. A special heart-felt thank you to all the contributors for sharing their experiences in a way that allowed this book to develop in its own time, but especially for the patience and kindness they showed when the project dragged on past many self-imposed deadlines. This book was made possible by the enriching intellectual relationships and connections with the contributors, who offered comments and advice on earlier versions of these chapters. Also, I want to thank Sara Wallin, James Brassett, Hugh Wilmott and James Woods for their extensive and helpful suggestions.

Finally, my deepest appreciation and thanks are reserved for my family. After beginning work on this project, I became pregnant with my second child and shortly after she was born my mother was diagnosed with terminal liver cancer. My husband, Sam, gladly took every bit of extra work with the house, the kids, whatever I needed, to get this book finished. Without his dedication, my own would not have been enough. I am most grateful for my family's support because this project, and much besides, could have easily been lost in my bereavement. My father reminded me that my mother had always wanted to publish a book but never did, I would like to dedicate this volume to her.

1
REIMAGINING CRITICAL METHODS

Johnna Montgomerie

This book was inspired by my curiosity about the social life of methods within the critical political economy tradition, by how it demands a new reflexivity about our methods in critical research. What began as a group of International Political Economy scholars, from both the political and cultural economy traditions, became an effort to advance our collective study of political economy. First by looking inward to examine the research practices proliferating within the critical school – in particular those in politics and international relations – which includes both political economy and cultural economy as separate but cognate forms of inquiry (Jessop and Sum 2003; Best and Paterson 2010). Then by looking outward to the wider social sciences to understand how methods continue to shape our collective study of capitalism, or the 'the economy', if you prefer. Political economy exists outside the academic discipline of Economics; it shares an understanding of capitalism that is not reducible to rational actors, market mechanisms or an inherently equilibrating macro-economy, and it cuts across a wide range of academic disciplines. However, united in opposition does not mean united in purpose – this book starts a conversation, it does not define an entire field of study.

As such, this book initiates a dialogue for those wanting to know more about how to go about *doing critical political economy*. For students wanting guidance on how to conduct critical research – from those starting out with a dissertation or honours essay to doctoral candidates beginning their professional journey with the research project that defines them as a scholar – this book wants to speak to those with a desire to do empirical research (be it qualitative or quantitative). You may be interested in key theories, issues or topics that shape the wider debates within the critical school but have no experience in engaging these questions empirically, but want to consider how it might be done. Also, this book is an invitation to colleagues at all levels of professional standing – post-doctorate to professor – to engage reflexively on methods and their role in shaping your critical research, career trajectory and/or ability to make expert claims within our shared institutions (Departments, PhD programmes, conferences, journals, professional associations, etc.). Making reflexive space for methods, especially for those engaging in social research, is necessary to advance the contemporary study of political economy.

What makes this book different is that it does not simply provide an overview of pluralist methodology or different types of method; rather, it engages directly with researchers in the field to reflect on how they 'do' critical political economy and what they have learned in the process. Beginning a conversation about methods as a shared experience is a new path forward, steering us away from our well-rehearsed disagreements into a collaborative engagement that could prove rewarding. Namely, by considering how methods shape what is critical about a piece of research, not just the researcher's ontological position or theoretical approach. It is one thing to acknowledge that methods are relevant and important, quite another to put methods centre stage. In doing so the effort is to countermand the relegation of methods as less important than theoretical understandings of what constitutes knowledge. It begins by accepting the methodological pluralism of the critical school and acknowledging our shared orientation – the remaking of capitalism. My hope is that by engaging in a dialogue about how political economy is a pluralist methodology we can forge a collaborative effort in the mutual pursuit of different, overlapping forms of analysis capable of interrogating something as complex as capitalism.

Why it matters

The rationale for advancing a pluralist methodology is to respond to the deepening crisis of positivist social science (Savage and Burrows 2007) by creating a platform of engagement in the hope of forging new terrain. We can readily observe multiple forms of crises – economic, ecological and social (Fraser 2014) – roll across the globe with no end in sight (Gamble 2014). The recent public crisis of economics begins with the failure to interpret the signs of a bubble that led to the 2008 financial crisis (Bryan et al. 2012; Davies and McGoey 2012). This inability to understand, interpret and analyse the causal mechanisms of the 2008 global financial crisis was neatly summarised by Queen Elisabeth II's simple question 'how did you not see it coming?' Despite the considered response by professional economists at the time (British Academy 2009; Coyle 2012), the discipline of Economics continues to suffer a profound crisis of credibility (Chakrabortty 2014; Chang 2014). This is laid bare for all to see by economics undergraduate students from across the globe campaigning to have economics reflect the world outside the classroom window with the slogan: 'The way economics is taught needs to change!' (Husnain and Parekh 2013; 'The PEPS Manifesto' 2014). What a hereditary monarch and a bunch of teenagers have in common is that they are articulating what critical political economy has been saying for years: contemporary economic orthodoxy is not fit for purpose. Real-world economic conditions continue to challenge established *a priori* assumptions about individual rationality and markets.

In the midst of this deepening crisis there are many prospects for change. For critical political economy to continue offering relevant and meaningful accounts of contemporary capitalism it must also change. We must abandon the 'orthodox' and 'critical' dichotomy that always leaves critical as 'anti' or in opposition to positivist social science and/or orthodox neoclassical economics. Of course, critical political economy and cultural economy eschew sterile formalism. Both agree that explaining the social world primarily in terms of the degree of relationship between variables based on *a priori* assumptions about individuals and markets is not particularly useful for understanding how the economy works or why it is in perpetual crisis. Critical scholars did, on many occasions and in many different ways, understand and diagnose the 2008 financial crisis (Palan 2009); moreover, critical political economy routinely advances current understandings of ecological and social crises (Gills 2010; Brand and Wissen 2013; Griffin 2007; Elias and Rai 2015). Triumphalism is not enough, we need more.

This book is an invitation to take a confident step forward by no longer defining 'critical' as in opposition to positivism, orthodoxy, mainstream, neoclassical economics, methodological individualism, and the list goes on and on. It is also a call to move beyond defining 'critical' strictly in terms of different ways of 'thinking'; that is in relation to various theoretical and philosophical traditions: Marxism, Feminism, Post-Modernisms, Constructivism, Post-Colonialism, and the list of 'isms' also goes on and on. Instead we need to foster a collaborative research agenda that explores the critical methodologies and heterodox methods that make up the critical school. This means treating methods as objects of inquiry to make visible the transformative dialectic between the explicit and implicit in process of knowledge creation (Savage 2013). By doing so we enrich our collective understanding of what critical political economy *does* – methods are no longer simply tools to validate theoretical claims (that exist independent from the method a researcher chooses); instead methods are the very doing of social research, where theoretical claims are made through a process of discovery, not yet foretold by hypothesis.

Doing critical political economy

By focusing on methods and methodologies we can forge a new terrain within the critical school. Scores of methods textbooks exist in every discipline and sub-discipline of the social sciences, and they typically present methods through dry descriptions of different qualitative and quantitative techniques. Standard research methods textbooks offer a generic schema for research design based on established categories of quantitative methods, qualitative methods or mixed methods. These are particularly useful as manuals for particular types of research. A big problem with this schema is that actually doing 'research' always comes after reading the textbook. Many researchers, like undergraduate economics students, realise that what is described in a textbook does not help you directly engage with the world outside the classroom window. A typical methods textbook offers a highly formalised schema for research design that explains the form it takes, not the substance of the research itself. Textbook 'methods' are not adaptive and certainly not transformative.

In politics and international relations methods texts (for example, Lamont 2015; Gowan 2011) adhere to a standard schema that explains ontology, epistemology and theory as a metaphysical distinction between positive and interpretive social science. Only then are different types of 'method' features, but mainly as tools for uncovering the metaphysical truth. Methods are what come after ontology, epistemology and theory. A fundamental weakness of framing methods using a first-principles approach is that it eliminates the researcher as an embodied person – that is, the individual doing the research is somehow not relevant to how that research is conducted. It is assumed that an academic researcher has an ontology (what the world consists of) and acknowledges his/her epistemology (what is considered knowledge) which exist *a priori* to methods. Ultimately the customary Ontology → Epistemology → Theory framework ensures that method always comes after metaphysics (Hollis 1981; Jackson and Sørensen 2015).

Methodology is the interface between ontology (how the world is), epistemology (how the world can be known), substantive theory (how the world is understood) and method (how the world is examined); for some methodology also culminates in etiology (what are the world's underlying causes) although not necessarily. Methodology is where method, theory and epistemology coalesce in an overt way in the process of directly investigating specific instances within the social world (Harvey 1990). Here, political economy is the methodology; and method, in this context, is ways of collecting empirical evidence that range from asking questions, through reading documents, to observation of both controlled and uncontrolled situations. While some methods lend themselves more readily to certain epistemological perspectives, no method of data collection is inherently positivist, phenomenological or critical. As such, methodology grounds inquiry in empirical evidence in a way that makes explicit the presuppositions that inform the knowledge claims, which were generated by the researcher's act of inquiry in the first place.

In this context, political economy as methodology foregrounds methods when doing critical research. However, I want to explicitly avoid making methods no more than sets of predefined tools used to find 'truth' or representations of truth in a specific cultural context. By treating method as a set of unchanging tools we confuse the device with the process of 'doing' research. In practice the very act of going out into the world to collect empirical evidence unsettles, disrupts and, more often than not, undermines the original research question and design beyond all recognition. If methods are tools, then it must be acknowledged they are often changed by the materials they interact with. Doing social research is messy (Law 2004) and we must also consider that when using methods as tools we might actually create social reality, rather than simply uncover it.

It is not clear how to move away from atomised ways of understanding the role of methods within social research. This makes writing a book about 'doing' critical research difficult because I want to explicitly avoid being prescriptive about how research should be done – especially without knowing what the research is, or who is doing it. Therefore, I have chosen to contextualise 'methods' within its institutional and social existence – as part of professional practices of contemporary academia in North America and Europe. The post-war era brought substantial public investment in universities, which went on to create a larger Higher Education sector. The resulting professionalisation of academic work meant that achieving qualifications and advancement is based on creating knowledge claims and expertise (Bourdieu 1988). Acknowledging the role of work practices is essential to understanding how methods shape research – this is the social stuff of research. As we will see throughout this volume, the working practices within the academic department of the contemporary university are an ever-present reality. It shapes how a PhD student conducts research, how research methods courses are taught, how grant applications are made and how work is valued by the department and wider community of scholars, such as the professional associations, national and international networks, funding bodies and leading disciplinary journals. Each of these academic institutions has their own set of practices, norms and ideas about what constitutes knowledge claims and expertise shapes how academics conduct research and make knowledge claims. All of these social relationships, institutions and cultures are acting upon the researcher's methods in different ways.

Pluralism in action

No definition of critical political economy is uncontroversial or authoritative, but for the purposes of this book it encompasses activities directed toward establishing an understanding of how capitalism is made and remade through social processes. Therefore, the economy is not axiomatic; it is made through social relations that are remade across time and space. Capitalism is technically complex, understanding the interaction between the unfolding of history – which creates recognisable forms of continuity – and human progress – which creates recognisable forms of socio-cultural change – makes the concept itself difficult to grasp. These social complexities reflect and refract in ways that ensure capitalism is not a determined process. Capitalism is an enigma (Harvey 2011) precisely because it is not a thing or a set of observable/predictable relationships; rather it is a constantly moving and dynamic process that is always in flux. This overarching view shapes how the critical academic researcher understands the very act of 'doing' critical research – how do you engage with a world historical process that necessarily exceeds your capacity to know it? The *de facto* answer has been to use a pluralist methodology. A pluralist political economy methodology offers a human-centred ontology (the social world is made of human understandings of it) and epistemology (knowledge is structured by existing sets of social relations) in which methods provide the evidence that makes visible these prevailing social processes.

Pluralism is a defining feature of the critical school; however, this is often regarded as weakness not strength because of the enduring practice of understanding 'critical' in opposition to positivism. As a result, very little consideration is given to what pluralism means in practice. Calls for a tolerance of methodological pluralism are not the same as being able to identify the practices of pluralism that make up cultural political economy. The former accepts each different methodology as 'separate but equal'; the latter seeks to forge a methodology for investigating capitalism that builds a comprehensive, although not necessarily coherent, understanding from a diversity of corroborating sources.

In short, capitalism is made and remade through institutions, structures, ideas and cultural practices that we can engage with empirically. Understanding the meaning of empirical evidence within a pluralist methodology requires us – again – to reclaim this concept from positivist social science. Empirical evidence is defined as human observation, experience and experiment – it is subjective, messy and creative. Positivism, empiricism and orthodox economics regularly use 'empirical' to mean large quantitative data sets and abstract econometric models that have only fantastical links to actual human experience or observation. Consequently, we must embrace the long-standing tradition of using human experience as (empirical) evidence to uproot deeply established dogma, which only exists to perpetuate established power structures. Accepting this principle does not require us to accept a singular way to determine what is (and what is not) considered empirical evidence. Rather, we can accept *prima facie* evidence of human experience as worth considering or evaluating, without conflating this with the value of the expert claims derived from this evidence.

For most researchers existing capitalist social structures are observed and experienced, in one way or another, as oppressive structures enacted through social process of gender, race and class. Investigating these oppressive structures empirically using a critical political economy or cultural economy lens makes visible how established categories of 'the economy' – namely, forced separation between politics and economics, states and markets, national and global, micro and macro – obfuscate the deeply social process of oppression imbued within it. Therefore, a significant element of critical political economy is about engaging empirically with aspects of social life that remain unseen, unheard, uncounted or unacknowledged within prevailing understandings of capitalism. Another important element of critical research is exploring the 'gaps', the tensions and inconsistencies in dominant accounts of established categories, models and variables.

The very acts of seeking, exploring, experimenting and drawing on experience challenges the oppressive social structures often lurking unnoticed in existing knowledge claims. Doing so means critical political economy can claim to do empirical research but cannot claim to be value-free. The belief that value-free observation is even possible is the crux of the disagreement between positivism and the rest of the social sciences (and humanities) who argue that most research is motivated by larger social purposes and, therefore, cannot be ever truly value-free. Lee Harvey (1990) is worth quoting at length to explain how critical methodologies use value-laden research to advance collective human knowledge:

Critical social research involves an epistemological perspective in which knowledge and critique are intertwined. Indeed, it is arguable that for a critical methodologist, knowledge is critique. A critical research process involves more than merely appending critique to an accumulation of 'fact' or 'theory' gathered via some mechanical process, rather it denies the (literally) objective status of knowledge and concerns itself with the processural nature of knowledge. Knowledge is a dynamic process not a static entity. Knowledge is not a bucket into which grains of information are dropped in the hope that they somehow coalesce into some kind of explanation of the world. For critical methodologists, knowledge is a process of moving towards an understanding of the world and of the knowledge which structures our perceptions of that world.

(p.3)

Critical political economy is explicit about its ethical and political stance to seek out and challenge prevailing orthodoxy. As such, this book accepts that knowledge about the political economy is a dynamic process that seeks an understanding of the remaking of capitalism as well as advancing the knowledge that structures our perception of it. In this pursuit method is the messy part. Engaging with a social political economic world knowing you cannot be a neutral observer offering a value-free analysis is a too often under-appreciated, and even un-recognised challenge. Especially when we account for the reality in which critical political economy scholars exist – a professional academic environment that demands knowledge claims and expertise that are structured by ideas of neutrality and value-free analysis. It is important to unpack the ways in which professional practice acts upon the academic researcher as well as constitutes what is valued (not value-free) academic knowledge or expertise.

A method for researching critical methods in practice

Promoting the reimagining of methods and pluralist methodology within cultural and critical political economy requires some imagination and a great deal of determination. My principal aim is that the key themes, concepts and ideas are forged through the same process of dialogue and debate this book seeks to foster within the critical school. To accomplish this, I decided to focus on answering one simple question: how do you go about 'doing' critical political economy? I found the answer by engaging directly with the people doing critical research, not just as technical practice but also as lived experience. The academics that contributed to this volume are my interlocutors, guiding me through the complex ways in which an academic charts his or her professional journey. The method used to produce this volume is a combination of 'collaborative encounter' and autobiography. As such, this book offers real-life examples of critical methodologies at work; in turn, allowing for collective reflection on how methods shape research agendas within critical political economy. This is a unique experiment in knowledge creation because it seeks to further methodological innovations within the critical school, especially with respect to promoting new forms of empirical research.

The research strategy was informed by the discussions, debates and visualisations of participants at two workshops held at the International Studies Association (March 2012) and the University of Manchester (September 2012). Small academic workshops create a unique space for intellectual engagement freed from the conventions of professional association meetings and/or collective publishing activities (like journal special issues or edited volumes) because they allow for open and honest discussion of issues. In both workshops I used the 'Collaborative Encounters' model developed at my research centre (CRESC 2013) which promotes a method of peer-based interaction that disrupt linear inside-to-outside and top-down models of knowledge transfer. In particular, this model adapts Open Space Technology as the organising principle of these workshops in order to allow participants to create the agenda (Owen 2008). This was a deliberate effort on my part to vanquish the standard 15–20 minute presentation (expert talking to audience) followed by brief discussion or question period. A key problem I faced was that most critical scholars would not present a paper on methods, in other words do not claim expertise on methods, but would spend a day with their peers learning more about it.

Open Space technology gave me a method for making a workshop that would reflect the questions, problems and issues the participants consider most relevant (not what I thought most relevant when inviting them to 'give a paper', as is normally done). On the practical side, for those that are unfamiliar with Open Space, it operates on a 'self-organisation' principle and is designed with experts in mind; it promotes attendees to move freely between breakout sessions and encourages them to engage only those topics that excite them (Olson 1996). Participants can 'vote with their feet' by leaving a discussion that no longer interests them and instead dedicate their efforts to debating and discussing the issues that matter most to the people in the room (Frey, Bird and Willoughby 2013). The advantage of Open Space is that it reorganises workshops to allow participants to create the agenda. In this case, we asked attendees to devise a workshop on methods that reflected the questions, problems and issues they considered most relevant. Using a self-organising form of engagement allowed participants to interact as embodied researchers, to debate and discuss the issues that mattered most to them. Both the ISA and Manchester workshops had rapid-fire (5-minute) presentations and used collaborative poster making to facilitate debate and discussion. Most workshop participants were unfamiliar with Open Space; some had reservations, while others jumped right in. Importantly, the self-organisation principle limited avenues of discussion that failed to advance a wider agenda on methods in the critical school.

This experiment in co-creation of knowledge sought to further methodological innovations within the critical school, especially with respect to promoting new forms of empirical research. Focusing on a collective output – this volume – put creativity and inventiveness at the centre of each day's events. In practice, the collaborative encounter facilitated a robust investigation into the actual sites, techniques and relationships within political and cultural economy as cognate fields of study. The workshop setting is particularly conducive to capacity building by offering a reflexive space to explore both the opportunities for and barriers to developing a collaborative research agenda on methods and methodologies of critical political economy. In doing so we explored how and when critical research can be culturally and socially transformative.

A clear limitation emerged after the collaborative encounters that immediately narrowed the scope of inquiry: there was not enough representation of quantitative methods. Within the workshops quantitative methods were relatively equally represented, giving fascinating detail on how methods inform the participants' research, which prompted rich and engaging discussion. However, after the workshops ended those participants using quantitative methods did not carry through to the next stage, which was to contribute an autobiographical vignette. As a result, the direction of travel of the research shifted dramatically, away from a plurality of methods towards a distinct focus on qualitative methods. In part, I was disappointed because I regularly use descriptive statistics and engage with regression analysis, and other quantitative methods, in my research in global finance. There are a good number of people working within the critical school using or engaging with quantitative methods, and not having them represented in a volume about critical methods seemed inappropriate. For some time, I tried inserting quantitative methods into the developing project, but it was forced and it showed. At this juncture I decided to focus on the developing autobiographies as a method and to let the evidence produced from those lead and shape the ultimate content of the book. Quantitative methods can be an important means to identify a relationship that is beyond that of qualitative research, but qualitative research can be used to explain that relationship further. My hope was that quantitative methods could be another volume or iteration of this project, because I believe the critical scholars that use quantitative methods offer important insight into pluralist methodology.

Developing the autobiography element of this project was initially inspired by a chance encounter with Kruzel and Rosenau's (1989) *Journey through World Politics*, which presented a series of autobiographical chapters from leading scholars of International Relations and International Political Economy. I was struck by how effective autobiography was in explaining how a field of study was forged through converging professional 'journeys'. Then, Inayatullah's (2010) *Autobiographical International Relations: I, IR* provided a more recent and truly creative volume that explicitly links the professional practices of teaching IR with being an expert in it. I was amazed at his question 'what does the topic of your study mean to you as a person?' (p.10); I had never, until that point, ever considered this question in my own research because it did not seem relevant, but it clearly is. With every chapter I was prompted to consider *my* personal connection to *my* research. Taken together, I began to reflect on my professional journey that brought me from an undergraduate degree at Simon Fraser University (Vancouver, Canada) through my graduate studies at the University of Sussex (Brighton, England) to a Research Fellowship at the Centre for Research on Socio-Cultural Change (CRESC) at the University of

Manchester, then on to a Senior Lectureship on a newly created Politics Philosophy and Economics degree at Goldsmiths, University of London, and on how this shaped what this book means to me, namely that I want to share the positive experience of being able to study political economy from a multi-disciplinary perspective. My professional journey led me to see the intellectual purchase of political economy, and my experience as part of two different interdisciplinary research centres showed me the widespread respect for critical political economy that exists outside the disciplinary walls of Politics and International Relations. It was these experiences that informed this book project and my commitment to avoiding continually redefining 'critical' in perpetual opposition to positivism.

Looking beyond Politics and International Relations, the disciplinary home of this volume, I drew on compelling examples of using autobiography as method (Majima and Moore 2009; DeVault 1999; Ullrich 1954). My excitement for autobiography was that it afforded me the most direct route out of evaluating methods using first-principles and because it made possible the breaking down of the imposed barrier between the rational and creative self that is implicitly or explicitly accepted by academic researchers. Autobiography makes trouble because it runs between fact and fiction (Coslett, Lury and Summerfield 2002); it disrupts established norms of the public-facing intellectual and the private thoughts and choices that make up the work-based practices of academic research.

The autobiographical vignettes offer testimony to how methods are used in practice and demonstrate how methods of social research are agents of social change (though in variable, complex and unanticipated ways), with values embedded in them. The authors of the autobiographical vignettes were invited to contribute to this volume by answering three specific questions: (1) What is your research expertise? (2) Why and how did you choose 'your' method? (3) How does your method/methodology shape how you 'do' research? Authors were asked to make direct reference to their own work as well as referencing the texts that most informed their method/methodological thinking and/or practice. We can observe how critical scholars interpret the ways in which social science methods shape – and are affected by – economic, social and cultural change across time and space. More importantly, by sharing their experiences, academics at all career stages offer new resources and guidance on the design and execution of a wide array of research projects. As such the autobiographical vignettes became part of the evidentiary base of this book; the accounts of how theory informs practice, how ethical challenges shape research, how research disrupts established certainties – and many others – informed the reflexive moves that refined the initial project to the final stages.

To organise and analyse this information I looked to the emerging methodological debates within *critical security studies*, a pseudo cousin of 'critical' sub-disciplines of International Relations. Drawing on the methods of identification and quantification that make visible the process of geopolitical transformation, 'critical' security studies seeks to overcome the positivist orthodoxy within International Relations.

More specifically, Laura Shepard's (2013) edited volume *Critical Approaches to Security: An Introduction to Theses and Methods* outlines not only the mutual constitutiveness of critical security studies and its methods but also the constitutive relationship between those methods and contemporary geopolitics. Also, Mark Salter and Can Mutlu's (2013) *Research Methods in Critical Security Studies* offers a reflexive approach to the different methodological 'turns' – ethnographic, practice, discursive, corporeal, material – that advance critical theory as a way of understanding power in the study of international relations and national security. Both volumes provided a rich resource to inform my own thinking about how methods are part of critical inquiry.

From this I developed a scheme to code and analyse the autobiographical vignettes in a way which ensured that I used this testimony to inform the writing of the book. At first blush the structure of the book suggests the chapters authored by me are distinct from the 'supplementary' autobiographical vignettes offered by the contributors; but, this is misleading because the autobiographies are integral pieces of evidence that articulate how academics do their critical research. By comparison to Shepard (2013), Salter and Mutlu (2013) compile a series of methods chapters from different academics in their professional network using these methods in practice; the rationale is that there are substantive generalist chapters and then expert chapters, so the reader can see both the big picture of how critical securities studies use methods and then follow up with the specific types of method the reader is interested in knowing more about. Overall, this style of approaching methods offers an innovative and engaging format that moves beyond the dry format of traditional methods textbooks. However, I did not replicate this approach; instead, I decided to use the autobiographical testimony as evidence and, then, developed that evidence to start a conversation about methods as transformative agents.

As such, I claim authorship of this book in the sense that its interpretations and arguments are my own, developed through engagement with my professional network and out of the evidence academics gave about their methods of doing political economy. Not all vignettes claim expertise in one type of method; but each offers a unique perspective on the strategies of doing critical research as well as detailed bibliographies of the author's research publications and key citations from the literature that most inform their methodological thinking. The autobiography is a stylised account of each author's professional journey, and are there for the reader to engage with and draw conclusions from, as I did. What follows seeks to contribute to methodological innovation within the critical school, especially with respect to promoting new forms of empirical research as well as enhancing and shaping methodological practices. By sharing the experiences of researchers in the design and execution of a wide array of research projects we explore how critical political/cultural economy methods are implicated in the organisation and administration of social and economic life. We see the many ways in which methods of social research are themselves agents of social change, with values embedded in them.

How to use this book

By initiating a conversation this book seeks to create a comprehensive platform for integrating discussions of methodology and methods into critical research practice. Of course, I expect the nature of the conversation will be different for those at the early stages of a research project, or career, and those in the latter stages. For students of political economy wanting to explore how methodology and method could help with critical inquiry chapters three, four, five offer a detailed account of how framing political economy as a pluralist methodology provides a framework for integrating the critical research ethic into the doing of academic inquiry. For those with established professional research careers, these same chapters are an invitation to make space for a reflexive critical research ethic within our professional understandings of how research can be done. Similarly, students will find the autobiographical vignettes useful to understanding how key figures in the field have built their professional journey through research that engages both key theoretical questions and material realities, as well as finding it useful for practical advice on key readings. For those more established in their respective professional journeys the vignettes are an invitation to reflect on which methodology and/or methods have shaped or been shaped by the subject and object of study. For example, this reflexivity is echoed in autobiographical accounts offered by Anne Sisson Runyan's 'Self-reflections on "the methods question" in feminist IR/IPE', Naeem Inayatullah and David Blaney's 'Tea and text: cultivated intuition as methodological process' and Christopher May's 'Norms, political economy and serendipity: thinking pragmatically about IPE'.

Similarly, chapter two speaks more directly to those readers that already identify their professional research within the field of International Political Economy to address directly our shared acts of discipline making. This chapter makes the case for setting a course away from the disciplinary routines that enforce particular ways of understanding the role of methods within the critical school by forging a new path towards an understanding of political economy as methodology not a discipline. Disciplinary approaches only lead to circular definitional debates seeking to impose boundaries on what we study – political economy, critical political economy, IPE, global political economy, cultural economy and cultural political economy – these are each a path to further division, foreclosing the forging of common ground or collaborative innovation. By changing the direction of travel, a new vision for paths to renewal can be glimpsed. Echoing the theme of new paths the autobiographical vignettes by Robbie Shilliam's 'Redemptive political economy', Dimitris Stevis' 'Investigating those you love: labour and global governance', John Hultgren's 'Discourse, nature and critical political economy: American environmentalists debate immigration' each provide a different perspective on pioneering a new direction of travel in their respective specialities.

Chapter three moves to the explanatory by focusing on developing an idiomatic framing of methods within the critical school. It does so by examining the 'social life of methods' as a way to consider more closely how to advance the pluralism of political economy. In particular, this chapter reflects on how methodological pluralism affects scholars' research ethics and how experts' pragmatic and/or judgement-based claims influence what we count as evidence. The autobiographical vignettes that form part of this collection enable us to see how we can develop and engage with a new idiom of methods to articulate the role of pluralism in professional practice. As such, three articulate accounts of professional journeys detail exactly how the academic, in practice, creates a unique idiomatic framing of methods to narrate and contextualise his or her critical research process: Kia Hall's 'Agility, intersectionality and deliberation: my path to an adaptive and transformative research process', Nicola Smith's '(Dis)embodied methodology in International Political Economy' and Samuel Knafo's 'Critical methodology and the problem of history'.

Chapter four puts forward an explicit iterative research strategy developed from Ackerly and True (2010), which involves being willing and able to recognise and take advantage of 'deliberative moments' that shed light on the rationale of one's research. Explicitly narrating the key choices and judgements that inform one's final argument requires a new way of articulating how knowledge claims emerge from the methods one uses to address the research puzzle at hand. This characterises critical research as a craft that depends on the constant evaluation of what certain methodologies do and how they do it. We place much-needed emphasis on the personal and professional contexts that inform how we negotiate choices, trade-offs and judgements. The strategy and craft of research are made explicit in the autobiographical accounts offered by Nicola Phillips' 'Doing research in the shadows of the global political economy', Chris Rogers' 'Reflections on the archive as a critical resource' and Ian Bruff's 'Qualitative research practices and critical political economy'.

Chapter five extends the reflexive practices of the iterative research strategy outlined in chapter four to include how evidence is mobilised in research practice and how writing brings into focus the long trajectory of research-led inquiry. In particular how being reflexive about how evidence is selected and mobilised inflects the new dialogue about critical methods with an in-built acknowledgement of the messiness and contingencies of critical social research (Jarvis 2013). In particular, I suggest a set of questioning practices that reiterate the dual movement of methods in a way that makes visible how evidence is made, not simply observed. More specifically, the first movement is to contextualise the evidence by accounting for *what kind of evidence is mobilised and what are its limits?* The second move opens this up by asking: *What is it evidence of?* in order to prompt the link between theory or evidence claims about social phenomenon. These explicit tensions are echoed in Liam Stanley's 'Everyday economic narratives' and Matthew Paterson's 'Social network analysis and critical political economy'.

Finally, the book concludes by revisiting how methodologically informed ways of researching, enriched by real-life accounts from academics doing empirical research, critiques the dominant frameworks, theories and modes of political economy that directly innovate this particular style of pluralism. Critical methods within political economy as methodology goes against the grain, but it makes space for the epistemological commitments of critical methodological practice. A move to opening up evidence could serve to better articulate how to make connections to the knowledge claims, be they theoretical interventions, conceptual development or evidentiary claims about the causes or consequences of social phenomena. Forging this path brings possibilities for collaboration and innovation within the study of cultural political economy that are foreclosed by attempts to impose disciplinary definitions on what critical or cultural political economy *is*; rather than what it studies and how.

Bibliography

Ackerly, Brooke, and Jacqui True. 2010. *Doing Feminist Research in Political and Social Science*. New York: Palgrave Macmillan.

Best, Jacqueline, and Matthew Paterson. 2010. *Cultural Political Economy*. London: Routledge.

Bourdieu, Pierre. 1988. *Homo Academicus*. Translated by Peter Collier. Stanford, CT: Stanford University Press.

Brand, Ulrich, and Markus Wissen. 2013. 'Crisis and Continuity of Capitalist Society–Nature Relationships: The Imperial Mode of Living and the Limits to Environmental Governance'. *Review of International Political Economy* 20 (4): 687–711. doi:10.1080/09692290.2012.691077.

British Academy, ed. 2009. 'The Global Financial Crisis – Why Didn't Anybody Notice?' http://www.britac.ac.uk/sites/default/files/03-Besley.pdf.

Bryan, Dick, Randy Martin, Johnna Montgomerie, and Karel Williams. 2012. 'An Important Failure: Knowledge Limits and the Financial Crisis'. *Economy and Society* 41 (3): 299–315. doi:10.1080/03085147.2012.661632.

Chakrabortty, Aditya. 2014. 'University Economics Teaching Isn't an Education: It's a £9,000 Lobotomy'. The Guardian, 9 May, sec. Comment is Free. www.theguardian.com/commentisfree/2014/may/09/university-economics-teaching-lobotomy-non-mainstream.

Chang, Ha-Joon. 2014. *Economics: A User's Guide. A Pelican Introduction*. London: Penguin Books.

Coslett, Tess, Celia Lury and Penny Summerfield. 2002. *Feminism and Autobiography: Texts, Theories, Methods*. London: Routledge.

Coyle, Diane. 2012. 'Economics Education after the Crisis: Are Graduate Economists Fit for Purpose?' Royal Economics Society, April.

CRESC. 2013. '(Un)doing Collaboration: Reflections on the Practices of Collaborative Research'. CRESC Working Paper Number 127.

Davies, William, and Linsey McGoey. 2012. 'Rationalities of Ignorance: On Financial Crisis and the Ambivalence of Neo-Liberal Epistemology'. *Economy and Society* 41 (1): 64–83. doi:10.1080/03085147.2011.637331.

DeVault, Marjorie L. 1999. *Liberating Method: Feminism and Social Research*. Philadelphia, PA: Temple University Press.

Elias, Juanita, and Shirin Rai. 2015. 'The Everyday Gendered Political Economy of Violence'. *Politics & Gender* 11 (2): 424–29. doi:10.1017/S1743923X15000148.

Fraser, Nancy. 2014. 'Can Society Be Commodities All the Way Down? Post-Polanyian Reflections on Capitalist Crisis'. *Economy and Society* 43 (4): 541–58. doi:10.1080/03085147.2014.898822.

Frey, J., C. Bird, and C. Willoughby. 2013. 'Smart Meeting Spaces for Knowledge Transfer'. *Smart Innovation, Systems and Technologies* 18: 31–38.

Gamble, Andrew. 2014. *Crisis Without End?: The Unravelling of Western Prosperity*. Basingstoke: Palgrave Macmillan.

Gills, Barry K. 2010. 'Going South: Capitalist Crisis, Systemic Crisis, Civilisational Crisis'. *Third World Quarterly* 31 (2): 169–84. doi:10.1080/01436591003711926.

Gowan, Peter. 2011. *Research Methods in International Relations: A Guide for Students*. London: Routledge.

Griffin, Penny. 2007. 'Refashioning IPE: What and How Gender Analysis Teaches International (Global) Political Economy'. *Review of International Political Economy* 14 (4): 719–36.

Harvey, David. 2011. *The Enigma of Capital: And the Crises of Capitalism*. London: Profile Books.

Harvey, Lee. 1990. *Critical Social Research*. Crows Nest, NSW: Unwin Hyman.

Hollis, Martin. 1981. *Explaining and Understanding International Relations*. New edn. New York: Oxford University Press.

Husnain, Mahim, and Rikin Parekh. 2013. 'Economics Students Demand an Education that Reflects Post-Crash World'. The Guardian, 13 November, sec. Guardian Sustainable Business. www.theguardian.com/sustainable-business/economic-students-demand-education.

Inayatullah, Naeem, ed. 2010. *Autobiographical International Relations: I, IR*. London: Routledge.

Jackson, Robert, and Georg Sørensen. 2015. *Introduction to International Relations: Theories and Approaches*. Oxford: Oxford University Press.

Jarvis, Lee. 2013. 'Conclusion: The Process, Practice and Ethics of Research'. In *Critical Approaches to Security: An Introduction to Theories and Methods*, edited by Laura J. Shepherd. Abingdon: Routledge.

Jessop, Bob, and Ngai-Ling Sum. 2003. 'On Pre- and Post-Disciplinarity in (Cultural) Political Economy'. *Economie et Société-Cahiers de l'ISMEA* 39 (6): 993–1015.

Kruzel, Joseph, and James N. Rosenau. 1989. *Journeys through World Politics: Autobiographical Reflections of Thirty-Four Academic Travelers*. Lanham, MD: Lexington Books.

Lamont, Christopher. 2015. *Research Methods in International Relations*. London: Sage.

Law, John. 2004. *After Method: Mess in Social Science Research*. Hove: Psychology Press.

Majima, Shinobu, and Niamh Moore. 2009. 'Introduction: Rethinking Qualitative and Quantitative Methods'. *Cultural Sociology* 3 (2): 203–16. doi:10.1177/1749975509105531.

Olson, Linda. 1996. *Open Space Technology and Self-Organization: A Case Study*. Pepperdine University, research project (MSOD).

Owen, Harrison. 2008. *Open Space Technology: A User's Guide*. Oakland, CA: Berrett-Koehler Publishers.

Palan, Ronen. 2009. 'The Proof of the Pudding is in the Eating: IPE in Light of the Crisis of 2007/8'. *New Political Economy* 14 (3): 385–94. doi:10.1080/13563460903087540.

PEPS-Économie. 2014. 'The PEPS Manifesto'. http://pepseco.wordpress.com/peps-in-english/manifesto/.

Salter, Mark B., and Can E. Mutlu. 2013. *Research Methods in Critical Security Studies: An Introduction*. London: Routledge.

Savage, Mike. 2013. 'The "Social Life of Methods": A Critical Introduction'. *Theory, Culture & Society* 30 (4): 3–21. doi:10.1177/0263276413486160.

Savage, Mike, and Roger Burrows. 2007. 'The Coming Crisis of Empirical Sociology'. *Sociology* 41 (5): 885–99. doi:10.1177/0038038507080443.

Shepherd, Laura J. 2013. *Critical Approaches to Security: An Introduction to Theories and Methods*. London: Routledge.

Ullrich, LeRoy Wensel. 1954. *Value of the Educational Autobiography as a Method of Studying Occupational Interest Patterns and Adjustment of College Students*. Madison: University of Wisconsin Press.

SELF-REFLECTIONS ON 'THE METHODS QUESTION' IN FEMINIST IR/IPE

Anne Sisson Runyan

Growing up in the midst of the Vietnam and Cold Wars and during the concomitant revival of the peace, (New) Left and feminist movements, I was immersed in a heady mixture of alternative educational, cultural and political spaces, spaces that the American feminists of my generation were using to (re)learn and debate the relationships (or unhappy marriages) between feminist, socialist and peace politics. Witnessing the differing referents – sexism, capitalism and war – these politics challenged through analysis and activism, I could not help but wonder how they could be apprehended in relation to each other. What orthodoxies about these phenomena not only kept them in place but also prevented our ability to see their possible relationships? Among the orthodoxies challenged in those days was 'the woman question' in Marxism. At the time, those of us who were thinking about what constituted socialist feminism began to sense that women were not the problem standing in the way of post-capitalist (and post-militarist) futures. Rather, as activists and scholars began theorizing the gendered nature of productive and reproductive relations integral to capitalism (and nationalism/imperialism/militarism), women's struggles for liberation came to appear fundamental to the fight for social justice.

By the time I entered a doctoral program in International Relations (IR), a field that I had mistakenly assumed allowed a space for thinking about relations of inequality and injustice on an international scale, I was surprised to learn that 'the woman question' itself, even in its most rudimentary form, was absent. Although sympathetic advisors permitted me to go my own way, I had little to guide me epistemologically or methodologically in IR proper and instead relied on extra-disciplinary feminist literature and methods to craft what may have been the first feminist IR dissertation. Over the ensuing thirty years, the woman question has been deeply problematized in feminist studies, including feminist IR and

International Political Economy (IPE), with the rise of feminist intersectional, post-colonial, post-structural, queer and transgender approaches. But just as these approaches have destabilized the woman question, they too have complicated 'the methods question.' Although still wavering between, on the one hand, an interest in making feminist approaches intelligible to current and future (feminist) scholars within the IR and IPE disciplines and, on the other hand, a suspicion of any method as a disciplining apparatus that seeks to tame approaches willing to 'wrestle with questions of global justice' (Ackerly & True 2006, pp. 245–46), some cadres of contemporary feminist IR/IPE scholars have recently begun to articulate the various methods used by feminists in the field. In this piece, I attempt to situate some of my earlier work in relation to the feminist IR/IPE methods that are now being articulated and codified.

Contemporary thinking about feminist IR/IPE methods

Second-generation feminist IR/IPE scholars, some of whom I have mentored and/or worked with, have taken up the methods question for the training of new generations of scholars. Brooke Ackerly and Jacqui True (2010, p. 7), for instance, argue that feminist inquiry cannot be reduced to any single method or 'political, ideological agenda'; nor, they contend, can such inquiry be dictated by any particular 'kind of world we would like to bring about,' as 'feminist goals are plural and contested.' Nevertheless, feminist inquiry can be guided by a feminist research ethic that is concerned with 'silences,' 'absences' and 'marginalizations,' as well as with the structures and processes, including feminist epistemologies, 'that cause and sustain them' (ibid.). Remaining critical of critical feminist epistemological perspectives requires recognizing when and how particular feminist perspectives become privileged, normalized and/or silenced; it also requires a research ethic that is 'always listening to new voices, always (respectfully) hearing cacophony, always suspicious of harmonies or recurring themes' (Ackerly & True 2010, p. 23). Such attentiveness to new voices to disrupt what Marysia Zalewski (2006) refers to as 'comfort texts' allows us to disturb (old and new) conceptual orthodoxies and boundaries and to eliminate the blindspots arising from our social situatedness. As this concerns feminist methodologies, the kind of self-reflexivity that Ackerly and True (2010) advocate is not so much intended to root out bias and achieve objectivity as it is concerned with resisting practices of othering and silencing in the face of difference. To understand the relational nature of research, we must reflect on and account for self/other constructs and dynamics, whether they occur between the researcher and the researched or among researchers.

Zalewski (2006, p. 61) argues that 'telling the story of feminist methodology lies in the narrating of the search for it, and the practice of it, which, although demanding responsibility, does not allow the comfort of finality.' In what follows, I offer some stories related to my search for a feminist methodology and the practices I have adopted both within and outside feminist IR/IPE.

Searching for feminist IR/IPE methods: a retrospective

When I began searching in the early 1980s for ways of challenging seemingly genderless IR/IPE worldviews and practices, there were no roadmaps. Yet, as I look back at my early work through the prism of recent articulations of feminist methods, I find I was engaging in many of the practices that are now being cataloged. My dissertation challenged problematic associations, both patriarchal and feminist, between women and peace (and men and war) that undermined a more diverse and cacophonous feminist peace politics. In my case study analysis of international feminist peace organizing, I was guided not by any singular tradition or approach but rather by a threefold commitment: first, to seek IR knowledge in marginalized spaces to counter hegemonic understandings of security; second, to excavate the varied historical and contemporary contributions that feminists in the Global North and South have made to peace and justice through thought and activism; and third, to engage in critique not with the aim of adjudicating opposing positions but instead with the goal of discouraging silencing and the imposition of normativities within feminist peace politics.

Valuing both structural and emergent post-structural feminist epistemologies, I adopted methodologies that were necessarily eclectic and unusual. Indeed, at a time when there was little place in IR for social movement analysis, as opposed to analyses of states and markets, my methods seemed to border on the unacceptable. With little formal training in the issues that concerned me and without a community of feminist IR scholars with whom I could connect, I found myself relying on a mixed-method form of data collection that involved, among other things, using feminist political theory to deconstruct realist assumptions, consulting feminist histories of women in war and peace, researching feminist theorizations of violence and non-violence, collecting emergent UN data on women, reading feminist utopian fiction and conducting case study analysis through participant observation, archival work, and interview and survey research.

Although I lacked guides within IR proper, I did benefit in my research from the feminist interdisciplinary literature in which I had been steeping myself independently for some time. I also had Maria Mies's *Fighting on Two Fronts: Women's Struggles and Research* (1982), from which I absorbed not only the permission to situate but also the necessity of situating myself within the constellation of activists whom I was studying and to whom I felt keenly accountable. In retrospect, I have come to realize that I was experimenting with what is now referred to in the literature of feminist IR methodology as the deconstruction of 'master frames,' frames that 'constrain our ways of thinking' about a particular phenomenon and delimit what is and is not to be taken seriously (Ackerly & True 2010, p. 211).

My first joint endeavor with Spike Peterson (see Runyan & Peterson 1991) came about in the wake of the feminist post-structural turn that highlighted both the power of symbolic/narrative/representational practices to constitute social/material realities and the discursive methods that demonstrate those practices. Spike and I drew from feminists in literary fields who were influenced by the semiotics work of Saussure and Barthes, which argued that hierarchical binaries as encoded in 'signifiers' constitute the deep structure of meaning-making in a particular social order and act to sustain that order regardless of intent (Hawkesworth 2006, p. 104). French psychoanalytic feminist theorists – most of whom were influenced by Lacan's notion of the (phallo-logocentric) Symbolic Order that is based on the repression of desire and difference – had posited that 'the feminine' has 'a particular kind of discursive effect or as the "radically repressed" provides insights into the gendered nature of subjectivity and culture' (Hawkesworth 2006, p. 106). It was this notion of the 'feminine' (not 'woman' or 'feminine values') as 'the other' – that is, as a site of disorder, even madness, that had to be controlled or reduced to tamed 'femininity' and thereby devalued – which provided us with a jumping-off point to 'subvert' IR theory. But it was also Sandra Harding's *The Science Question in Feminism* (1986) that helped us to re-frame feminist analysis for IR and IPE. In particular, we were influenced by Harding's argument in favor of post-positivist orientations toward both a feminist 'standpoint' and 'postmodern' approaches, with the latter acting as a check on essentializing and universalizing claims about women, gender *and* feminism.

As we began work on our first project, Spike and I also decided to write together and viewed this decision as a methodological one with both practical and political implications. Seeing our task as a broad feminist re-writing of IR and IPE that would be accessible to students new to the study of world politics, we hoped to introduce critical perspectives early and centrally in ways that would destabilize students' assumptions not only about the world but also about themselves. From a practical standpoint, writing together made sense, as Spike and I were junior scholars undertaking a large project and treading on unfamiliar, even unwelcoming ground. But writing together also made 'feminist sense,' as it compelled us to enact a form of and a commitment to relational and collective knowledge production. That commitment extended to organizing a community of feminist IR and IPE scholars to further the project of expanding and complicating feminist IR/IPE knowledge.

Over our decades-long collaboration on *Global Gender Issues* (1993, 1999, 2010, 2014), our goal has been to make visible and intelligible the deep structure and structuring gender binaries that significantly account for the blindness and outright resistance to old and new forms of empirical evidence, whether qualitative or quantitative, produced by critical (or post-positivist) feminist IR/IPE scholars. In the process of re-framing and translating existing world-ordering frames, we extended the concept of the gendered division of labor to include gendered (and, later, racialized and sexualized) divisions of power, violence and resources and argued that such divisions feed off each other in ways that privilege one side of a binary in the construction of an 'interpretive grid' (Balkin 2003). Identifying the 'power of gender' as one such interpretive grid (or meta-lens) that constitutes a globalized dominant or master frame rooted in western metaphysics, we later complicated our argument to take better account of the simultaneously reinforcing and disruptive powers of other master frames, each of which intertwines with gender to order thought and social relations. As we contended, dominant political, geopolitical and economic arrangements achieve their taken-for-granted-ness or hegemony through association with the naturalized hierarchical dichotomies or binaries of gender as it is mediated through race, class, sexuality and nation. At the same time, however, we followed feminist authors whose work on the instabilities of masculinities was informed by Derrida's focus on the instability of meaning. Relying on these works, we made the case that the deconstruction or 'the critical interrogation of binaries' is not about simply flipping a binary to privilege the subordinated side but rather about recognizing 'contradictions, lacunae, false totalities, and homogenizations' (Hawkesworth 2006, p. 105) in master frames (including feminist ones) as a means of displacing them and their ordering power.

While feminist post-colonial scholarship was complicating my thinking about gender and IR generally speaking, work by post-positivist feminist economists provided some of the impetus behind the feminist challenge Marianne Marchand and I subsequently offered to the 'one true story' of neo-liberal globalization, a story that involved globalization being characterized as a universal and universalizing *force majeure* to which there were no alternatives. In our first edition of *Gender and Global Restructuring* (Marchand & Runyan 2000), we reconceived neo-liberal globalization as a 'global restructuring,' a phrase that was intended to underscore the multi-speed, multi-sited, multi-scale, uneven and disjunctive process unaccounted for in the dominant discourse of globalization as a coherent and totalizing unfolding. Focusing on the problematics of economism and teleology in globalization discourse, we posited that certain 'feminizing' discursive frames undergird and naturalize neo-liberal ideology and policies, which come to appear both common-sensical and inexorable. In particular, we considered how globalization discourse 'feminizes' – that is, renders as devalued, weak, anachronistic or sentimental – the state in relation to the market, certain state sectors (welfare) in relation to other state sectors (finance), manufacturing in relation to finance and workers in the old economy in relation to workers in the new economy. When Marianne and I began working on the second edition of our book (2011), our concerns shifted in response to the rise of feminist and queer scholarship on the Foucauldian biopolitics of global governance and its attendant necropolitics (Mbembe 2003), particularly in the post 9/11 context. Continuing to look for openings that would displace the production of neo-liberal subjectivities (and their relation to post-9/11 securitized subjectivities) within the (global) 'governance of intimacy' – a form of governance in which gender and sexual relations themselves are being neo-liberalized – we brought together work that highlighted the incompleteness of and thus resistances to the inculcation of such subjectivities. We also signaled the rise of neo-liberalized and securitized feminism in the new millennium. However, as Marysia Zalewski and I have recently argued in 'Taking Feminist Violence Seriously in Feminist International Relations' (Zalewski & Runyan 2013), feminism has never been innocent of productive and destructive power. While Marysia and I recognize this, we also contend that feminism need not be abandoned, as it is a theoretical site subject to constant epistemological and thus methodological reinvention. Furthermore, relying on a methodological innovation we call following 'the trail of blood,' which we use to detect discourses of female embodiment in representations of feminism, we argue that anxieties about the declining counter-hegemonic efficacies of feminism spring from the association of feminism with the violated and/or decaying female body; as we suggest, it is this association, rather than feminism itself, that should be abandoned. This is not to say that no promise exists in the method of embodying capitalism. The 2008 financial crisis constituted a particularly spectacular event of excess, uncontrollability and fallibility, an event during which the supposedly hard, impenetrable and rational body of capitalism was exposed as vulnerable.

A conclusion without finality

What has emerged for me in this selective self-reflection on 'the methods question' in feminist IR/IPE is that the search for methods is really a continuous search for discontinuities – for those ideas, practices, collaborations and demands for inclusion and disruption that unsettle well-worn paths, comfort zones and easy conclusions within a field and one's own work. For me, a basic critical 'method' in IPE thus involves being constantly vulnerable to rethinking, reworking and reimagining the search for global justice while being open to, cultivating, learning from and putting in relation new and multiple critical voices from across a range of social and disciplinary locations.

Works cited

Ackerly, BA & True, J 2006, 'Studying the struggles and the wishes of the age: feminist theoretical methodology and feminist theoretical methods,' in BA Ackerly, M Stern & J True (eds.), *Feminist methodologies for international relations*, Cambridge UP, Cambridge, pp. 241–61.
Ackerly, B & True, J 2010, *Doing feminist research in political and social science*, Palgrave Macmillan, New York.
Balkin, K (ed.) 2003, *Poverty: opposing viewpoints*, Greenhaven Press, San Diego.
Harding, S 1986, *The science question in feminism*, Cornell UP, Ithaca, NY.
Hawkesworth, M 2006, *Feminist inquiry: from political conviction to methodological innovation*, Rutgers UP, New Brunswick, NJ.
Marchand, MH & Runyan, AS (eds.) 2000, *Gender and global restructuring: sighting, sites, and resistances*, Routledge, London.
Marchand, MH & Runyan, AS (eds.) 2011, *Gender and global restructuring: sightings, sites, and resistances*, 2nd edn, Routledge, London.
Mbembe, A 2003, 'Necropolitics,' *Public Culture*, vol. 15, no. 1, pp. 11–40.
Mies, M 1982, *Fighting on two fronts: women's struggles and research*, Institute of Social Studies, The Hague.
Peterson, VS & Runyan, AS 1993, *Global gender issues*, Westview Press, Boulder, CO.
Peterson, VS & Runyan, AS 1999, *Global gender issues*, 2nd edn, Westview Press, Boulder, CO.
Peterson, VS & Runyan, AS 2010, *Global gender issues in the new millennium*, 3rd edn, Westview Press, Boulder, CO.
Runyan, AS & Peterson, VS 1991, 'The radical future of realism: feminist subversions of IR theory,' *Alternatives*, vol. 16, pp. 67–106.

Runyan, AS & Peterson, VS 2014, *Global gender issues in the new millennium*, 4th edn, Westview Press, Boulder, CO.

Zalewski, M 2006, 'Distracted reflections on the production, narration, and refusal of feminist knowledge in international relations,' in BA Ackerly, M Stern & J True (eds.), *Feminist methodologies for international relations*, Cambridge UP, Cambridge, pp. 42–61.

Zalewski, M & Runyan AS, 2013, 'Taking feminist violence seriously in international relations,' *International Feminist Journal of Politics*, vol. 15, no. 3, pp. 293–313.

TEA AND TEXT

Cultivated intuition as methodological process

Naeem Inayatullah and David Blaney

> *He who tastes, knows ... Instead of talking about the celestial beverage, offer it at your banquets. Those who like it will ask for more. Those who do not will show they are not fitted to be tea drinkers. Close the shop of argument and mystery. Open the teahouse of experience.*
>
> (from Idries Shah's (1969) 'The Story of Tea')

We read texts. More specifically, we read theorists who treat capitalism as foundational in three senses: they examine the ethical and political problems capitalism creates; they treat capitalism as something with an identifiable and coherent logic; and they study capitalism's history as something structured and palpable that unfolds and changes in space/time. We read texts that consider capitalism ethically, logically and historically.

We exclude theorists who treat capitalism's ethical and political difficulties as either positively or negatively resolved. We also exclude those theorists who are unconcerned with, or opposed to, treating capitalism as having a logic and those who ignore the global historical structures capitalism creates. In practice, this means we exclude theorists influenced by contemporary neo-classical economics and those who, in Richard Ashley's (1983) terms, participate in 'logical economism.'

These exclusions leave us with an abundance of theorists. We favor members of the Scottish Enlightenment (Adam Smith, Adam Ferguson, James Steuart and John Millar), as well as Hegel, Marx and Karl Polanyi. We also favor the contemporary theorist (and our former teacher) David P. Levine. We are still pondering if a reading of the foundational authors of marginalist economics fits our concerns. We might say that much that we have wished to learn lies in the overlap of these texts and our contemporary life experiences.

Why these theorists? The Scottish Enlightenment figures are central for obvious reasons. They were keen observers of the origins of capitalism. Their theorization faced and probed ethical dilemmas, including the examination of economic problems via textual narratives, instead of relying on equations, graphs and technical jargon. And they are inherent multi-disciplinarians or even, perhaps, pre-disciplinarians. Their texts involve a richness of observation, a conceptual precision and a judicious circumnavigation of politics/ethics.

Hegel draws us for three reasons. First, he develops a historical dialectics that influenced Marx, who is by far the greatest explicator of capitalism we have read. Second, despite, or perhaps because of, Marx's towering achievements, Hegel's examination of capitalism remains undervalued. His development of the concept of property and his exploration of how needs must multiply as production expands were later taken up by Thorsten Veblen, Robert Heilbroner and David P. Levine. Hegel famously regarded poverty as the necessary product of modernity and civil society and therefore saw it as unable to be eliminated within capitalism. Poverty remained the one issue that Hegel knew he did not solve, even as he understood that it threatened the entire edifice of his social theory. His prescience on the knottiness of poverty remains astounding.

Marx hardly needs comment, except perhaps to say that we read him as the greatest *pro*ponent of capitalism. In contrast to Marx's work, Hayek's and Friedman's polemical endorsement of capitalism leads them to hide its essential fissures. Marx is committed to no such endorsement, and as a result, he sheds a clear and sober light on capitalism's achievements. Understanding capitalism without Marx is possible but unnecessarily challenging. Doing so might be akin to charting the structure of the human psyche without attending to Freud.

Polanyi banks on Marx. He shows how humans resist the abstract punishment and disciplining of market society and how this resistance tempers capitalism's attack on life. Human defenses partially humanize capitalism, but they also prolong capitalism's longevity. Polanyi's richest contribution is that he refuses the stage theory that tempts Marx. Instead, he complicates the structure of history and everyday life such that the past, the present and the future reveal themselves as coeval. On Polyani's account, the future of the Third World is not pre-ordained to replicate the present of the First World. Rather than supporting stage theory and sovereign boundaries, which are the non-overlapping Euclidian twins of time and space, Polanyi imagines others' cultural differences as a challenge to capitalism and as resources for those occupying a world within and beyond capitalism.

A few early marginalist economists just might pass muster. Though often working urgently to close the fissures and resolve uncertainties created by nineteenth-century capitalism, they – as founders – debated foundational issues. W. Stanley Jevons explained and justified the utilitarian assumptions of his political economy instead of presuming them, while Alfred Marshall, with explicit reference to Hegel, saw his static models as part of a science that comprehended the unfolding of human consciousness. In addition, A. C. Pigou strove to advance an economic viewpoint in the face of Christian and Nietzschean ethics. All three men worked to establish a new science against the backdrop of evolutionary theories and struggled to reconcile equilibrium metaphors with processes unfolding in time. What may be most interesting, however, is the way modern economics, despite the work of these early economists, was founded precisely by the conscious closing of questions related to history and culture. Today, few economists speak to such foundational issues.

How do we read the theorists we have mentioned? Like all analysts of texts, we search for logical flaws and contradictions. That said, we also treat such contradictions as necessary. We imagine that the theorist is attempting something difficult by trying to stay true to multiple but opposing theoretical insights or by bridging opposing aspects of reality. When we interact generously with our sources, their logical flaws, contradictions and mistakes seem less like hard nuggets to collect than mysteries to fathom. Instead of insurmountable obstacles, flaws, contradictions and mistakes become tensions, tonal shifts and bumps that we can locate as the necessary result of some essential structural problem. We allow these tensions, tonal shifts and bumps to lead us to the fundamental difficulties with which the theorists wrestle. Ascertaining these foundational difficulties allows us to chart the horizons of the writers' theoretical and existential world. For example, the problem for sixteenth-century European theorists was how to think about the sudden discovery of the Amerindians given that their primary ethnographic source, the Bible, did not account for them. Were Amerindians human? If so, how to explain their seeming lack of civilization? If not, what responsibilities did Europeans have to these creatures?

We consider the contradictory structure of authors' texts not as distortions but as lenses through which they struggled to make sense of the world. Our first task is to try to see the world as they saw it. We then compare their horizon with our own, and through this comparison, we learn lessons about our present moment. Do the authors we read have ethical problems similar to ours? Do their proposed solutions differ from ours? What can we learn from such textual time travel? Quentin Skinner, John Pocock and the Cambridge school of 'contextual' history have led the way in such methods (Skinner 2000). We have taken some of our inspiration from their work.

Having noted our relation to existing authors and schools of thought, we believe that our theoretical contribution, to the degree we have one, is two-fold. First, we bring a Lacanian/Žižekian interpretation to our readings. For us, the emergence of capitalism wounds life. Those who primarily extol the virtues of capitalism deny the pain of this wounding; those who primarily emphasize the pain (see our treatment of Richard Ashley as an exemplar) deny why the wound might nevertheless be worth suffering (Blaney & Inayatullah 2010). Our interpretation aims at avoiding both blind spots. We regard the wound as a *whole* and as a *hole* around which we circle. Encircling the wound of capitalism, we aim to foreground the ethical debates it produces, even as we note how our capacity to live within capitalism depends on avoiding those debates and covering that wound.

Second (and simultaneously), we locate themes in the works of (dead, white, male) political economists that can be read to support a third-world perspective. Given our own historicity, we cannot avoid highlighting those works' racism, sexism, classism and first-world-ism. Yet we also uncover alternative themes that work against our immediate interpretations. For instance, Smith and his Scottish Enlightenment counterparts can be read as offering a haunting critique of capitalism; Hegel's treatment of poverty can be perceived as clearer and more honest than anything we have read in our own period; Marx can be read as following a comparative method that goes against his own expressed methodological predilections; and Polanyi's critique of the great European transformation can be understood as working in intimate tandem with his excavation and partial endorsement of non-capitalist third- and fourth-world economic systems. We believe that texts are worth reading when the presence of counter-themes upsets and upends any smooth textual journey.

Our preference for reading, appreciating and analyzing texts against the grain arises from a combination of Hegel's practice of immanent critique (as learned from David P. Levine), the psychoanalytical approach of Lacan and Žižek and the profound insights and the deft reading practices of Ashis Nandy. How did we 'choose' our method? This question makes us uncomfortable because it seems more apropos to say that the method chose us. In part, we reacted to our graduate training in the 1980s at the University of Denver. While the faculty taught positivist methods, most of the students explored approaches that were more qualitative and philosophical. Both of us started in development economics probing questions of international inequality. We regarded our interests in political theory, international relations and comparative politics as intertwined. Our attempt to see these sub-disciplines as a whole led us to investigate the history of economic thought and then to consider ethnographic approaches to economics. Polanyi's influence on us was pivotal, as he married his critique of historical capitalism with an excavation of the benefits of non-capitalist economies. Today, we tend to think of ourselves as ethnologists of capitalism who specialize in that part of the western white canon that explains and defends capitalism.

Imagining we could have chosen or foretold such a journey turns the precariousness of our path into a smooth, hardened, pre-existing motorway. The limits of our method are easy to diagnose but difficult to overcome. We have no data, no archive, no delimited field that we can claim to represent or about which we can speak as experts. Indeed, it seems as if we have no empirical or actual referent. Although we write to understand the actual world and to shift our relations to that world through our understanding, we also recognize that we may be criticized for assuming that working on texts is the same as working on the world.

In addition, our focus on political economy's western white canon reveals an absence of explicit black and brown theorists. As a result, we have been admonished for attempting to represent third-world concerns without incorporating third-world voices. These are weaknesses of which we are aware.

These flaws also present strengths, strengths to which we are wedded. To be more precise, we locate third-world voices within political economy's western white canon. We aim to show how this canon – despite its racism, its support of imperialism and its justification of capitalism – nevertheless produces sub-themes that subvert its more well-known and explicit claims. By uncovering these sub-themes within the canon, we hope to find some purchase in the move from text to actuality. In reading the western white canon, our aim is not merely to hear the voices of third-world others but also to create solidarities between those voices and the canon in question. In Ashis Nandy's (1987) terms, we strive to identify 'civilizational allies.' We believe this strategy has more potential than the usual juxtaposition of western and non-western voices.

How does this method shape our 'doing' of research, and how does the 'doing' of research shape us? We feel uncertain about these questions' meaning. For us, the 'doing' of research is inseparable from our method. Perhaps we feel this way because our research (and, therefore, our method) is inextricable from the texts we have been drawn to read (or that have chosen us). We are tempted to say that our method of researching is inspired intuitively by the urgency of our questions and by our attempt to reach out toward what we cannot yet say. We also recognize that these intuitions are cultivated by drinking the tea and asking for more.

Works cited

Ashley, R 1983, 'Three modes of economism,' *International Studies Quarterly*, vol. 27, pp. 463–96.

Blaney, D & Inayatullah, N 2010, *Savage economies: wealth, poverty and the temporal walls of capitalism*, Routledge, New York.

Nandy, A 1987, *Traditions, tyranny, and utopias*, Oxford UP, Delhi, p. 55.

Shah, I 1969, *Tales of the dervishes: teaching stories of the sufi masters over the past thousand years*, E.P. Dutton, New York, p. 89.

Skinner, Q 2000, *Visions of politics. Volume I: regarding method*, Cambridge UP, Cambridge.

Further reading

Nandy, A 1983, *Intimate enemy: loss and recovery of self under colonialism*, Oxford UP, Delhi.

Inayatullah, N & Blaney, D 2004, *International relations and the problem of difference*, Routledge, New York.

Inayatullah, N & Blaney, D 2012, 'Liberal fundamentals: invisible, invasive, artful, and bloody hands,' *Journal of International Relations and Development*, vol. 15, no. 2, pp. 290–315.

Levine, DP 1978, *Economic theory: the elementary relations of economic life*, Routledge & Kegan Paul, New York.

Todorov, T 1984, *The conquest of america*, Harper and Row, New York.

NORMS, POLITICAL ECONOMY AND SERENDIPITY

Thinking pragmatically about IPE

Christopher May

Before entering the academy, I worked for fifteen years in the private sector, including a period running my family's (very) small business. As a result, I had extensive experience of the ways in which diverse forms of evidence and analysis inform any practical decision. These experiences stayed with me as I pursued my PhD studies at Nottingham Trent University, worked for eight years at University of the West of England and then became a Professor at Lancaster University. My earlier work focused on the political economy of intellectual property rights (IPR), while my current project concentrates on the (not un-related) questions of how and why the rule of law seems to have become the 'common sense' of global politics. Despite the differences in these projects, my method has remained the same.

The most influential scholars and works on my method have been Susan Strange (1988), Paul Feyerabend's *Against Method* (1993) and Margaret Archer (1988, 1995). My first published article sought to establish a methodological link between Strange and Feyerabend as a grounding for critical political economy (see May 1996). In different ways, Strange and Feyerabend seem to adopt similar methodological norms. Feyerabend's position has its anchor in professional ethics; his concerns relate to acceptable practices of scientific analysis rather than to a strict concentration on one or another set of analytical grounds. As for Strange, the pluralism that often leads scholars to criticise her 'slackness of method' actually allows her work to remain open to diverse sources of insight. In my previous work on IPR and in my ongoing project, I always start my analysis with a consideration of the sets of norms that shape, justify and legitimate behaviour/actions in the global political economy. At the centre of my work is the attempt to analyse the character and content of dominant norms and then to examine how these norms are (re)produced. My approach starts from the assumption that norms importantly define and influence a system of power relations. Although I draw on Strange's (1988) notion of the four structures of power – security, finance, production and knowledge – that reinforce each other,

I have personally remained most interested in the knowledge structure. This is not to say that I view material capabilities as unimportant. Rather, having observed scholars' concentration on those forms of power, I have felt that the role of ideational power in the knowledge structure is under-discussed in global political economy.

My collaboration with Susan Sell on the history of IPR (May & Sell 2005) led me to develop a fruitful and informative interaction with Archer (see May & Sell 2005, Chapter Two; May 2010, Chapter One), who pushed me to think seriously about the ways in which norms play a role in the behaviour of social actors. My reading of Archer focuses on the desire of individuals to bring their practices and activities (their material existence) into line with their understanding of the world. More specifically, I consider how norms and ideational commitments shape individuals' depiction of the world and how change is achieved by the contradiction between norms and the world as people find it. With this in mind, I have argued that changes in regulations and political settlements in intellectual property are driven by the tension between the narratives of justification and the *actual* effects of making knowledge into property. Where robust norms can cause us to change our actions to match the way we understand the world, weaker norms – or perhaps 'stronger' social practices – can lead us to bend and re-shape the norms themselves so that they align with social actions. When norms and actions/practices are already aligned or, in Archer's phrasing, 'complementary', then both norms and actions are reinforced. That said, change is still possible in complementary norm/practice structures, as actors can redefine how practices are understood and can successfully criticise the meaning or value of norms. In such cases, change is brought about by the interaction of norms and practices, but that interaction is determined or affected by the role of individuals alongside structures. In my own work, I thus focus on how the norm of the rule of law is being inculcated in global elites and how such inculcation affects policy formation, especially in developing countries.

Over many years, my influences have allowed me to develop something akin to my own method, which informs what I do when researching. The tenets, if you will, of my method are as follows:

> *Cui Bono?* Susan Strange made this her key question for any analysis, and it remains my mobilising inquiry. My analysis always starts with the question of who is benefiting, and not only economically, from social, political or economic arrangements. Such a consideration proved especially useful in my work on IPR, as it revealed a gap between, on the one hand, the narratives of justification commonly promoted at the World Trade Organisation and elsewhere (through programmes of (re)production) and, on the other hand, the way in which IPR affects those who might want to utilise protected and commoditised knowledge.
>
> *Pluralism in sources, data and information.* I avoid privileging specific kinds of data over others and prefer a diverse diet of information as the basis for social science practice. Diverse sources may provide corroboration for my ideas or suggest gaps between norms and outcomes that subsequently become the

subject of my analysis. While one form of evidence may need to be privileged over others at certain stages in the analysis process, we should never privilege one form of evidence to the exclusion of all others. Indeed, it is useful to understand why different modes of evidence/analysis may lead to different conclusions about the case/issue/problem being explored. For instance, by focusing on formal elements of the rule of law (the existence of courts and clear laws), we may conclude that the rule of law clearly exists; however, if we focus on justice, equality or law's often posited substantive elements, we may conclude that regimes seemingly governed by law are not as close to our presuppositions about the normative value of the rule of law.

Good faith use of diverse sources. If we are to utilise diverse streams of information and diverse methods of analysis, we must do so in good faith. As analysts, we need to set out clearly how we establish criteria, evaluate information and weigh elements of analysis when developing an argument. Although it is unlikely that anyone can escape entirely from accusations of selective citation or distorting others' arguments, we need to try to retain the nuanced character of our analysis and the uneasy fit that may obtain between that analysis and evidence. Remembering Feyerabend's claim that 'anything goes', we should never decide on any method prior to considering a problem, nor should we forget that the recognition of the problem and its analysis are mutually constitutive.

Embracing serendipity. One of the advantages of methodological monism (or at least a clear privileging of one method) is that the choice of sources is largely pre-decided. However, pluralism also comes with advantages, as openness to diverse sources means that insight can be found anywhere. Like Strange, I take my luck as I find it in unearthing new and unforeseen sources. Although following up on unexpected 'leads' may result in nothing, doing so may illuminate a new realm of work that can then be brought into the purview of one's own analysis. The key is never to dismiss anything until you have had a look. The most personal example of serendipitous discovery I can provide relates to the time shortly after my father's death. From him, I inherited a large and varied library of books, among which was an extensive collection of volumes by Lewis Mumford. Something suggested to me that I should look at those volumes rather than sell them, and in doing so, I came across Mumford's analysis of the history of technology. Prior to reading that analysis, I had known Mumford only as an analyst of the city; yet after reading his work on technology, I used it as the analytical core of my second major monograph, *The Information Society: A Sceptical View* (May 2002).

Clarity of argument. Finally, there is an evident need to present analysis in a clear and accessible language. Specialised terminology may be required, not least because it may be the *lingua franca* of the field being analysed; however, we should take care to explain why we are using the terminology we are, and we should use specialised language sparingly. I am firmly convinced that complex analysis does not necessarily require complexity of presentation or a proliferation of neologisms.

In one sense, my approach suggests a bias toward coherence, as it is built on the notion that social agents will seek to bring normative and material elements into line. However, the sheer complexity of the world, which involves possible tensions between different normative/material alignments, makes arriving at overarching analytical coherence difficult, if not impossible. Within the global political economy, the routines and practices of individuals, organisations and institutions are the sites where normative settlements are almost unconsciously reproduced; as a result, looking beyond an overarching approach to the modern system of neo-liberalised capitalism requires us to recognise the vast divergences in practices and norms that inform our own and others' actions and beliefs. Although we should always strive for internal/technical coherence when developing our account of the global political economy, we should also accept that a coherent account, say, of capitalism will be too general and abstracted to account fully for actual social practice. Following Strange, I do not underestimate the use of abstract models for illuminating practice; yet I also recognise that the most fruitful analysis frequently arises when we explore the gaps between our models and actual practice.

Precisely for this reason, my work on intellectual property focused on the gap between well-established analytical claims about the benefits of adopting and deploying IPR and the observable effects of IPR across the global system. Meanwhile, my current work on the rule of law examines that norm's construction by specific agents rather than accepting it as an emergent political value. In particular, my focus on the role of norms, the manner in which they are (re)produced and their political impact leads me to conclude that the critique of normative settlements may have some impact on social practices and the norms themselves by potentially feeding into the processes of normative (re)production. For critical analysts, it is not uncommon to sense a divide between critical and problem-solving analyses. In sensing that divide, however, we should follow Robert Cox (1996) in choosing not to privilege one type of analysis over the other. To be more precise, we cannot exclude ourselves from the practices of understanding the world; indeed, the paradox of social *science* is that by examining and discussing our subject, we become part of the social development of the understanding of that subject. In my work, for instance, I have become part of the processes that I (following Archer) have placed at the centre of the analytical project of (my) IPE.

In sum, my work, based as it is on a critique of dominant norms, locates the transformative potential of analysis in its ability to effect normative change. With that belief in mind, the issue of clarity of communication becomes paramount. If we understand our task to be a transformative one, then we need to be able to communicate with those who are not ensconced in the academy but rather are out in the (sometimes brutal) world of neo-liberalised capitalist economic relations. Failing to attempt to communicate clearly to non-academics is, to my mind, a decision to forego the development of a transformative critical theory. While our analyses certainly need not be crude or simplified, they do need to be explained clearly and in 'real-world' English.

Works cited

Archer, M 1988, *Culture and agency: the place of culture in social theory*, Cambridge UP, Cambridge.
Archer, M 1995, *Realist social theory: the morphogenetic approach*, Cambridge UP, Cambridge.
Cox, RW (with Timothy J Sinclair) 1996, *Approaches to world order*, Cambridge UP, Cambridge.
Feyerabend, P 1993, *Against method*, 3rd rev. edn, Verso, London.
May, C 1996, 'Strange fruit: Susan Strange's theory of structural power in the international political economy', *Global Society*, vol. 10, no. 2 (spring), pp. 167–89.
May, C 2002, *The information society: a sceptical view*, Polity Press, Cambridge.
May, C 2010, *A global political economy of IPRs: the new enclosures*, 2nd rev. edn, Routledge, London.
May, C & Sell, S 2005, *Intellectual property rights: a critical history*, Lynne Rienner Publishers, Boulder, CO.
Strange, S 1988, *States and markets: an introduction to international political economy*, Pinter Publishers, London.

2
FORGING NEW PATHS IN THE CRITICAL SCHOOL

Johnna Montgomerie

Let us begin by openly acknowledging that academic knowledge production occurs in institutional contexts, specifically those that create and police the contemporary academic 'discipline' (Bourdieu 1988; Becher and Trowler 2001). Like all institutions, academic disciplines change over time. Only a few decades ago, Political Economy was an academic discipline in its own right, the advent of neoclassical economics led to the separation of the study of economics as a science from the study of politics, which was Americanised into political science. The institutional separation of politics and economics reflects how academics *themselves* defined their disciplines and what constituted their claims of expertise. Positioning this book as part of the *Review of International Political Economy* (RIPE) series thus gives it an academic home in Politics' or Political Science's already defined sub-discipline of International Relations. Seen through this lens, International Political Economy (IPE) is a sub-set of a sub-discipline, a sub-set located at the margins of a more important discipline. If we put the word 'critical' in front of 'international political economy', we are essentially referring to a sub-discipline of a sub-discipline, which suggests even further degrees of irrelevance.

This chapter, however, strives to recast the current disciplinary framing of critical political economy (CPE) as the product of well-rehearsed disagreements that ultimately lead down blind alleys. Mapping the limits of a discipline involves ritualistic efforts to identify, define and qualify key debates within a community of scholars; the result is often a tendency to agree in predictable ways and to disagree in highly structured ways. Here, we look at two of the well-rehearsed disagreements that define the boundaries of CPE as a discipline. In doing so, though, our purpose is not to intervene in the disagreements or offer answers to resolve them; rather, we wish to provide an alternative route to new intellectual frontiers.

By simply acknowledging the role of academic discipline formation in International Political Economy, we run the risk of believing there is nothing new about the professionals carving out or inventing areas of claimed expertise (Saks 1983; Seabrooke 2011). Accepting the reality of work-based professional practice as the driving force of knowledge creation, curation and, ultimately, justification allows us to conceptualise the role academics play in making knowledge claims – not in the underlying validity of the claims themselves – as an organising force (Clark 1987; Musselin 2008; Ricci 1987). Cultivating such a conceptualisation allows us to reflect on how an academic 'discipline' is created and enforced, not to mention how it is opposed and reinvented. Academic discipline formation is, after all, a social process, not an objective metaphysical given. This chapter is thus an invitation to look at critical political economy as both a form of inquiry and a method of research. It is, of course, difficult to try to reimagine CPE without conceiving of it as existing in a perpetual state of opposition. Indeed, such reimagining requires us to look beyond our current disciplinary horizons. Nevertheless, this kind of diversity is a strength in an academic environment that celebrates interdisciplinary research and cross-disciplinary collaboration; yet it is also weakness in an academic world where departments, journals, conferences and professional associations are all organised in terms of 'established disciplines'. CPE should avoid disciplinary silos while also recognising that it suffers from having no formal academic home.

On discipline formation

Let us take as our starting point the contemporary academic discipline, which can be seen as forms of professional practice that provide established frameworks by which people agree or engage in highly structured disagreements. Agreements within disciplines often relate to their key delineating factors. That is, what can, by general consensus, be placed under the umbrella of political economy within the study of Politics and International Relations. Whatever cannot be put under such an umbrella belongs to another discipline, such as sociology or geography. Within any discipline, there are recognisable theoretical camps and different methodological approaches that require critiques of both dominant theory and methods. Highly structured disagreements are well known to those within a discipline as the key 'debates'. Such debates, or well-rehearsed points of controversy, usually involve contesting boundaries about what is included or remains excluded from the disciplinary 'cannon' (Hyland 2004). In International Relations, the primary field of study is the State (Waltz 1959; Jessop 1990; van der Pijl 2007); therefore, the sub-discipline of International Political Economy is the study of States and Markets (Strange 1996; Lindblom 2001; Boyer and Drache 1996; Palan 2003). There are, of course, different well-established theoretical understandings of the state and its relationship to the market (Bonefeld and Holloway 1995; Castles 2007; Clarke and Newman 1997; Moran 2003; Poulantzas 1978) and different methods for making knowledge claims about that relationship (Cameron and Palan 2004; Fine and Lapavitsas 2000; Frieden and Lake 2005; Gilpin 2001). Delineating States and Markets as the disciplinary province of IPE creates a recognisable border between what *is* and, perhaps more important, what *is not* the subject matter of this sub-set of a sub-discipline.

Within its established boundaries, IPE frequently engages in two highly ritualised debates. The first of these debates involves delineating between mainstream and critical IPE, while the second involves determining what 'critical' IPE actually is. In the remainder of this chapter, I want to analyse these highly controlled and well-rehearsed debates as integral processes of discipline-making that succeed in enforcing hierarchies within professional networks without necessarily proving successful in creating new knowledge claims. One can find evidence of the centrality of these debates in the frequent publication of 'state of the art' special issues, edited volumes or handbooks related to IPE topics, issues and theories. As a student of IPE, one might believe in reading these debates that they reflect the field's most up-to-date innovations. Reading these debates as academic professionals, however, we understand the institutional context in which such knowledge is produced.

Acknowledging the actual process of knowledge creation – or the method by which a 'state of the art' survey is curated – is important. By regarding disciplinary debates as part of an academic network's professional practice, a practice through which individuals seek to establish the credibility of their expert claims among like-minded peers, we can effectively reframe the meaning of these debates. Recreating these highly structured disagreements involves a messy process of sorting ideas, theories and methods into a typology that ranks knowledge production hierarchically (Jarvis 2000) and necessitates assigning degrees of coherence that do not exist in practice. Such sorting, ranking and assigning only serve to create caricatural versions of difference that never stand up under scrutiny.

Mainstream versus critical International Political Economy

The first ritualised disagreement within International Political Economy involves the separation between 'mainstream' and 'critical' approaches to the discipline. At any given time, the location of the separation point between the two approaches depends almost entirely on perpetual debates within International Relations itself, debates that are then simply transposed into the study of the interplay between politics and economics at the international level. The origins of this well-rehearsed debate arguably begin with Kenneth Waltz's (1979) *Theory of International Politics*, which makes a clear case for International Relations as a positive science. Robert Cox's (1981) seminal critique, 'Social Forces, States and World Orders: Beyond International Relations Theory', challenges the dominant assumption that the study of world politics can adhere to the value-free observation of facts required of positivist social science. Arguing that '[t]heory is always for someone and for some purpose' and that '[a]ll theories have a perspective' (p. 128), Cox proceeds to call into question the very notion of the unitary state (capable of action) that underlay Waltz's desire to create laws and theories of international politics.

Over the next thirty years, this debate played out again and again, with 'mainstream' IR approaches privileging positive social science methodology and 'critical' IR approaches focusing on the normative dynamics of world order. Frieden and Lake (2005) provide a good summary of how International Political Economy is understood in terms of the dominant debates of the 1970s and 1980s. As they note, IPE placed and continues to place emphasis on the interplay of economics and politics in inter-state relations and enforces the demarcation between 'normative' and 'empirical' scholarship as alternative views. Frieden and Lake's discussion of the shape of IPE is largely framed by Robert Keohane's (1986) characterisation of the IR discipline as the study of inter-state power relations, a study that does not claim to be a value-free explanation of world politics; instead, IR has value as a theory because of its robust ability to explain state action in the pursuit of wealth and power and to do so under a variety of different conditions (p. 5). The process of discipline-making reinforces the distinction between rationalist approaches, which are most associated with positive social science, and reflectivist approaches. The distinction between these two approaches continues to hold sway, with 'critical' IPE acting as the opposition to mainstream positivist social science as it is applied to the study of inter-state politics.

B. J. Cohen (2008, 2009) offers the most recent iteration of the condition of the field by framing the division between critical and mainstream IPE in terms of a 'transatlantic divide'. In his account, the American School emphasises positivism and empiricism, while the British School concentrates on the 'Really Big Questions' of how the world operates and changes. Cohen takes a novel approach to well-known disagreements by offering an intellectual history of IPE that focuses on the ideas and careers of key thinkers whom he dubs 'the Magnificent Seven' (p. 8): Robert Cox, Robert Gilpin, Peter Katzenstein, Robert Keohane, Charles Kindleberger, Stephen Krasner and Susan Strange. Cohen is refreshingly honest when outlining how he came to choose these key thinkers. As he explains, he emailed his extensive network of sixty-seven IPE professionals to ask for their expert opinions and then made a judgement call based on his long career as a professor in the field (pp. 9–10). If nothing else, Cohen's selection process repeats in shorthand what we already know about disciplines: namely, that professional networks and rank are important elements of institutional hierarchies and go far in lending validity to academic expertise claims.

While there is little doubt that Cohen's intervention makes a meaningful contribution to our collective understanding of IPE as a contemporary discipline, subsequent debates have become mired down by latching on to the word 'Transatlantic' to signify the same old division between, on the one hand, positive, empirical and rationalist (American) IPE and, on the other hand, critical, normative and pluralist (British) IPE. As so often happens in the academy, the publication of Cohen's survey on the state of the field was followed by a flood of other similar publications. The *Review of International Political Economy* (2009 16:1), for instance, published a special issue entitled 'Not So Quiet on the Western Front: The American School of IPE', while *New Political Economy* (2009 14:3) put forth its own special issue entitled 'The "British School" of International Political Economy'. These were compiled in Phillips and Weaver's (2010) follow-up compilation, which, like the volumes before it, continued to characterise mainstream IPE as positivist and empirical and critical IPE as 'the opposite'.

Perhaps the most important thing the state of the art shows is how academics underwrite the validity of their claims to expertise by mobilising professional networks. My frustration in reading these debates is that they rarely yield new knowledge; instead they act as ritualised border patrols. While some scholars certainly view rehearsing familiar debates as a celebration of the discipline, others feel that doing so reinforces academic tribalism and forestalls intellectual development. For those in the latter camp, the first step in building a critical school should undoubtedly be an acknowledgement of the predictable outcome of continuously reinforcing existing disciplinary boundaries: namely, the foreclosure of innovation.

What is 'critical' International Political Economy?

This same process of discipline-making is internalised and reproduced in ritualistic debates identifying, defining and qualifying what it means to be 'critical' within IPE. One consequence of this focus on the meaning of 'critical' is that it leads to highly structured disagreement *between* critical approaches. The debate about various critical approaches plays out in different (but not dissimilar) professional networks of people, who meet at international conferences or department-sponsored workshops to exchange papers and collaborate in finding publication outlets. Yet one of the absurdities of this debate, not to mention the larger one behind it, is the very use of the term 'critical'. What expert's claim to expertise does not have its root in 'being critical'? Indeed, the idea of an academic describing his or her expert knowledge as deriving from 'an uncritical acceptance of the *status quo*' beggars belief.

While it is certain that academic critique is not the same as critical social inquiry (Callinicos 2006), it is worth emphasising how the adoption of labels within and across professional academic networks is a fraught process of brand management with no clear exit. Ultimately, attempts to define what is 'critical' serve the purpose of gatekeeping (both within and outside the discipline) more than they do the purpose of self-identification. More specifically, journals, articles and volumes that seek to define different theoretical camps – or what, in this volume, Nicola Smith calls different 'bodies of thought' – reproduce the hierarchy of framing knowledge claims. And behind each series of publications, of course, there is a set of related conference panels and email threads between collaborating scholars who are seeking to shape the boundaries of their discipline. Remembering Higgott and Watson (2007), we should recognise that divisions within IPE are too often conceptually problematic and theoretically overplayed. Ritual 'state of the discipline' debates as forms of discipline-making ensure that the vainglory of small differences will force 'critical' approaches into a perpetual state of opposition, regardless of whether those approaches are opposed to positivism (empiricism, orthodoxy) or other forms of critical research.

Although it would be impossible to give a full and faithful account of each iteration of the 'What is critical IPE?' debate (for example see: Jones 2001; Bruff and Tepe 2011; Worth 2011; Belfrage and Worth 2012), we can trace a clear line of descent from Robert Cox's (1981) early distinction between problem-solving and critical theory as a constructive framework to the most recent work by Shields et al. (2011), which frames critical IPE in terms of 'dis-sensus' and argues for a common ground on which diverse critical approaches can coexist without necessarily agreeing. On the branches of the Cox–Shields et al. genealogical tree, of course, various debates take place between different theoretical camps. Marxist critiques of International Political Economy abound (for just a few see: Burnham 2001; Drainville 1994; Cammack 2007; Dunn 2009), either deriding the whole endeavour or advocating the adoption of more theoretically rigorous concepts (Burnham 1994; Drainville 1994; Fischer and Tepe 2011; Worth 2012). Meanwhile, Gramscian alternatives (Gill 1993, 1995; Sassoon 1998; Bieler and Morton 2001; Morton 2003) reply with new ways of re-conceptualising class struggle in a global economy (Overbeek 2001; van der Pijl 2005; Cox and Sinclair 1995; Bieler and Morton 2001), a proposed re-conceptualisation that is accompanied by its own detailed critique (Burnham 1991; Germain and Kenny 1998; Ayers 2013). What comes from these debates is a pluralist understanding of 'critical' (van Apeldoorn, Bruff and Ryner 2010) that depends on contestation between those who call themselves 'critical'.

For many, 'critical' represents a normative commitment to expose exploitation and the power relations at the core of contemporary capitalism; for others, 'critical' is understood in terms of the ability to demonstrate an adherence to a particular theoretical framing of contemporary capitalism. What should be noted, however, is that even these seemingly benign understandings point to knowledge-producing hierarchies within the discipline. In other words, by cordoning off sections of the field that are legitimately 'critical', IPE academics repeat the epistemological gate-keeping they elsewhere decry.

Although it is undeniable that creating and defending a discipline (or a theory, for that matter) requires a degree of sectarianism and that academic sectarianism lends disciplines coherence and rigour, we should note that the prominence of sectarian concerns also forces us to lose a great deal. We need, for instance, only look to the continued exclusion of feminist, cultural and ecological approaches to political economy to see how disciplinary debates about and within critical IPE reproduces hierarchies that destroy the normative commitment of critical social inquiry – that is, the commitment to expose exploitative power relations in order to end them. Most efforts to define critical political economy still stubbornly ignore the gendered dimensions of exploitation in favour of class or state power relations (Griffin 2007; Waylen 2006). Rather than following the lead of Anthropology, Sociology, Geography and Cultural Studies (Jones, Nast, and Roberts 1997; Gibson-Graham 2006; Hesse-Biber 2011), IPE follows International Relations, Political Science and Economics in its persistent silence on gendered issues, even though there is ample empirical evidence of its existance (Bakker 2003; Bedford and Rai 2010; Griffin 2007; Peterson 2003). Simultaneously, key twentieth-century theoretical innovations that are widely accepted across the social sciences and humanities, including the cultural turn toward accepting the ecological limits of the global system, remain firmly on the margins of critical IPE debates. This is a significant failure, one that demonstrates how the established frameworks of IPE as an academic discipline impede its willingness to innovate or fulfil its normative commitment.

Can we find common 'critical' ground?

This is precisely why, I contend, focusing on established shared methods and methodologies provides a collaborative means of both engaging different theoretical camps within the critical school and reaching across formal disciplinary boundaries to advance our understanding of political economy. Forging a new path does not entail a rupture with the past; rather, the aim is to make a useful contribution to the critical school of political economy. A dedication to pluralism or 'dis-sensus' means we must openly acknowledge the significant theoretical differences between 'camps' within the school. Established distinctions between different critical theories are just that: established. Instead of continuing to engage in highly structured and ritualised disagreements, let us follow the example set by Best and Paterson (2014), who quote Zygmunt Bauman's (1987) metaphors of gardening in discussing disciplinary practices within IPE:

> [We considered] gatekeeping and gardening as modes of governing. Gatekeeping governing seeks to define who is to be included in and excluded from IPE as a field. A gardening metaphor is much more apt for what we were trying to do and how we might use the various ideas in what gets called IPE: as spades, trowels and rakes that enable us to carefully sow seeds, tend and nurture them, identify weeds and bugs that need to be removed, and reap the rich harvest, in a process of iterative, reflexive learning about the world.
>
> (p. 739)

Pursuing the collaborative 'garden' route offers potential new ways for developing a pluralist methodology that transforms theoretical differences into meaningful advancements in our collective field of study.

Curating our intellectual traditions

Accounts of the classical tradition of political economy generally begin with Adam Smith, David Ricardo, John Stuart Mill and Karl Marx. These figures are then shown to have influenced another generation, from Weber and Schumpeter to Veblen, Polanyi and Keynes. Classical political economy is our shared intellectual history that tries to understand the emergence of capitalism. Contemporary political economy draws from these rich political, economic, social and cultural/aesthetic accounts of the emergence of market civilisation; it then combines those accounts with clear methodologies and different methods for investigating social phenomena. We can see such a project in Kees van der Pijl's (2009) excellent open-access intellectual history of the pre-disciplinary boundaries of political economy. In each chapter van der Pijl adopts the classical works of political economy into an explicit methodological frame (ontology + epistemology) in order to explain how 'classical' political economy becomes 'global' political economy. Another approach of note is Matthew Watson's (2005a) detailed argument in support of using classical political economy methodology for studying economic relations as a potential 'foundation' of international political economy. Watson's subsequent journal articles demonstrate the analytical purchase of his methodological approach of adapting classical political economy to offer detailed empirical evaluation of contemporary financialised economy (Watson 2013b, 2005b, 2013a). In this connection, Colin Hay (2002) also merits attention for explicitly outlining a *via media* methodology for critical political economy that bridges Positivism and Interpretivism by drawing on the pre-disciplinary traditions of early political economy (for an excellent review see: Clarke 2009).

Framing the 'critical school' in terms of its rich pluralist antecedents helps us to develop a shared methodological orientation that can incorporate a heterodox set of methods for evaluating capitalism. Andrew Gamble (1995) echoes this sentiment when he writes that current articulation of political economy is 'interesting precisely because it is methodologically diverse, can make links between many disparate literatures and approaches … [and] offer[s] the best hope of emerging from some of the intellectual and policy straitjackets of the recent past' (p. 518). We must continue to develop a practical understanding of the pluralist methodology used within cultural political economy, a methodology that will allow culture to be analysed as aesthetics (Belfrage 2012), ethics (Brassett and Holmes 2010) or moral economy (Stanley, Deville and Montgomerie 2016). More broadly, we must emphasise that the context within which a society operates influences the functioning of its markets and other social processes. This is a lesson that the classical tradition taught us long ago in its refusal to separate culture from economics and politics (Belfrage and Hauf 2015).

At this point, we must confront the elephant in the room: the role of Marxism in the methods and methodologies of critical political economy. This is a difficult tight-rope to walk; by this, I mean to acknowledge that Marxism is its own discipline, its own field of study and its own theoretical tradition, and in many ways, that discipline does not engage with those portions of Marx's work that discuss 'political economy' (e.g., Marx's detailed empirical investigation, analysis and abstraction of modes of production). That said, most people within the critical school consider themselves Marxist, which means that Marxism plays a significant role in shaping any shared methodologies (Fine and SaadFilho 2010). A problem arises, however, when the Marxist fusion of theory and method (Harvey 2012) becomes a means of excluding other theoretical approaches that are considered either too Marxist or insufficiently Marxist (Burnham 1994; Cammack 2007). The present chapter, for instance, would fail to meet the epistemological test set by much Marxist critical political economy. Then again, the goal of the chapter is not to pass a test but rather to demonstrate how divisions within the critical school prohibit intellectual advancement. Suffice it to say that we recognise Marxism as a central pillar of the critical school (Milonakis and Fine 2009; Gruffydd-Jones 2012; Starosta 2015) and acknowledge the robustness of its methodology in providing conceptual and empirical tools for the analysis of unequal power relations (Harvey 2011), the organisation and constitution of the state (Jessop 1982), and the role consumption plays in shaping the material cultures of contemporary capitalism (Fine 2002).

We need only look to the important contribution Gramscian inspired political economy has made to contemporary political economy to understand the rich and varied influence of Marx and Marxism with the critical school. For instance, Robert Cox's (1993) 'essay on method' decisively outlined how to analyse the historical changes in ideas, institutions and material capabilities; these three concepts became the sites of inquiry that informed an entire generation of critical IPE scholars (Cox 2009). Most notable is Stephen Gill's (1993) use of this method to inform his rich empirical investigation into the Trilateral Commission; which, later developed into a powerful conceptual framing of disciplinary neoliberalism as discursive practice and new constitutionalism as an institutional process of creating new material capabilities (Gill 1995). Similarly, Kees van der Pijl's neo-Gramscian method for empirically investigating transnational class formation (1984) informed the wider Amsterdam Project in international political economy (Overbeek 2004).

Pushing our progressive innovations

However important our intellectual traditions are they cannot stand in the way of progress and innovation within the critical school. As noted previously, critical IPE often considers gender a less essential component of its studies. While critical political economy certainly shares the emancipatory agenda of feminism, it frequently does not use its heterodox and flexible set of methods to offer empirically rich and plausible accounts of gendered capitalism (for a more comprehensive account see: Waylen 2006; Peterson 2003). Nevertheless, feminist political economy has explicit methods and methodological framings for making visible and analysing the power relations of gender, race and class within contemporary capitalism. Anne Tickner (2005b, 2005a), for instance, calls out those who seek to impose positivist framings of gender; instead, she encourages methodological orientations that are useful for understanding the gendering of international politics. Therefore, gender, race and class are the linkages between everyday lived experiences and the constitution and exercise of political economic power at the state and global levels. Her work thus reconfigures what is considered a legitimate contribution within knowledge hierarchies (Weber 1994). More specifically, feminist methodology reframes the old positivist/interpretivist debate by embracing their heterodox, pluralist and interpretivist methods as innovations. In the words of Soreanu (2010), criticism needs to be seen 'as [playing] an active part, [as work] that does and is not only being done'.

This is precisely the objective of this book. We need to think about how we 'do' critical political economy in order to break free from our preoccupation with our difference from Economics, Political Science or International Relations. We also need to re-visit the idea of what it 'is' to be critical.

Political economy is a methodology capable of investigating hierarchies of power, not simply degrees of relationships between variables. Drawing on the interdisciplinary strength of feminist methods and methodologies (Harding 1987; Ackerly and True 2010; DeVault 1999; Naples 2013) brings new potential to critical social research (Ramazanoglu and Holland 2002; Reinharz 1992). More specifically, the study of CPE must integrate the seminal feminist critique of economics and political economy in order to *count* (Waring 1989), let alone *account* for, the unpaid reproductive labour in the 'home' that is a necessary condition for the paid productive labour in the 'market' (England and Folbre 1999; Himmelweit 2002). Before contemporary political economy struggled to address gender issues, classical political economy struggled to conceptualise sex and biological reproduction (Folbre 1992). In both cases, scholars were (or are) willing to accept the existence of unequal power relations but wary of adopting gendered methods for evaluating them. This is a serious problem that must be remedied. We need only look at Elson and Cagatay's (2000) 'The Social Content of Macroeconomic Policies' to glimpse the potential methodological advancement feminist political economy promises the wider critical school. Other conceptual and analytical work done on the 'care economy' (Folbre 2006; Donath 2000) and 'social reproduction' (Bakker 2007; Young 2003) makes a similar case for embracing the methodologies of feminist political economy (Fraser 2014). In sum, engaging with feminist methodology offers innovative new ways of analysing the unequal and often unseen power dynamics within contemporary capitalism (Bakker and Gill 2003; Elias and Rai 2015; Rai and Waylen 2013; Roberts 2012).

Cultivating our cultural roots

Best and Patterson's (2010) *Cultural Political Economy* is the most comprehensive articulation of the cultural economy research agenda within the discipline of International Political Economy. The collection of essays demonstrates how detailed analysis of the cultural constitution of economic practices offers an alternative analytical framing that denies any separation between culture and economy. In some of the later essays, Best and Paterson argue that paying attention to the role of culture in political economy allows a better understanding of multiple different empirical phenomena by resisting narrower forms of causal analysis; for that reason, they embrace a methodology that analyses the cultural constitution of economic practices (Best and Paterson 2014).

The growing literature on cultural political economy incorporates key methodological experiments in 'using social theory' (Pryke, Rose and Whatmore 2003). Foucauldian inspired IPE is an expansive body of literature that engages a plurality of sources using genealogy as method to make very clear interventions that advance theory and method. For example, in the realm of contemporary finance, we might mention de Goede's (2004, 2005) and Langley's (2002, 2008) accounts of the everyday life of finance. Also, the cultural economy of Brassett and Rethel's

(2015) critical analysis of gendered narratives of global finance. Alternatively, we can look to Blaney and Inayatullah's (2010) *Savage Economics*, the method (p. 5) of which relies on unpacking the complex lattice of power relations whereby culture constitutes the process of wealth accumulation.

Looking to the wider multi-disciplinary field of cultural economy, it offers a decidedly contemporary approach to understanding the decentred networks of human, non-human and technological interaction that constitute economic activities and relations (du Gay and Pryke 2002). As a research programme, cultural economy 'seeks to understand why and how market processes work within specific cultural contexts' (Chamlee-Wright 2010, p. 16). Culture provides context for our shared understanding of 'the global economy'; it is not a static object but a continuously evolving process that both shapes and is shaped by human action. Cultural economy, as a field, recognises the evolving nature of culture and investigates how culture constitutes the global economy in practice; in doing so, however, cultural economy does not do away with the thematics of political economy but rather inflects them differently. Indeed, the methodologies of political and cultural economy both reject a pre- (or non-) social concept of the economy and consider that discourses, ideas and culture are at least partially constitutive of economic social relations, processes and frames (Beer and Burrows 2013).

A clear methodological framing of cultural political economy is offered by the 'Lancaster school', which combines the classical political economy and moral economy of Andrew Sayer (1992, 2007, 2000, 2001) with Jessop and Sum's unique synthesis of neo-Gramscian regulation theory with a methodology for investigating discursive and material transformation (for further details, see Jessop and Oosterlynck 2008). In Sayer's work, emphasis is placed on the social and cultural embedding of capital accumulation within the Elites (Sayer 2015), which allows us to see how the unequal power relations within capital accumulation have powerful disembedding and disruptive effects (Sayer 2010). Meanwhile, the cultural political economy of Jessop and Sum (2010) uses semiosis 'to interpret and, in part, explain events, processes, tendencies, and emergent structures in the field of political economy'. As they explain, 'Semiosis involves the social production of inter-subjective meaning and, as such, is a foundational moment of all social practises and relations.' In consequence, they advocate a 'version of CPE [that] makes a methodological and, more importantly, ontological turn'. For Jessop and Sum, then, the study of political economy depends as much on an historical tradition of inquiry as it does on a pluralist methodology with considerable explanatory power. Indeed, they conclude that the critical school is self-consciously *post-disciplinary* in substance and forms of engagement precisely because it is inspired by the *pre-disciplinary* study of classical political economy (see also Sayer 2001).

When seen through the lens of critical methods and methodologies we can begin to perceive how to 'do' critical political economy; which can help us bridge the deep theoretical division that has so far impeded sustained collaboration across the critical school.

Conclusion

In order to build a methodological platform for collaboration across the critical school of political economy, there must be a wholesale integration of feminist and cultural economy methodologies into the widely accepted *pre-disciplinary* tradition of political economy, which includes Marxism. Such a step is necessary if we wish to stop the policing of CPE as an academic discipline along the binary lines of mainstream/critical, interpretvist/positivist social science, and heterodox/orthodox economics. While such binary caricatures continue to exist, a meaningful discussion of methods is prevented. We cannot deny ourselves closer consideration of our methods simply because they have become guilty by association with empiricism, positivism and orthodox economics. Unlike other social science disciplines – Sociology, Anthropology, Politics, Geography, to name few – which are defined by the object of their collective study – society, humanity, politics – Economics defines itself as a commitment to methodological individualism in the search for causal relationships that can explain social phenomena. As a result, much of Economics is not about 'the economy' at all but rather about offering mathematical proof of the causal relationships that exist between units of analysis. Placing critical political economy in permanent opposition to positivism fails to acknowledge the diversity and richness of our field of inquiry and forecloses the possibility that we will be methodologically innovative. This cuts us off from quantitative methods as a useful way of engaging different types of evidence to understand the unfolding of global capitalism. We can no longer leave methods firmly in the domain of Economics or positivism. After all, political economy is about disrupting, challenging and, in some cases, uprooting established orthodoxy.

Bibliography

Ackerly, Brooke, and Jacqui True. 2010. *Doing Feminist Research in Political and Social Science*. Basingstoke: Palgrave Macmillan.

Ayers, Alison J., ed. 2013. *Gramsci, Political Economy, and International Relations Theory: Modern Princes and Naked Emperors*. Basingstoke: Palgrave Macmillan.

Bakker, Isabella. 2003. 'Neoliberal Governance and the Reprivatization of Social Reproduction'. In *Power, Production, and Social Reproduction*, edited by Isabella Bakker and Stephen Gill, 66–82. New York: Palgrave Macmillan.

Bakker, Isabella. 2007. 'Social Reproduction and the Constitution of a Gendered Political Economy'. *New Political Economy* 12 (4): 541–56.

Bakker, Isabella, and Stephen Gill, eds. 2003. *Power, Production and Social Reproduction: Human In/security in the Global Political Economy*. Basingstoke: Palgrave Macmillan.

Becher, Tony, and Paul Trowler. 2001. *Academic Tribes And Territories: Intellectual Enquiry and the Culture of Disciplines*. McGraw-Hill Education (UK).

Bedford, Kate, and Shirin M. Rai. 2010. 'Feminists Theorize International Political Economy'. *Signs* 36 (1): 1–18. doi:10.1086/652910.

Beer, David, and Roger Burrows. 2013. 'Popular Culture, Digital Archives and the New Social Life of Data'. *Theory, Culture & Society* 30 (4): 47–71. doi:10.1177/0263276413476542.

Belfrage, Claes. 2012. 'For a Critical Engagement with Aesthetics in IPE: Revitalizing Economic Imagination in Times of Crisis'. *International Politics* 49 (2): 154–76.

Belfrage, Claes, and Felix Hauf. 2015. 'Operationalizing Cultural Political Economy: Towards Critical Grounded Theory'. *Journal of Organizational Ethnography* 4 (3): 324–40. doi:10.1108/JOE-01-2015-0002.

Belfrage, Claes, and Owen Worth. 2012. 'Critical International Political Economy: Renewing Critique and Ontologies'. *International Politics* 49 (2): 131–35. doi:10.1057/ip.2011.39.

Best, Jacqueline, and Matthew Paterson. 2010. *Cultural Political Economy*. London: Routledge.

Best, Jacqueline, and Matthew Paterson. 2014. 'Towards a Cultural Political Economy – Not a Cultural IPE'. *Millennium – Journal of International Studies* 43 (2): 738–40. doi:10.1177/0305829814557063.

Bieler, A., and A. D. Morton. 2001. 'The Gordian Knot of Agency-Structure in International Relations: A Neo-Gramscian Perspective'. *European Journal of International Relations* 7 (1): 5–35.

Blaney, David L., and Naeem Inayatullah. 2010. *Savage Economics: Wealth, Poverty and the Temporal Walls of Capitalism*. London: Routledge.

Bonefeld, W. Holloway, J., eds, 1995. *Global Capital, National State and the Politics of Money*. London: St. Martin's Press.

Bourdieu, Pierre. 1988. *Homo Academicus*. Translated by Peter Collier. Stanford, CT: Stanford University Press.

Boyer, R., and D. Drache. 1996. *States against Markets: The Limits of Globalization*. Hove: Psychology Press.

Brassett, James, and Christopher Holmes. 2010. 'International Political Economy and the Question of Ethics'. *Review of International Political Economy* 17 (3): 425–53. doi:10.1080/09692290903507201.

Brassett, James, and Lena Rethel. 2015. 'Sexy Money: The Hetero-Normative Politics of Global Finance'. *Review of International Studies* 41 (3): 429–49.

Bruff, Ian, and Daniela Tepe. 2011. 'What Is Critical IPE?' *Journal of International Relations and Development* 14 (3): 354–58. doi:10.1057/jird.2011.7.

Burnham, Peter. 1991. 'Neo-Gramscian Hegemony and the International Order'. *Capital & Class* 15 (3): 73–92. doi:10.1177/030981689104500105.

Burnham, Peter. 1994. 'Open Marxism and Vulgar International Political Economy'. *Review of International Political Economy* 1 (2): 221–31. doi:10.1080/09692299408434277.

Burnham, Peter. 2001. 'Marx, International Political Economy and Globalisation'. *Capital & Class* 25 (3): 103–12. doi:10.1177/030981680107500109.

Callinicos, Alex. 2006. *The Resources of Critique*. Cambridge: Polity.

Cameron, A., and R. Palan. 2004. *The Imagined Economies of Globalization*. London: Sage.

Cammack, Paul. 2007. 'RIP IPE'. SSRN Scholarly Paper ID 1526759. Rochester, NY: Social Science Research Network. http://papers.ssrn.com/abstract=1526759.

Castles, G. 2007. *The Disappearing State?: Retrenchment Realities in an Age of Globalisation*. Cheltenham: Edward Elgar Publishing.

Chamlee-Wright, Emily. 2010. *The Cultural and Political Economy of Recovery: Social Learning in a Post-Disaster Environment*. London: Routledge.

Clark, Burton R. 1987. *The Academic Profession: National, Disciplinary, and Institutional Settings*. Berkeley: University of California Press.

Clarke, Chris. 2009. 'Paths between Positivism and Interpretivism: An Appraisal of Hay's Via Media'. *Politics* 29 (1): 28–36. doi:10.1111/j.1467-9256.2008.01335.x.

Clarke, John, and Janet Newman. 1997. *The Managerial State: Power, Politics and Ideology in the Remaking of Social Welfare*. London: Sage.

Cohen, Benjamin J. 2008. *International Political Economy: An Intellectual History*. Princeton, NJ: Princeton University Press.
Cohen, Benjamin J. 2009. 'Striking a Nerve'. *Review of International Political Economy* 16 (1): 136–43. doi:10.1080/09692290802524166.
Cox, Robert W. 1981. 'Social Forces, States and World Orders: Beyond International Relations Theory'. *Millennium Journal of International Studies* 10: 127–55.
Cox, R. W. 1993. 'Gramsci, Hegemony and International Relations: An Essay in Method'. In *Gramsci, Historical Materialism and International Relations*, edited by Stephen Gill, 49–66. Cambridge: Cambridge University Press.
Cox, Robert. 2009. 'The "British School" in the Global Context'. *New Political Economy* 14 (3): 315–28. doi:10.1080/13563460903087441.
Cox, Robert W., and Timothy Sinclair. 1995. *Approaches to World Order. Cambridge Studies in International Relations*. Cambridge: Cambridge University Press.
De Goede, Marieke. 2004. 'Repoliticizing Financial Risk'. *Economy and Society* 33 (2): 197–217.
De Goede, Marieke. 2005. *Virtue, Fortune, and Faith: A Genealogy of Finance*. Minneapolis: University of Minnesota Press.
DeVault, Marjorie L. 1999. *Liberating Method: Feminism and Social Research*. Philadelphia, PA: Temple University Press.
Donath, Susan. 2000. 'The Other Economy: A Suggestion for a Distinctively Feminist Economics'. *Feminist Economics* 6 (1): 115–23. doi:10.1080/135457000337723.
Drainville, André C. 1994. 'International Political Economy in the Age of Open Marxism'. *Review of International Political Economy* 1 (1): 105–32. doi:10.1080/09692299408434270.
Du Gay, Paul, and Michael Pryke. 2002. *Cultural Economy: Cultural Analysis and Commercial Life*. London: Sage.
Dunn, Bill. 2009. *Global Political Economy: A Marxist Critique*. London: Pluto Press.
Elias, Juanita, and Shirin Rai. 2015. 'The Everyday Gendered Political Economy of Violence.'. *Politics & Gender* 11 (2): 424–29. doi:10.1017/S1743923X15000148.
Elson, Diane, and Nilufer Cagatay. 2000. 'The Social Content of Macroeconomic Policies'. *World Development* 28 (7): 1347–64.
England, Paula, and Nancy Folbre. 1999. 'The Cost of Caring'. *The Annals of the American Academy of Political and Social Science* 561: 39–51.
Fine, Ben. 2002. *The World of Consumption: The Material and Cultural Revisited*. Hove: Psychology Press.
Fine, Ben, and Costas Lapavitsas. 2000. 'Markets and Money in Social Theory: What Role for Economics?' *Economy and Society* 29 (3): 357–82.
Fine, Ben, and A. SaadFilho. 2010. *Marx's "Capital"*. 5th edn. London: Pluto Press.
Fischer, Anita, and Daniela Tepe. 2011. '"What's 'Critical' about Critical Theory": Capturing the Social Totality (das Gesellschaftliche Ganze)'. *Journal of International Relations and Development* 14 (3): 366–75. doi:10.1057/jird.2011.12.
Folbre, Nancy. 1992. '"The Improper Arts": Sex in Classical Political Economy'. *Population and Development Review* 18 (1): 105–21. doi:10.2307/1971861.
Folbre, Nancy. 2006. 'Measuring Care: Gender, Empowerment, and the Care Economy'. *Journal of Human Development* 7 (2): 183–99. doi:10.1080/14649880600768512.
Fraser, Nancy. 2014. 'Can Society Be Commodities All the Way Down? Post-Polanyian Reflections on Capitalist Crisis'. *Economy and Society* 43 (4): 541–58. doi:10.1080/03085147.2014.898822.
Frieden, Jeffry A., and David A. Lake. 2005. *International Political Economy: Perspectives on Global Power and Wealth*. London: Routledge.

Gamble, Andrew. 1995. 'The New Political Economy'. *Political Studies* 43 (3): 516–30. doi:10.1111/j.1467-9248.1995.tb00320.x.

Germain, Randall D., and Michael Kenny. 1998. 'Engaging Gramsci: International Relations Theory and the New Gramscians'. *Review of International Studies* 24 (1): 3–21.

Gibson-Graham, J. K. 2006. *The End of Capitalism (as We Knew It): A Feminist Critique of Political Economy; with a New Introduction*. Minneapolis: University of Minnesota Press.

Gill, Stephen. 1993. *American Hegemony and the Trilateral Commission*. Cambridge: Cambridge University Press.

Gill, Stephen. 1995. 'Globalization, Market Civilization, and Disciplinary Neoliberalism'. *Millennium Journal of International Studies* 2 (4): 399–423.

Gilpin, R. 2001. *Global Political Economy: Undestanding the International Economic Order*. Princeton, NJ: Princeton University Press.

Griffin, Penny. 2007. 'Refashioning IPE: What and How Gender Analysis Teaches International (Global) Political Economy'. *Review of International Political Economy* 14 (4): 719–36.

Gruffydd-Jones, Branwen. 2012. 'Method of Political Economy'. In *The Elgar Companion to Marxist Economics*, edited by B. Fine, A. Saad Filho, and M. Boffo, 220–26. Cheltenham: Edward Elgar Publishing.

Harding, Sandra G. 1987. *Feminism and Methodology: Social Science Issues*. Bloomington: Indiana University Press.

Harvey, David. 2011. *The Enigma of Capital: And the Crises of Capitalism*. Reprint edn. Oxford: Oxford University Press.

Harvey, David. 2012. 'History Versus Theory: A Commentary on Marx's Method in Capital'. *Historical Materialism* 20 (2): 3–38.

Hay, Colin. 2002. *Political Analysis: A Critical Introduction*. Basingstoke: Palgrave Macmillan.

Hesse-Biber, Sharlene Nagy. 2011. *Handbook of Feminist Research: Theory and Praxis*. London: Sage.

Higgott, Richard, and Matthew Watson. 2007. 'All at Sea in a Barbed Wire Canoe: Professor Cohen's Transatlantic Voyage in IPE'. *Review of International Political Economy* 15 (1): 1–17. doi:10.1080/09692290701751241.

Himmelweit, Susan. 2002. 'Making Visible the Hidden Economy: The Case for Gender-Impact Analysis of Economic Policy'. *Feminist Economics* 8 (1): 49–70. doi:10.1080/13545700110104864.

Hyland, Ken. 2004. *Disciplinary Discourses*. Michigan Classics edn: Social Interactions in Academic Writing. Minneapolis: University of Michigan Press.

Jarvis, D. S. L. 2000. *International Relations and the Challenge of Postmodernism: Defending the Discipline*. Columbia: University of South Carolina Press.

Jessop, Bob. 1982. *The Capitalist State: Marxist Theories and Methods*. Oxford: Wiley-Blackwell.

Jessop, Bob. 1990. *State Theory: Putting the Capitalist State in its Place*. Cambridge: Polity Press.

Jessop, Bob, and Stijn Oosterlynck. 2008. 'Cultural Political Economy: On Making the Cultural Turn without Falling into Soft Economic Sociology'. *Geoforum* 39 (3): 1155–69. doi:10.1016/j.geoforum.2006.12.008.

Jessop, Bob, and Ngai-Ling Sum. 2010. 'Cultural Political Economy: Logics of Discovery, Epistemic Fallacies, the Complexity of Emergence, and the Potential of the Cultural Turn'. *New Political Economy* 15 (3): 445–51. doi:10.1080/13563461003802051.

Jones, John Paul, Heidi J. Nast, and Susan M. Roberts. 1997. *Thresholds in Feminist Geography: Difference, Methodology, Representation*. Lanham, MD: Rowman & Littlefield.

Keohane, Robert O., ed., 1986. *Neorealism and its Critics*. New York: Columbia University Press.

Langley, Paul. 2002. *World Financial Orders: An Historical International Political Economy*. London: Routledge.
Langley, Paul. 2008. *The Everyday Life of Global Finance: Saving and Borrowing in Anglo-America*. Oxford: Oxford University Press.
Lindblom, Charles E. 2001. *Politics and Markets: The World's Political Economic System*. New York: Harper Collins.
Milonakis, Dimitris, and Ben Fine. 2009. *From Political Economy to Economics: Method, the Social and the Historical in the Evolution of Economic Theory*. London: Routledge.
Moran, M. 2003. *The British Regulatory State: High Modernism and Hyper-Innovation*. Oxford: Oxford University Press.
Musselin, Christine. 2008. 'Towards a Sociology Of Academic Work'. In *From Governance to Identity*, edited by Alberto Amaral, Ivar Bleiklie and Christine Musselin, 47–56. Higher Education Dynamics 24. Dordrecht: Springer.
Naples, Nancy A. 2013. *Feminism and Method: Ethnography, Discourse Analysis, and Activist Research*. London: Routledge.
Overbeek, Henk. 2001. 'Transnational Historical Materialism: Theories of Transnational Class Formation and World Order'. In *Global Political Economy: Contemporary Theories*, edited by Ronen Palan, 168–83. London: Routledge.
Overbeek, Henk. 2004. 'Transnational Class Formation and Concepts of Control: Towards a Genealogy of the Amsterdam Project in International Political Economy'. *Journal of International Relations and Development* 7 (2): 113–41. doi:10.1057/palgrave.jird.1800011.
Palan, R. 2003. *The Offshore World: Sovereign Markets, Virtual Places, And Nomad Millionaires*. Ithaca, NY: Cornell University Press.
Peterson, V. Spike. 2003. *A Critical Rewriting of Global Political Economy: Integrating Reproductive, Productive, and Virtual Economies*. Hove: Psychology Press.
Phillips, Nicola, and Catherine Weaver. 2010. *International Political Economy: Debating the Past, Present and Future*. London: Routledge.
Poulantzas, N. 1978. *State, Power, Socialism*. London: NLB.
Pryke, Michael, Gillian Rose and Sarah Whatmore. 2003. *Using Social Theory: Thinking Through Research*. London: Sage.
Rai, Shirin M., and Georgina Waylen. 2013. *New Frontiers in Feminist Political Economy*. London: Routledge.
Ramazanoglu, Caroline, and Janet Holland. 2002. *Feminist Methodology: Challenges and Choices*. London: Sage.
Reinharz, Shulamit. 1992. *Feminist Methods in Social Research*. Oxford: Oxford University Press.
Ricci, David M. 1987. *The Tragedy of Political Science: Politics, Scholarship, and Democracy*. New Haven, CT: Yale University Press.
Roberts, Adrienne. 2012. 'Financing Social Reproduction: The Gendered Relations of Debt and Mortgage Finance in Twenty-First-Century America'. *New Political Economy* 18 (1): 21–42. doi:10.1080/13563467.2012.662951.
Saks, Mike. 1983. 'Removing the Blinkers? A Critique of Recent Contributions to the Sociology of Professions'. *The Sociological Review* 31 (1): 3–21. doi:10.1111/j.1467-954X.1983.tb00677.x.
Sassoon, Ann S. 1998. 'Family, Civil Society, State: Is Gramsci's Concept of Societa Civile Still Relevant?' *Philosophical Forum* 29 (3–4): 206–17.
Sayer, Andrew. 1992. *Method in Social Science: A Realist Approach*. Hove: Psychology Press.
Sayer, Andrew. 2000. 'Moral Economy and Political Economy'. *Studies in Political Economy* 61: 79–104.

Sayer, Andrew. 2001. 'For a Critical Cultural Political Economy'. *Antipode* 33 (4): 687–708. doi:10.1111/1467–8330.00206.
Sayer, Andrew. 2007. 'Moral Economy as Critique'. *New Political Economy* 12 (2): 261–70.
Sayer, Andrew. 2010. 'Class and Morality'. In *Handbook of the Sociology of Morality*, edited by Steven Hitlin and Stephen Vaisey. Handbooks of Sociology and Social Research. New York: Springer New York.
Sayer, Andrew. 2015. *Why We Can't Afford the Rich*. Bristol: Policy Press.
Seabrooke, Leonard. 2011. 'Economists and Diplomacy: Professions and the Practice of Economic Policy'. *International Journal* 66 (3): 629–42.
Shields, Stuart, Ian Bruff, and Huw Macartney. 2011. *Critical International Political Economy: Dialogue, Debate and Dissensus*. Basingstoke: Palgrave Macmillan.
Soreanu, Raluca. 2010. 'Feminist Creativities and the Disciplinary Imaginary of International Relations'. *International Political Sociology* 4 (4): 380–400. doi:10.1111/j.1749-5687.2010.00112.x.
Stanley, Liam, Joe Deville, and Johnna Montgomerie. Forthcoming. 'Digital Debt Management: The Everyday Life of Austerity'. *New Formations*.
Starosta, Guido. 2015. *Marx's Capital, Method and Revolutionary Subjectivity*. Leiden: Brill.
Strange, Susan. 1996. *The Retreat of the State: The Diffusion of Power in the World Economy*. Cambridge: Cambridge Univesity Press.
Tickner, J. Ann. 2005a. 'What is Your Research Program? Some Feminist Answers to International Relations Methodological Questions'. *International Studies Quarterly* 49 (1): 1–22. doi:10.1111/j.0020-8833.2005.00332.x.
Tickner, J. Ann. 2005b. 'Gendering a Discipline: Some Feminist Methodological Contributions to International Relations'. *Signs* 30 (4): 2173–88. doi:10.1086/428416.
Van Apeldoorn, Bastiaan, Ian Bruff, and Magnus Ryner. 2010. 'The Richness and Diversity of Critical IPE Perspectives: Moving beyond the Debate on the "British School"'. In *International Political Economy: Debating the Past, Present and Future*, edited by Nicola Phillips and Catherine Weaver, 215–22. London: Routledge.
Van der Pijl, Kees. 1984. *The Making of an Atlantic Ruling Class*. London: Verso.
Van der Pijl, Kees. 2005. 'A Theory of Global Capitalism: Production, Class and State in a Transnational World'. *New Political Economy* 10 (2): 273.
Van der Pijl, Kees. 2007. *Nomads, Empires, States: Modes of Foreign Relations and Political Economy*. London: Pluto Press.
Van der Pijl, Kees. 2009. 'A Survey of Global Political Economy'. Scribd. www.scribd.com/doc/63641502/A-Survey-of-Global-Political-Economy-Kees-Van-Der-Pijl.
Waltz, Kenneth N. 1959. *Man, the State and War: A Theoretical Analysis*. New York: Columbia University Press.
Waltz, Kenneth N. 1979. *Theory of International Politics*. Long Grove, IL: Waveland Press.
Waring, Marilyn. 1989. *If Women Counted: A New Feminist Economics*. London: Macmillan.
Watson, Matthew. 2005a. *Foundations of International Political Economy*. Basingstoke: Palgrave Macmillan.
Watson, Matthew. 2005b. 'What Makes a Market Economy? Schumpeter, Smith and Walras on the Coordination Problem'. *New Political Economy* 10 (2): 143–61.
Watson, Matthew. 2013a. 'Competing Models of Socially Constructed Economic Man: Differentiating Defoe's Crusoe from the Robinson of Neoclassical Economics'. *New Political Economy* 16 (5): 609–26. doi:10.1080/13563467.2011.536209.
Watson, Matthew. 2013b. 'The Eighteenth-Century Historiographic Tradition and Contemporary "Everyday IPE"'. *Review of International Studies* 39 (1): 1–23.

Waylen, Georgina. 2006. 'You still Don't Understand: Why Troubled Engagements Continue between Feminists and (Critical) IPE'. *Review of International Studies* 32 (1): 145–64. doi:10.1017/S0260210506006966.

Weber, Cynthia. 1994. 'Good Girls, Little Girls, and Bad Girls: Male Paranoia in Robert Keohane's Critique of Feminist International Relations'. *Millennium – Journal of International Studies* 23 (2): 337–49. doi:10.1177/03058298940230021401.

Worth, Owen. 2011. 'Where Did the Critical Go?' *Journal of International Relations and Development* 14 (3): 358–65. doi:10.1057/jird.2011.8.

Worth, Owen. 2012. 'Accumulating the Critical Spirit: Rosa Luxemburg and Critical IPE'. *International Politics* 49 (2): 136–53. doi:10.1057/ip.2011.44.

Wyn Jones, Richard. 2001. *Critical Theory and World Politics*. Boulder, CO: Lynne Rienner Publishers.

Young, B. 2003. 'Financial Crises and Social Reproduction: Asia, Argentina and Brazil'. In *Power, Production and Social Reproduction*, edited by Isabella Bakker and Stephen Gill, 103–23. New York: Palgrave Macmillan.

REDEMPTIVE POLITICAL ECONOMY

Robbie Shilliam

My long-term research project is to rethink the relationship between the market and (un)freedom. Spanning the study of classical political economy and histories of Atlantic slavery, my work undertakes a hermeneutical retrieval of the enslaved and their various descendents' traditions of thought and action. Rather than a set of tools that I put to work to produce knowledge, my methodology is a sensibility through which I cultivate knowledge. I would describe it as a *redemptive political economy*. There are two broad aspects to my project, which might be useful to sketch out before turning to my methodology itself.

The first aspect is a rethinking of classical political economy in light of its engagement with, but disavowal of, Atlantic slavery as contemporaneous with the rise of capitalism in Europe. Crucially, the classical relationship proposed between property, labour and freedom – a relationship in regard to which liberal, Marxist and Foucauldian approaches typically situate themselves – must be reconceived when the alienation of labour power (capitalism) is considered alongside what Aimé Césaire (2000, p. 42) called the 'thingification' of labouring persons (African enslavement). While the alienation of labour power is performed upon and through a person who retains his/her personhood in the eyes of the law (especially under natural law), thingification is a radical alienation of both labour power and personhood itself. In this respect, plantation slavery in the Americas, not industrial factories in Europe, epitomise the fundamental relationship between capital and (un)freedom. Adam Smith and many other philosophers of the age grappled with this problem; indeed, many classical political economists were also abolitionists. Yet specific engagements with capital and (un)freedom as they pertain to enslavement have been marginalised in subsequent interpretations of this tradition (Shilliam 2012a).

The second aspect of my project is to redeem cosmological understandings of the relationship between the market and (un)freedom, understandings that have been cultivated by enslaved Africans and their formally free descendents. These understandings resonate with key themes of classical political economy but not through a social-scientifically disenchanted hermeneutic of profane needs and necessities. I therefore describe these understandings as cosmological because their broaching of needs and necessities are incorporated within understandings of time, space and relation that do not segregate the profane and sublime (Shilliam 2013a). To be more precise, these traditions, unlike political economy, strive to cut a liberatory path through impossibly oppressive terrains, and in doing so, they rely on the use of cognitive tools that go beyond material cause and effect (see Shilliam 2012b). For example, the enslaved who won their freedom in the Haitian Revolution knew themselves to be driven by the spiritual agencies of their African family and ancestors (Hutton 2007). If they had not known that, they would not have flung themselves on the French plantations, planters and soldiers. To fight and live was to liberate oneself in the Americas, but to fight and die was to liberate oneself by returning to Guinea, the land of the living that existed under the sea. Un-modern cosmologies are effective. Yet in most approaches to political economy, they are disdained as pre-modern, un-reflexive, reactionary or opiate. For just this reason, my project aims to retrieve the radical intent of 'subaltern studies' – that is, to decolonise privileged epistemes – before it morphed into a post-structurally inclined obsession with the master grammar of colonial archives (Shilliam 2013b).

I did not choose my methodology; in both intellectual and personal terms, it chose me. I came to university as a mature student who had left school early. In the intervening period, I had been an amateur academic who mainly bought books from charity shops, and what I read tended to reflect my immediate environment and the peoples, issues and ideas that populated it. Black Power, Rastafari, message-by-music, social justice and unemployment were some of the key notes that resonated in this space. More specifically, I sensed that the underlying thematic of my environment was influenced by the living legacies of African slavery in present-day western culture and economy. During my undergraduate years, I was introduced primarily to critical theory – especially Marx and the capital relation – and to methods related to historical sociology, methods that mainly, but not entirely, focused on European narratives.

Although the University of Sussex was an excellent institution where I could hone my critical faculties in political economy, I always hoped that, at some point, the issues and concerns of my lived environment would be able to join step with my university studies. I was lucky to have pursued my undergraduate degree in the now-defunct school of African and Asian Studies (AFRAS); the legacies of liberation struggles could still be felt on the reading lists of that school. Within political economy courses, however, I saw fewer openings for the issues and concerns that I had brought with me, even though Gramsci and Trotsky tried their best to provide some space (Shilliam 2004). When I finally began writing my DPhil on nineteenth-century German philosophies of history (Shilliam 2009), I also decided to return to research and writing on Marcus Garvey (Shilliam 2006) and to study further the hermeneutics of Black Power and Rastafari. After I finished my PhD in 2005, I left its content and method almost entirely behind. Since then, I have concentrated on redeeming the experience of African enslavement, which depended on creative survival within and resistance to the plantation system, a system that, like reservations, lays bare the relationship between the market and (un)freedom.

As I suggested at the beginning of this piece, a redemptive political economy cultivates knowledge instead of producing it. Looking at the Latin roots of 'produce' and 'cultivate', we could say that to produce knowledge is to lengthen, prolong or extend, whereas to cultivate knowledge is to till and turn matter around so that it folds back on itself to encourage growth. In this respect, and prompted by a conversation with Naeem Inayatullah, I consider knowledge production to be less a creative endeavour than a process of accumulation (knowledge for knowledge's sake), a process that either consistently defers politics or places them further down the road as the culmination or consequence of extended intellectual activity. In contrast, a redemptive political economy requires the scholar to turn over and oxygenate living and retrievable pasts as a means of cultivating liberatory knowledge for present-day practices (Nandy 1983). Yet cultivation also implies habitation, which means that knowledge is creatively released as scholars enfold themselves in the matter of their inquiry (see Brodber 1990). Within such a process, politics are not deferred but rather sprout up at every stage of knowledge cultivation.

The methodology I am sketching here is one in which the scholar, guided by a redemptive ethics, creatively re-inhabits the matter of inquiry. The medieval Christian church colonised the notion of redemption and, settling it with concerns about original sin, made the redemptive act a super-human one. When I use the word 'redemption', I retrieve its older pre-Christian meaning, which places emphasis on gaining back – or being released from – a situation for a price, a price that need not be pecuniary. Though associated with the struggle against slavery, this older meaning is grounded in an ethics of reparative social justice and is practised by people across the world (Bogues 2003, p. 16). (For the Māori of Aotearoa, New Zealand, the practice of redemption/return is termed *utu*, which has been mischievously translated by settler populations into emotive 'revenge'. In addition, during the struggle against Apartheid, the Zulu term *mayibuye* gained provenance: 'Let it [the humanity that preceded Apartheid] return.') What should be stressed is that oppressors, as much as the oppressed, are open for redemption. Where the oppressed seek with great difficulty to redeem themselves (or gain something back) from what has been detrimental, oppressors can seek to redeem (or release) themselves from their privilege. Because each of us might conceivably be viewed as both oppressed and oppressor, we all need to attend to various combinations of these redemptive acts (Nandy 2007). This is especially the case when we inhabit the privileged sphere of academia and pursue a redemptive ethics therein (see West 1993).

I should now make it clear that the personal story I related above was not meant to be an auto-biography. Methodologically, that story constitutes part of my cultivation of knowledge about the relationship between the market and (un)freedom, as well as about the seminal place that enslaved Africans and their various descendents occupy in that relationship. Personally implicated in this particular past and present,

I pursue two redemptions that constantly enfold me – turn me over – in the inquiry that I have no choice but to inhabit.

My first pursuit is to redeem slavery – that is, to affirm that enslaved peoples were never slaves but actively fought their legal and economic dehumanisation on a variety of planes with resources that were collectively handed down from pre-slavery arrangements (Stuckey 1968; Warner-Lewis 2003). With these resources, enslaved peoples and their diverse descendents have cultivated an ethos of liberation that clarifies the relationship between the market and (un)freedom far more acutely and insightfully than classical political economists have done, especially those economists who posit alienation – rather than thingification – as the hallmark of that relationship (see James 1993). My second pursuit is to redeem – release – myself from the oppressive tendencies of social scientific interpretation. What I refer to here is the nebulous notion of 'academic standards', the protection of which usually requires the maintenance of a cognitive distance between, on the one hand, the scholar and his/her collection of 'scientific' knowledge and, on the other hand, the 'object' of inquiry and his/her 'everyday'/'lay' knowledge. Those who police this distance justify their activities through a modernist valorisation of social scientific knowledge as more translatable and more extendable than lay knowledge. The attendant ideology of such distancing relies on the notion that where social scientists produce generalisable theories, lay scientists merely provide data (Shilliam 2011a). When this system of knowledge apartheid is applied to the study of slavery, only white abolitionists are considered to possess an ethos and moral philosophy worthy of redemption (Shilliam 2013c).

As an example of my redemptive pursuits, I will finish by discussing my engagement with Engels's ethnography of the English working class. Usually associated with the discipline of anthropology, ethnography demands that the scholar enter into the lifeworlds of a people in order to understand *their* understanding of their own experience. Ethnography is a method that in many ways led to the birth of critical political economy. Before beginning his lifelong collaboration with Marx, Engels sojourned with the English working class in Manchester in order to understand their conditions and, perhaps, potential for self-transformation. Yet long before Engels, ethnography, in the classical Greek sense, was already used to construct and encode distance, whether geographical or social, between home and abroad and between foreign peoples and native inhabitants (Buxton 1999). The restructuring of European academies to support colonial rule capitalised on this production of distance rather than on a cultivation of relation (see Shilliam 2011b). As a colonial tool, ethnographic field work does not encourage or sanction a *cultivation* of the relationship between a scholar and his/her interlocutors; rather, it requires that scholars *produce* knowledge about those interlocutors.

The limitations of ethnography having been noted, I would nevertheless argue that ethnography necessarily enfolds the scholar within his/her matter of inquiry. For a long time, anthropology could function only by the express disavowal of such necessary intimacy (Clifford 1986). The son of a Prussian manufacturer, Engels himself was forced to rethink his bourgeois pretensions to liberal freedom as pure hypocrisy in the wake of his sojourns with the Manchester working class. Recognising that bourgeois freedom was attained at the price of working class unfreedom, Engels had to redeem himself as a bourgeois businessman and scholar. It was that redemption, I would submit, that inspired Marx to clarify his key contribution to political economy: namely, his masterful hermeneutic movement from the familiar realm of exchange, equality and civil society to that other-worldly and grotesque realm of production, domination and exploitation (Marx 1990, p. 280). In this movement, we see bourgeois political economists, including Marx and Engels, enfolding themselves in their matter of inquiry. Indeed, the subtitle of the first volume of *Capital*, which reads 'A Critique of Political Economy', confirms just these reparative ethics.

And yet we should also note that Engels invests the proletariat not with an agency derived from his sociological appreciation of their condition but rather with the borrowed (and radical) agency of the African slave (Shilliam 2014). This borrowing, which might better be considered a robbery, is achieved by way of an analogical device that Engels learned from the Chartists and 'Tory Radicals'. More specifically, Engels labelled the working class 'Sklave', a term by which he meant to suggest that that class was enslaved to the capitalist class, entirely immiserated and thus possessing nothing to lose and everything to gain by their resistance. Through Engel's (1971) suggestive sketch of the 'Communist Credos', the radical agency of the 'Sklave' is appropriated to fuel the world-historical mission of the proletariat (or 'Knecht') in the *Communist Manifesto*. The enslaved are subsequently ejected from the key dynamic of world history, their place taken by European factory workers. Responding to my work, many colleagues have told me or intimated to me that the relationship of race to class is first and foremost an analytical issue. But I have to say, I take it to be an ethical issue first and foremost, one which addresses a politics of exclusion; and it is this politics that must be analysed. How dare Engels rob enslaved Africans of their ethos of liberation! This is a racist act – let us state it clearly. Was there really nothing to learn about (un)freedom from those who had not just been alienated but, more so, thingified by the market ... and yet were fighting back?

When is it that knowledge cultivation petrifies and turns into knowledge production? Why is it that knowledge production for and on behalf of some can undermine knowledge cultivation by others? My redemptive political economy strives to testify to these breaches as a means of repairing them. My aim is to take the tradition of political economy, till it, turn it over some more and oxygenate it with the liberation ethos of enslaved Africans and their various descendents.

Works cited

Bogues, A 2003, *Black heretics, black prophets: radical political intellectuals*, Routledge, New York.

Brodber, E 1990, 'Fiction in the Scientific Procedure', in S Cudjoe (ed.), *Caribbean women writers: essays from the first international conference*, Calalous Publications, Amherst, pp. 164–68.

Buxton, RGA 1999, 'Monsters in Greek ethnography and society in the fifth and fourth centuries BCE', in RGA Buxton (ed.), *From myth to reason? studies in the development of greek thought*, Clarendon Press, Oxford, pp. 197–214.

Césaire, A 2000, *Discourse on colonialism*, Monthly Review Press, London.

Clifford, J 1986, *Writing culture: the poetics and politics of ethnography*. University of California Press, Berkeley.

Engels, F 1971, 'The Communist Credos', in DJ Struik (ed.), *Birth of the Communist Manifesto*, International Publishers, New York, pp. 162–87.

Engels, F 1987, *The condition of the working class in England*, Penguin, London.

Hutton, C 2007, *The logic and historic significance of the Haitian Revolution and the cosmological roots of Haitian freedom*, Arawak, Kingston.

James, CLR 1993, *American civilization*, Blackwell, Cambridge, MA.

Marx, K 1990, *Capital: a critique of political economy, vol. 1*, Penguin, Harmondsworth.

Nandy, A 1983, *The intimate enemy: loss and recovery of self under colonialism*, Oxford UP, Delhi.

Nandy, A 2007, 'Traditions, tyranny, and utopias: essays in the politics of awareness', in *A very popular exile*, Oxford UP, Delhi.

Shilliam, R 2004, 'Hegemony and the problematic of primitive accumulation', *Millennium*, vol. 33, no. 1, pp. 59–88.

Shilliam, R 2006, 'What about Marcus Garvey? Race and the transformation of sovereignty debate', *Review of International Studies*, vol. 32, no. 3, pp. 379–400.

Shilliam, R 2009, *German thought and international relations: the rise and fall of a liberal project*, Palgrave Macmillan, New York.

Shilliam, R 2011a, '"Open the Gates Mek We Repatriate": Caribbean slavery, constructivism and hermeneutic tensions', in *ISA Asia Pacific Regional Conference*, Brisbane, *Conference Proceedings from the International Studies Association*.

Shilliam, R 2011b, 'Decolonising the grounds of ethical inquiry: a dialogue between Kant, Foucault and Glissant', *Millennium*, vol. 39, no. 3, pp. 649–65.

Shilliam, R 2012a, 'Forget English freedom, remember Atlantic slavery: common law, commercial law and the significance of slavery for classical political economy', *New Political Economy*, vol. 17, no. 5, pp. 591–609.

Shilliam, R 2012b, 'Civilization and the poetics of slavery', *Thesis Eleven*, vol. 108, no. 1 (1 February), pp. 99–117.

Shilliam, R 2013a, 'The spirit of exchange', in S Seth (ed.), *Postcolonial theory and international relations*, Routledge, London, pp. 166–82.

Shilliam, R 2013b, 'Redemption from development: Amartya Sen, Rastafari and promises of freedom', *Postcolonial Studies*, vol. 15, no. 3, pp. 331–50.

Shilliam, R 2013c, 'Black redemption, not (white) abolition', in DL Blaney & A Tickner (eds), *Claiming the international*, Routledge, London, pp. 141–58.

Shilliam, R 2014, 'Decolonizing the *Manifesto*: communism and the slave analogy', in T. Carver & J. Farr (eds), *The Cambridge companion to the Communist Manifesto*, Cambridge UP, Cambridge, chapter 11.

Stuckey, S 1968, 'Through the prism of folkore: the black ethos in slavery', *The Massachusetts Review*, vol. 9, no. 3, pp. 417–37.

Warner-Lewis, M 2003, *Central Africa in the Caribbean: transcending time, transforming cultures*, University of West Indies Press, Kingston.

West, C 1993, 'The dilemma of the black intellectual', *The Journal of Blacks in Higher Education*, vol. 2, pp. 59–67.

Further readings

Blaney, D & Inayatullah, N 2010, *Savage economics: wealth, poverty and the temporal salls of capitalism*, Routledge, London.

Brodber, E 2003, *The continent of black consciousness: on the history of the African diaspora from slavery to the present day*, New Beacon Books, London.

Robinson, C 1983, *Black Marxism: the making of the black radical tradition*, Zed Books, London.

INVESTIGATING THOSE YOU LOVE

Labor and global governance

Dimitris Stevis

Throughout most of my professional life, I have been researching the governance of the world political economy, with particular attention to its democratization through labor and environmental regulation. To this day, the International Labour Organization (ILO) remains one of the world's few tripartite organizations, and a number of scholars see it as the model for a World Environmental Organization (WEO). Environmental governance, which, in contrast to labor governance, is decentralized, followed the formation of the ILO by decades, but its decentralized character has in large part led to the debate about a WEO. With increasing force, private governance has joined and often overshadowed public governance in recent decades. For some, this is evidence of an ontological shift in the global political economy; yet for critical political economists, this development has to be placed in relation to the dramatic shift toward hyper-liberal capitalism. To overemphasize the proliferation of governance schemes is to obscure that shift in social power. In order to capture both the architecture and the social purpose of governance, I have employed history and typology. My hope has been that history would allow me to trace governance, while typology would facilitate synchronic and diachronic comparisons.

A number of influences have shaped my thinking on what purpose these methodological tools should serve. As a graduate student in international politics, I was exposed to the literatures on dependency, trans-national politics, world order studies, hegemony and world systems. A graduate seminar on Marx and Weber persuaded me of the usefulness of typologies, provided they were not ahistorical reifications. During the late 1970s and early 1980s, a study group that brought together faculty and graduate students across the social sciences exposed me to a wide range of classical social theorists and to contemporary debates on social history, the state, power, hegemony, class and social organization. Since the late 1980s, I have read extensively about environmental politics and policy and have been motivated in this endeavor by a move to a department that specializes in these areas. During the early 1990s, another interdisciplinary study group allowed me to revisit some of the earlier thinkers and ideas I had encountered and encouraged me to explore agency and structure, post-structuralism and post-modernity, and democratic theory with a particular eye toward social democracy and radical democracy. Finally, I was influenced in a variety of ways by working for my partner in her long-term trans-disciplinary project on the contact period and the subsequent centuries in the Andes. The impacts of my experiences are too many to summarize here. For the purposes of this note, however, let me say that those experiences have allowed me to appreciate the generative powers of global divisions of labor and the contradictory ways in which such powers are manifested.

As a result of the aforementioned influences, I approached the study of political economy, in general, and governance, in particular, with a clear understanding that historical and typological methods needed to be sensitive to three parameters. First, the study of a particular governance arrangement had to capture, or at least be attuned to, the empirical spatial and diachronic boundaries of that arrangement. Historical materialists and historical structuralists have long highlighted the generative impacts of global and trans-national divisions of labor, as well as the trans-national and inter-temporal political relations that emerge from labor dynamics (Bukharin 1967; Cox 1987). Bertell Ollman's (1976) discussion of internal relations, though not about global and trans-national divisions of labor, has very much influenced me and has led me to treat divisions of labor as instances of internal relations.

Historical materialists and historical structuralists – among whom I include some of the prominent dependency theorists – do recognize that particular countries, regions and positions within the world political economy share common characteristics at particular points in time, characteristics that are shaped by historical divisions of labor. Because such divisions are historical, however, the more reflexive scholars in those fields do not reify them but instead remain alert to the possibility that divisions of labor change and that hegemonic and counter-hegemonic alliances cut across countries or regions.

Not only organizing people between social categories, such as countries, workers and nature, divisions of labor and governance arrangements also organize individuals within and across social categories (Harrod 1987). National systems of industrial relations do not simply arrange labor unions in relation to capital; they also arrange particular groups of workers in relation to each other. Manufacturing unions, for instance, dominated national and trans-national industrial relations during the last century, just as naturalists dominated environmental politics.

For me, understanding global governance and the prospects of its democratization entails two steps. First, it involves identifying the characteristics of governance at the levels of divisions of labor, geopolitical spaces and social categories. Second, and more important, it involves figuring out how these are mutually constituted and nested. In order to accomplish these goals, I have used a series of typologies, all of which are based on 'voice' and 'choice.' The form and content of these typologies were shaped by others' work on radical democracy and social democracy

(Esping-Andersen 1990; Young 1990; Bachrach & Aryeh 1992). Essentially, I have borrowed from others to make sense of what interests me.

'Voice' refers to both the range of stakeholders who can participate in governance and the ways in which they can do so. It is possible to have a broad range of stakeholders for the purpose of informing or consulting with them, but it is equally possible to have fewer stakeholders who can actually negotiate binding policies. Voice becomes more democratic when it includes more affected stakeholders, including the weak, and allows for the possibility of binding policy-making.

There is good reason to believe that governance is democratized when previously excluded stakeholders are brought in to the governing process. As noted above, however, no social category is monolithic. Bringing in labor unions, environmentalists or women's organizations compels us to consider who is recognized and why. What is the price of their recognition? What 'choices' must they abandon in order to be invited? Governance arrangements vary depending on what is on the agenda. Some arrangements allow discussion of a broad range of relevant issues among stakeholders while others permit narrower discussions.

Potential combinations of voice and choice are numerous. It is possible to have broader participation that can result in binding policies, albeit on less consequential matters. Indeed, precisely because broad participation tends to result in a focus on less consequential issues, radical movements and parties have historically contested parliamentary participation. It is also possible that everything can be on the table on the condition that no binding policy emerges. Markets allow broad voice (everybody who has money can buy) but limited choice in the sense that the consumer does not decide on what products will be produced and how. In contrast (and perhaps counterintuitively), authoritarian regimes have been known to adopt far-reaching reforms based on a combination of narrow participation and a broad range of options. Here, we need only think of Bismarck in Germany, Vargas in Brazil and Perón in Argentina.

One can create a simple 2×2 table based on voice and choice, and I have done so in the past (Stevis 2002). However, I think it is better to treat these dimensions as ordinal rather than nominal variables and to adjust them to the particular arrangement that is investigated. One can also treat emerging categorizations as dummy variables. To be clear, I do not think that only case studies are appropriate for this typology. One could look at union membership, for instance, to trace the standing of women workers across time, sector and country. In my own work, I have drawn on three sets of data: historical information, interviews and observation. As regards historical information, I have gathered it from two kinds of sources: publications that cover longer swaths of time and publications that emerged during particular periods. While I have been able to draw extensively from English, French and Spanish sources, I have been limited because I do not know German. My work on both labor and the environment has thus been handicapped to a certain extent.

Interviews have been another source of information. Over the last fifteen years, I have talked to many people, some of whom were involved in global labor politics. As a result of an ongoing project on global framework agreements, I have increasingly talked to labor people at the national and local levels, mainly in the USA. The information I have gathered from them is complemented by information from corporate management and government employees. I have also attended various meetings involving unions over the years. From a methodological point of view, however, what I do with the information I gather from interviews and observation is just as important as the identity of my interviewees and the content of my observations. How can I recognize the limitations imposed upon management by internal and external factors while also recognizing that management has more power than workers and unions? And how can I recognize that unions are often the cause of their own problems while remaining empathetic towards their fight for organizational existence and members' security? The typology I have adopted has forced me to reflect on the problem of both gathering and using information, but I doubt that I can avoid the methodological biases built into my modes of data collection and analysis.

What are the possible uses of my typological efforts and the emerging categories I identify (Kluge 2000; Elman 2005; Moses 2011)? I have to admit up front that I use typologies and the categories they reveal in order to remind myself that what I see before me is not necessarily all there is. While I view global framework agreements as an important step towards trans-national industrial relations, for instance, I also recognize the wisdom of remembering that not all unions along a company's production network are involved in negotiations about and implementations of those agreements and that many workers in a given network are not represented by unions (Stevis 2010).

The typologies I employ are also useful for classification. Since 1995, I have taught international law by organizing my discussions and lectures in terms of agents, subjects, objects and phantoms, all of which are specific categories that I have derived from the dimensions of voice and choice. Within international law, states and state agencies, IGOs, some churches and, increasingly, corporations have agency in that they can participate in making trans-national policy. While some states are weak by any standard, it is worth noting that even weak states can provide passports and nationality, which have well-known off-shoring implications. Increasingly, individuals are gaining subjecthood through trans-national courts; they are also gaining the ability in some countries' national courts to contest human rights violations anywhere in the world. Children and animals are protected in national and trans-national law but do not have a recognized voice in advancing their own rights. Meanwhile, phantoms, a category that includes trafficked persons and temporary workers, are entities in a social and legal grey area.

A similar set of categories has helped me in analyzing the internal governance of labor (Stevis & Boswell 2006). Although some workers and their unions are recognized and can participate in collective agreements, others who cannot negotiate such agreements can use provisions similar to human rights (e.g., prohibition of forced employment, wages, occupational health and safety) to protect themselves and improve their lives. For much of history, certain categories of workers, including slaves and women, were considered objects. This continues to be the case with underage workers and, one could argue, with workers employed under specific employment visas. Finally, some workers, including certain contract laborers and undocumented immigrants, are covered by none of the provisions listed above; these individuals can be considered indentured workers.

The typologies I use also serve explanatory purposes. The combinations of voice and choice allow for a closer understanding of the processes of decision-making and the nature of policy outputs, as distinguished from policy outcomes. The proliferation of experiments in governance offers many opportunities to examine those experiments' outcomes in depth. To my mind, such examinations are necessary, provided that one's starting point is an understanding of the architecture and social purpose of the deliberation process. While policy outcomes are often unintentional and shift path dependencies in unanticipated ways, it unlikely that any outcome can come from any output. An example of this has been the North American Commission for Labor Cooperation, an organization that was crafted to fail (Stevis & Boswell 2001). What we should keep in mind is that much of politics is about who makes policy, when they make it, how they make it and, I would add, why they make it.

To close, I continue to ponder whether the analytical dimensions on which I concentrate (i.e., participation and choice/options) are adequate and whether the categories I derive adequately reflect those dimensions. That said, I believe both the dimensions I examine and the categories I establish have helped me to avoid agent–subject or subject–object dichotomies without leading me to create an impossible list of categories. In addition, those dimensions and categories remind me that while hegemonic power relations involve subalterns contributing to their own oppression, power relations – and the governance arrangements they engender – do have directionality. Finally, my work with typologies has enabled me to explore specific instances of governance, such as global framework agreements, with a fuller understanding of their limitations and promise.

Works cited

Bachrach, P & Aryeh, B 1992, *Power and empowerment: a radical theory of participatory democracy*, Temple UP, Philadelphia.

Bukharin, N 1967, *Imperialism and world economy*, H. Fertig, New York.

Cox, RW 1987, *Production, power, and world order: social forces in the making of history*, Columbia UP, New York.

Elman, C 2005, 'Explanatory typologies in qualitative studies of international politics,' *International Organization*, vol. 59, no. 2, pp. 293–326.

Esping-Andersen, GS 1990, *The three worlds of welfare capitalism*, Princeton UP, Princeton, NJ.

Harrod, J 1987, *Power, production, and the unprotected worker*, Columbia UP, New York.

Kluge, S 2000, 'Empirically grounded construction of types and typologies in qualitative research,' *Forum Qualitative Sozialforschung/ Forum: Qualitative Social Research*, vol. 1, no. 1, art. 14.

Moses, J 2011, 'Epistemological and methodological foundations,' in *International Encyclopedia of Political Science*, Sage Publications, London.

Ollman, B 1976, *Alienation: Marx's conception of man in capitalist society*, Cambridge UP, New York.

Stevis, D 2002, 'Agents, subjects, objects, or phantoms? Labor, the environment, and liberal institutionalization,' *The Annals of the American Academy of Political and Social Science*, vol. 581, no. 1, pp. 91–105.

Stevis, D 2010, 'International framework agreements and global social dialogue: parameters and prospects,' Employment working paper, no. 47, International Labour Office, Geneva.

Stevis, D & Boswell, T 2001, 'Labor policy and politics in international integration: comparing NAFTA and the European Union,' in B Dobratz, L Waldner & T Buzzell (eds.), *The politics of social inequality*, JAI Press, Greenwich, CT, pp. 329–58.

Stevis, D & Boswell, T 2006, 'Globalising social justice all the way down? Agents, subjects, objects and phantoms in international labor politics,' in M Davis & M Ryner (eds.), *Poverty and the production of world politics: unprotected workers in the global political economy*, Palgrave, London, pp. 204–22.

Young, IM 1990, *Justice and the politics of difference*, Princeton UP, Princeton, NJ.

DISCOURSE, NATURE AND CRITICAL POLITICAL ECONOMY

American environmentalists debate immigration

John Hultgren

One of the booths at the 2006 Rocky Sustainable Living Fair was a clear outlier. While the majority of organizations in attendance handed out information on topics like community-supported agriculture, composting and environmental education, a group called Northern Coloradoans for Immigration Reduction (NCIR) was making the argument that immigration harmed the natural environment of the United States.

This was the first time that I had encountered debates over the environmental impacts of immigration. The presence of NCIR provoked a great deal of controversy among attendees, many of whom viewed environmental protection as an inherently progressive, cosmopolitan concern. It turned out that while several of the organization's members were environmentalists who were active with the Sierra Club and Audubon Society, others had darker ties to nativist and white nationalist organizations. After much consternation, the group was not invited back to subsequent fairs on the grounds that they 'were not acting in a respectful manner' (Park 2007). The debate, however, has continued on local editorial pages and public forums.

This local argument over the environmental impacts of immigration led me to take an interest in how individuals and organizations conceptualize nature and deploy it in attempts to reconfigure political institutions and concepts, such as sovereignty, the nation and the state. As I started exploring the immigration/environment debates further, I soon discovered that all the participants involved, whether environmental restrictionists or their opponents, recognize that 'nature' is in crisis; at the same time, I found little agreement on what, exactly, 'nature' is. In fact, even among the restrictionists themselves, there was widespread variability in the definition of 'nature.'

When I started looking into this matter, I was just beginning my doctoral studies in environmental politics. The case seemed to provide a fascinating lens into the social construction of nature and the concept's relation to changing ideals of sovereignty, political community, political economy and governance. The question I found myself asking was, 'How can I best study the complex ways that conceptions of nature intersect with knowledges, norms and institutions to produce social exclusion?' I ultimately decided to pursue *discourse analysis*.

Immigration and nature: a discursive intervention

As I began reading works emphasizing the social construction of nature (see Cronon 1996; Kosek 2006), I came to the conclusion that although non-human entities retain an autonomy and a materiality apart from human projects, human understandings of nature are intimately bound up in *discourse*, which Hajer (1995, p. 44) defines as the 'ensemble of ideas, concepts and categories through which meaning is given to social and physical phenomena and which is produced and reproduced through an identifiable set of practices.' Discursive constructions of nature vary widely: nature can be 'romanticized and aestheticized or villainized and deemed threatening; it can be rationalized and instrumentalized or sacralized and worshiped; it can represent an enclosed space of equilibrium or a wild space of untamed and overlapping flows' (Hultgren 2015, p. 7). In short, nature means different things to different people and is deployed to achieve a wide range of political ends.

Discourse analysis seeks to analyze the practices of representation through which various objects (e.g., 'the environment,' 'the immigrant,' 'America') are invested with meaning (Milliken 2001). Central to discourse analysis is a concern about how a particular 'regime of truth' makes it possible for certain individuals or groups to speak as authoritative agents on a particular issue, while relegating others to the status of mere objects who must be spoken of or for (Hultgren 2015, p. 7). For example, certain discourses construct nature through romantic epistemological practices that produce an ideal of wilderness closely entwined with cultural ideals of race and nationhood. Historically, such discourses have marginalized indigenous and minority populations or constructed them as 'savage' threats to the nation and its natural environment.

With regard to debates over the environmental impacts of immigration, discourse analysis allowed me to examine critically the ontological and epistemological assumptions that were embedded in previous efforts to grapple with the so-called 'immigration problem.' As I began looking into these debates, it became clear that positivist modes of analysis were dominant and that restrictionists and opponents alike were asking themselves, 'What are the impacts of immigrants on the environment of the United States?' In this framing, the debate about the environmental impacts of immigration is effectively reduced to an 'empirical' question about whether or not immigration causes environmental degradation in a particular, bounded territorial area (Squalli 2010; Price & Feldmeyer 2012).

Relying on discourse analysis enabled me to recognize that there are normative assumptions embedded in such regimes of truth. For example, positivist discourse on the environment insists that the health of nature can be measured through national-level proxies (e.g., American carbon-dioxide emissions). Such a discourse effectively transforms socially constructed borders into natural facts while *a priori* eliminating any eco-systemic or trans-national forms of analysis. Implicit here is a claim that the nation-state is the appropriate lens through which environmental impacts can be examined and understood. And while those employing this form of discourse highlight the impact that the trans-national movement of bodies has on environmental health, they also cleanse the analytical terrain of the trans-national political economic logics, processes and institutions that push forward migration and, in many cases, environmental degradation (Hultgren 2015, p. 24). With all this in mind, I ultimately came to the conclusion that those who are concerned about the exclusionary social implications of environmental restrictionism but who continue to employ positivist analyses, effectively allow their opponents to set the terms of the debate on the relationship between immigration and the environment.

Surprisingly enough, however, I also found myself at odds with the mode of analysis adopted by several opponents of environmental restrictionism. Although opponents attempt to denaturalize borders and call attention to the power of global capitalism, they continue to adopt an uncritical perspective with regard to nature. In their discourse, nature is an inherently global and cosmopolitan concern that should not be examined through the lens of the nation-state (Potok 2010; Ross 2010). Relying on this logic, opponents contend that anyone supporting environmental restrictionism is not a 'real' environmentalist but rather a xenophobe who is *appropriating nature* to advance alternative social goals. For example, Frank Sharry (as cited in Ludden 2008) of *America's Voice*, an organization that supports immigrants' rights, has argued that restrictionists are not genuine eco-centrists; instead, they are 'nativists in three-piece suits who are smart enough to figure out how to present a face that looks like they're progressive-minded.' While I sympathize with this sentiment, it underestimates the heterogeneity of American restrictionism and fails to consider how actual commitments to nature factor into the restrictionist movement. A characterization such as Sharry's unintentionally disables responses to environmental restrictionism's most sophisticated iterations, which are also the iterations most likely to persuade greens.

In attempting to ameliorate these deficiencies, I analyzed the discourses of environmental restrictionists using two primary forms of data collection: documents and interviews. First, I explored various restrictionist representations of nature, political community and governance on websites and in publications and media appearances. Second, I conducted interviews with individuals who had publicly voiced restrictionist positions. Applying discourse analysis to these 'texts' enabled me to unpack how links between certain representations of nature (Malthusian, Darwinian, Romantic, etc.) and particular populations ('Mexicans,' 'globalists,' etc.) or institutions ('the state,' 'the border,' etc.) figure into attempts to advance or reinforce normative visions of political community.

The promises and perils of discourse analysis

My application of discourse analysis to American debates over the environmental impacts of immigration has produced two key insights that other modes of analysis have missed. First, I have been able to specify how conceptions of nature deployed by restrictionists are imbricated in commitments to cultural ideals of nationalism, race and sovereignty. I have identified three discourses of environmental restrictionism – social nativism, eco-nativism and eco-communitarianism – each of which renders nature intelligible through different epistemological practices and in accordance with different strategies. These findings suggest that environmental restrictionism is more heterogeneous than previously thought; they also underscore the various ways in which proponents of restrictionism can strategically mold their arguments to attract adherents across the American political spectrum.

Second, I have uncovered a discursive shift that extant progressive critiques of environmental restrictionism have not recognized. In material geared toward public consumption, American restrictionists have strategically moved to a discourse of eco-communitarianism, a more nuanced narrative that resonates in important ways with the epistemological commitments of mainstream greens. Those commitments include a critique of neoliberalism, an emphasis on attachments to America's 'wild places' and an advocacy of global environmental stewardship. The eco-communitarian discourse, however, continues to assert that in a period of ecological crisis, 'our' normal political and ethical obligations to immigrants ought to be suspended in order to protect 'America's nature.' Such a discourse is most likely to influence liberal environmentalists, and it is against that discourse that progressive opponents ought to aim their critiques.

Like all methods, however, discourse analysis has its limitations. First, approaches emphasizing the social construction of nature often fail to take the materiality of the non-human realm seriously. Recent works in post-humanism have grappled with this problem by attempting to let non-humans communicate on their own terms (see, for instance, Haraway 2008). Nature may not be able to 'speak,' but as post-humanists suggest, eco-centrists may be able to cultivate a more generous ethos of engagement by listening more intently and differently. My future work will attempt to address the limitations of discourse analysis by focusing on the material realities of human and non-human migrants.

A second limitation of discourse analysis is its tendency to understate historical path-dependencies and institutional sedimentations. This limitation usually becomes clear in scholars' attempt to highlight the contingent discursive constructions upon which apparently immovable structures and institutions depend. In this vein, discourse analysis alone cannot explain the coercive force that the state wields against migrant bodies or the chains of production that connect migrant workers to American consumers, but it is still valuable in providing insight into the systems of meaning that these institutions depend on for their constant reproduction. American authorities, for example, have recently turned to environmental restrictionist logics in their attempts to justify the expansion of the US–Mexico border wall; according to their most frequently voiced arguments, the wall will prevent border crossings and the pollution of the natural environment that accompanies them (Sullivan 2007). In the face of such arguments, challenging discourses of environmental restrictionism is a necessary, though by no means sufficient, step towards destabilizing these institutional structures.

Conclusion

In a political environment dominated by neoliberalism, it is easy to see the appeal of nature. Indeed, my desire to protect nature led me to graduate school to study environmental politics.

I am convinced that nature is in crisis in myriad ways. Getting out 'into nature' provides me with a much needed escape from the pressures of day-to-day life. Hiking, running and skiing in natural areas are spiritual experiences to me – experiences that leave me with a deep appreciation and respect for the non-human. I think that many people share these sentiments; nature:

> provides a sense of place amid the dislocations of capital, a space of leisure to compensate for the increasing demands of work, a sense of tradition that answers yearnings for simpler times, and a symbol of purity at a time when seemingly little is sacred and all is commodified.
> *(Hultgren 2015, p. 4)*

A close examination of the discourses surrounding immigration and the environment, however, has demonstrated to me that nature's perceived location within progressive politics also enables it to be used for exclusionary purposes by a variety of actors who seek simultaneously to naturalize their own privileged location within the political community and to marginalize others. For such actors, nature becomes a progressive signifier that establishes an implicit connection between blood and soil, between 'simpler times' and 'whiter times' and between the purity of national culture and the purity of the natural environment.

The danger of such formulations is not that overt racists will succeed in appropriating nature to advance their xenophobic agenda; rather, the real threat is that environmentalists who view nature through epistemologies that are subtly entwined with cultural ideals of nation and race will be led astray. It is by challenging these narratives – narratives in which power functions insidiously through claims to objectivity and the naturalization of social norms – that discourse analysis is most valuable.

Featured work

Hultgren, J 2015, *Border walls gone green: nature and anti-immigrant politics in America*. University of Minnesota Press, Minneapolis.

Works cited

Cronon, W 1996, 'The trouble with wilderness: or, getting back to the wrong nature,' *Environmental History*, vol. 1, no. 1, pp. 7–28.

Hajer, M 1995, *The politics of environmental discourse: ecological modernization and the policy process*. Oxford UP, Oxford.

Haraway, D 2008. *When species meet*. University of Minnesota Press, Minneapolis.

Kosek, J 2006, *Understories: the political life of forests in northern New Mexico*, Duke UP, Durham, NC.

Ludden, J 2008, 'Ads warn that all immigration must be reduced,' *National Public Radio*, September 18, viewed April 12, 2012, www.npr.org/templates/story/story.php?storyId=94545604.

Milliken, J 2001, 'Discourse study: bringing rigor to critical theory,' in KM Fierke & KE Jorgenson (eds.), *Constructing international relations: the next generation*, M.E. Sharpe, Armonk, NY.

Park, B 2007, 'Friends in low places,' *The Rocky Mountain Chronicle*, viewed May 10, 2009, www.rmchronicle.com/index.php?id=1359&option=com_content&task=view.

Potok, M 2010, 'Executive summary,' in *Greenwash: nativists, environmentalism and the hypocrisy of hate*, Southern Poverty Law Center, Montgomery, AL.

Price, C & Feldmeyer, B 2012, 'The environmental impact of immigration: an analysis of the effects of immigrant concentration on air pollution levels,' *Population Research and Policy Review*, vol. 31, no. 1, pp. 119–40.

Ross, A 2010, 'Greenwashing nativism,' *The Nation*, August 16.

Squalli, J 2010, 'An empirical analysis of U.S. state-level immigration and environmental emissions,' *Ecological Economics*, vol. 69, pp. 1170–75.

Sullivan, E 2007, 'Chertoff defends border fence,' *Associated Press*, October 1, viewed January 31, 2012, www.huffingtonpost.com/huff-wires/20071001/border-fence/diff_D8S0NC000_D8S0ND480.html.

Further reading

Sandilands, C 1999, 'From natural identity to radical democracy,' in *The good natured feminist: ecofeminism and the quest for democracy*, University of Minnesota Press, Minneapolis.

3

DEVELOPING A LANGUAGE OF METHODS WITHIN THE CRITICAL SCHOOL

Johnna Montgomerie

This chapter makes the case for developing a shared idiom for methods and methodology within the critical school of political economy. In using the word 'idiom', I mean to acknowledge that a 'language' of methods – a language largely confined to positivist methodology – already exists. One benefit of developing a new critical idiom about methods is that doing so allows us to recognise the well-established methodological differences between positivism and pluralism without having to develop a whole new vocabulary to speak or write about how we do research. It should be noted that the language of methods currently used in connection with positivism and methodological individualism has a specific contextual meaning that does not pertain to the actual meaning. In terms of empirical analyses, for instance, the language of positivism uses 'empiricism' to mean the quantitative analysis of large datasets. More broadly, however, the meaning of the term empirical is 'evidence drawn from experience'. 'Rigour' is another word that can have different definitional inflections. In general terms, 'rigour' simply refers to how comprehensive and thorough the research process is; in academic practice, however, 'rigour' can mean anything from offering a comprehensive account of the entire scope of available knowledge on a topic to providing formal mathematical proofs.

In most cases, analytical rigour is judged by the disciplinary parameters of academic study. In the study of economics or politics and international relations, for instance, the dominance of positivism within the social sciences has led to a particular understanding of analytical rigour that reinforces positivism's hegemony and emphasises methodological individualism. Just like the US court ruling that found that obscenity could be determined on the basis of '*I know it when I see it*' (Gewirtz 1995), the final academic judgement on what counts as rigorous research is a cultural one made in the highly organised institutional structures of contemporary academic disciplines.

In trying to forge a new path beyond anti- or post-positivist positions, it is important that we acknowledge the ways in which methods are used within positivism as a means to an end. Within positivism, methods are devices of measurement and quantification that are judged based on their precision and used to inform generalisation and prediction. As such, methods are the language and intricate grammar of positivist social science, a language and grammar that inform more colloquial debates within economics, politics and international relations. Critiques of positivism have been appearing for decades, and as those critiques proliferate, we witness all the more clearly the *rigor mortis* (or, perhaps, the 'rigour' mortis) of orthodoxy setting in. We can continue to keep fighting with a dying beast, or we can decide to cover new terrain.

In the hopes of doing the latter, I suggest that we begin to develop our own idiomatic framing of methods within the critical school. The autobiographical vignettes that form part of this collection enable us to see how we can engage with and use an idiom of methods to articulate the role of pluralism in professional practice. This chapter is therefore dedicated to examining what has previously been called the 'social life of methods'. Such an examination allows us to consider more closely how to advance pluralism within political economy. In particular, this chapter reflects on how methodological pluralism affects scholars' research ethics and how experts' pragmatic and/or judgement-based claims influence what we count as evidence. Finally, the chapter considers how we can begin to reimagine our research processes and reconceive the ends to which we put our collected evidence.

The social life of methods in the critical school

I first came across the phrase 'the social life of methods' as a postdoc at the Centre for Socio-Cultural Change (CRESC) at the University of Manchester. The phrase denotes the different disciplinary approaches that are used to study socio-cultural change. Since my first exposure to the phrase, a fledgling literature has sprung up that recognises how methods both constitute and are constituted by the social world (Law, Ruppert and Savage 2011). The mutually constitutive relationship between methods and the social world becomes all the clearer when we realise that methods are developed and deemed (in)valid based on expert knowledge claims.

More recently, a research agenda has begun to be formed that seeks to experiment with the analytical purchase of the social life of methods (SLOM). The first iteration of this agenda appeared in a special issue of *Theory, Culture and Society* (30:4), which included a compelling series of articles exploring how SLOM informs a new methodological focus in social research. The theme of a mutual interchange between methods and the world was most clearly articulated in Savage's introduction to the special issue:

> My argument is that the 'Social Life of Methods' arises as part of a dual movement. These are, firstly, an increasing interdisciplinary interest in making

methods an object of study. Secondly out of the crisis, increasingly evident in the 'research methods community' regarding positivist forms of knowledge as forms of standardized data exceed the capacity of standard quantitative procedures to process and analyse them.

(Savage 2013, p. 4)

As Savage suggests, the shift away from positivism offers new prospects for an emerging dialogue about methods within the critical school. Within SLOM, positivism is already acknowledged as a dying orthodoxy. Echoing Steinmetz's (2005) claims about how the politicisation of methods occurs alongside positivism's colonisation of the social sciences, SLOM offers an interdisciplinary critique of positivism as a means of encouraging new ways of studying social change. In particular, SLOM strives to contextualise the forms of codification, standardisation, regression and 'the general linear model' (Abbott 2001) that have been taken for granted in the rise of positivist quantitative methods (Savage 2010). The larger aim of SLOM is to demonstrate that methods are both objects of analysis and devices of knowledge production that are embedded in a set of institutional and cultural practices that affect how research is 'done' in academic and political spheres. The most recent iteration of this way of thinking is the 'SLOM:Lab network', which consists of a group of researchers who focus their attention on 'both [their] own research methods and those of the people [they] work with' and who consider how such methods 'influenced [their] understandings of how to conduct social research' (SLOM:lab 2016). The goal of SLOM:Lab is to show that interdisciplinary, collaborative and innovative methods are crucial to successfully studying contemporary forms of social life.

I argue we should engage with the SLOM agenda to re-conceive the pluralist methodology used within the critical school. More specifically, my suggestion is that we use the social life of methods as a way of adding to our understanding of the constitutive role that methods play in contemporary political economy. Doing this requires that we build on the strong interconnections already existing between SLOM and the study of geopolitics. Critical security studies, for example, is currently developing a comprehensive dialogue on the social life of methods, a dialogue that describes how the methodological grammar of international security regimes turns bodies into things to be counted, measured, benchmarked and, ultimately, controlled. In particular, the extensive work of Louise Amoore (Amoore 2014; Amoore and Piotukh 2015) explores how calculative technologies and devices forge new socio-digital assemblages of neoliberal governance. Drawing heavily from the insights of Science and Technology Studies (STS), this critical engagement with methods as device (dispositif) foregrounds how human/non-human interconnections drive other social developments, in law, politics, public policy, ethics and culture. Importantly, STS takes head on that scientific facts and study of technological developments are the products of socially constituted forms of academic investigation rather than objective representations of nature or fact.

Using the social life of methods as a starting point for a new dialogue within the critical school offers a potentially fruitful avenue for moving beyond the seemingly endless critique of the obvious failings of positivist methodological apparatus. Choosing to forego the rehashing of well-worn critiques, SLOM cross-fertilises post-positivist thinking with radical and heterodox currents within political economy and cultural economy. By inaugurating an interdisciplinary conversation about how methods constitute our empirical understanding of contemporary capitalism, we can give our research new dimensions that exceed tired and highly structured disagreements. SLOM offers us a means of challenging intellectual jurisdictions rather than a tool for extending pre-existing critical frameworks to accommodate new objects of analysis. While it is important that we take advantage of the opportunity offered by the crisis of positivism, we should do so in a way that incorporates debates and conceptual innovations from cognate fields of 'critical' social research. Surpassing the disciplinary boundaries that rather wilfully segregate international relations and international political economy, we can usefully reconceive the meaning of the word 'critical' as it applies to our methodologies and the debates and collaborations that sustain them.

The self-imposed silence on methods within the study of cultural political economy poses many problems, not least of which is that our understanding of our own research practices can become obscured. The contributors to this volume make this point forcefully while simultaneously arguing that discussions of methods should not be curtailed because of the perceived links between methods and positivism, economics and methodological individualism. As Chris May articulates in his vignette, we can reject the essentialism of positivist methods without turning against methods themselves; after all, turning against methods altogether is an essentialist move in its own right. Aside from using methods instrumentally, then, we also need to keep in mind that methods have social agency. For example, using a debt-to-GDP ratio as a benchmark for economic stability means not just understanding 'what' is being measured but also recognising that this measure has the power to produce change within the political governance of contemporary capitalism.

In addition to being reflexive about the quantities, metrics and benchmarks that affect social change, SLOM literature reveals how expert knowledge claims make visible power relations, inequality, institutional practices and various other processes of socio-cultural change in ways that transform our understandings of global society. This is unique in that it invites us to explore how methods reveal the contours of the social world through different devices, calculative techniques and conceptual notions, including the notion that populations are delimited or constructed through cultural understandings of 'big data' (Ruppert, Law and Savage 2013; Housley et al. 2014). What we can take from SLOM is the idea that methods are fluid procedural frameworks, not static instruments or simple tools. Because a pluralist methodology is valuable and benefits from constant innovation, we need to radically energise the study of method by building on and combining the empirical strength of political and cultural economy. What's more, we need to be reflexive and critical about our own 'epochalist' thinking, which tends to reinforce specific narratives of history. As Shilliam, Hall, and Inayatullah and Blaney articulate in their respective vignettes, positivist methods are tied to the instrumentalisation of human life and thus contribute to the elevation of purely technical tools of analysis over methods that investigate, and place value on, the social dynamics of human affairs. We can productively work against positivism's influence by beginning a new conversation about how methods are social and constitute the social world.

One important step in starting such a conversation is developing a critical methodological idiom that challenges the rigid categories of political economy and remains open to alternative approaches. Traditionally speaking, the enforced divisions between economics, politics and culture are understood as a key disciplinary feature of the social sciences; in contrast, a pluralist methodology erases the dividing lines between those fields of study and recognises them as cognate expressions of human civilisation. Similarly, a host of antiquated liberal dichotomies – including those between the private and public spheres, states and markets, finance and the real economy, and the production of things and the reproduction of people – continue to obscure the deeply integrated social processes that underpin contemporary capitalism. Especially since the onset of the 2008 financial crisis, such dichotomies have declining analytical purchase and neglect to account for the machinations of global capitalism. By moving beyond the well-established liberal categories of political economy, we not only leave behind the oft-trodden ground of methodological debate but also uncover possible new ways of understanding and evaluating overlapping forms of inequality, such as income, wealth, gender, race and class inequality. To underscore the imbrication of such inequalities, we must transform our theoretical acknowledgements of power relations' intersectionality into actual methodological practices that make the geometries of power visible (Massey 1999; Bedford and Rai 2010).

Crafting a critical research ethic

In working to initiate a new dialogue about methods within the critical school, we must first cease thinking of political economy as a 'discipline'. The very idea of disciplinarity presupposes the establishment of boundaries and orthodoxy, both of which run counter to political economy's critical epistemological tradition. To escape the confines of disciplinarity, I suggest that we focus on the implicit pluralist methodology already used in cultural political economy to develop a clear research ethic for interrogating social phenomena. Specifically by integrating Ackerly and True's (2008) feminist research ethic into the practice of doing political economy as methodology, which means:

> The research ethic involves being attentive to (1) the power of knowledge, and more profoundly, of epistemology, (2) boundaries, marginalization, and silences, (3) relationships and their power differentials, and (4) our own situatedness as researchers. We need to be aware of how our own basket of privileges and experiences conditions our knowledge and research. However, the

feminist-informed researcher's commitment to self-reflection is not merely a commitment to reflecting on his identity as a researcher but rather, to noticing and thinking through silences in epistemology, boundaries, and power dynamics (of the research process itself) from a range of theoretical perspectives as he does his research.

(p. 695)

The articulation of a critical research ethic as a set of 'questioning practices' provides a push to commit to inquiry about how we inquire; in other words a feminist research ethic involves asking ourselves a set of questions that have no definitive answers. Within cultural political economy, this critical research ethic incorporates longstanding feminist challenges to the scientific claims of positivist research and how scientific method is adapted in social science in highly socio-cultural ways; as Ann Runyan articulates in her crafting of the critique of the 'master frame' in international relations. A central part of this is masking the researcher's subjectivity in the process of making knowledge claims; as such feminist research openly challenges epistemology. For pluralist political economy this means, 'recognizing that there are many epistemological perspectives each opening and foreclosing certain understandings of what it means to know and to contribute to shared knowledge enhances our study' (Ackerly and True 2008, p. 695). Longstanding struggles against positivist epistemology and the dominance of methodological individualism mean that we must forge a space for interrogating our own norms of knowledge creation. In the same way that we interrogate the established boundaries between economics, politics and culture or between states, markets and society, we must reflexively consider what we include and exclude from our study of cultural political economy. Sharing with feminism its investment in pluralism, a critical research ethic can benefit greatly from feminism's open and adaptive set of principles without necessarily advancing particular feminist theories (Ackerly and True 2008, p. 694).

As the various pieces in this volume suggest, attentiveness to boundaries is already a key feature of how many critical researchers engage with their central research focus; many contributors point in their own fashion to the need of hearing previously unheard voices, of seeing what has long remained hidden and of casting light into the shadows of the global economy. Because the investigation of the unexplored or purposely ignored involves entering unknown territory and doing so in unprecedented ways, such investigations, especially when set against traditional positivist practices of codification and standardisation, court disapproval and criticism. By cultivating a critical research ethic, however, we can go some way to forestalling the potential charges that may be levelled at critical investigation. To be more precise: elucidating a critical research ethic emphasising the mutually constitutive relationship between methods and the social world will enable us not only to innovate our research practices but also to make the foundations and aims of those practices clearer. We cannot feign ignorance or helplessness when it comes to investigating power and exclusion, the creation of divisions between 'us' and 'them' or the social and material manifestations of profit and loss. For just this reason, we must place methodological questions over ontological abstractions to ground our study of political economy upon a research ethic that asks specific questions about power, authority and justice. Such a grounding is paramount within critical scholarship because the researcher must be actively engaged with the world as events unfold within it.

In the broadest terms, then, a critical research ethic involves accounting for choices and practices. My insistence on such an ethic tallies with the central theme of this volume – that is, with its focus on both the act of 'doing' research and our desire to improve the quality of our scholarship's knowledge claims.

Ethics in practice

The autobiographical vignettes in this volume point to a sort of paradox. On the one hand, they underscore the self-imposed silence related to formal research ethics in political economy; on the other hand, they demonstrate the profound ethical commitments that underlie individual researchers' critical social research. One virtue of these vignettes is that they suggest our ability to confront perplexing ethical dilemmas without resorting to the universalisation of thought that methodological individualism is usually said to entail. The overwhelming focus of positivist research is the implementation of methodological individualism, this frames ethics as set of 'best-practice' guidelines for research on human subjects (Van Maanen 1983). It is clear that this seriously limits how critical researchers engage with formal ethics procedures. Most research within political economy, for instance, has no direct engagement with human subjects; as a result, discussions of ethics within the research process are few and far between.

When conversations about ethics are limited to the ethical treatment of human subjects, those conversations become constrained by a certain kind of language. More specifically, such conversations involve determining the integrity and objectivity of the researcher by evaluating his or her work according to formulaic criteria: whether the researcher avoids harming participants physically or emotionally; whether the researcher has obtained subjects' informed consent and voluntary participation; and, whether the researcher has ensured subjects' privacy and/or anonymity (Social Research Council 2016; Miller et al. 2012). These criteria are, in turn, inflected by certain methodological registers (Erikson 1967). A *situational* ethics provides a greater degree of flexibility in decision-making in order to respect that the kinds of deception social researchers practice are trivial compared to those perpetuated by institutions of power in modern society (Douglas 1976). Alternatively, an '*anything goes*' approach to ethics recognises that social methods are embedded in social practice that encourage minor transgressions, including researchers being dishonest in order 'to get an honest answer'. As such researchers are invited to study anyone in any setting provided that their research has a scientific purpose, does no harm to participants and does not deliberately damage the discipline (Denzin 1994).

There is a value in ethical formalism, but it does reproduce epistemological reductionism of methodological individualism; more importantly, this formalism is deeply embedded in bureaucratic practices that affect everything from PhD committees and research funding applications to administrative oversight and enforcement (Israel and Hay 2006). As the contributors to this volume so often suggest, the kinds of bureaucratic practice that stem from ethical formalism often fail to resonate with individual researchers' ethical commitments. Instead, the actual practice of ethics – and the practice of conducting ethical research – is overwhelmed by the paperwork that accompanies formalism.[1]

As most critical researchers will attest, the challenge of conducting research and ethically accounting for decisions and findings lies not just in 'doing no harm' but in making visible 'the harm being done' by agents, institutions and power structures. Shedding light on unseen or unacknowledged sources of harm within the global economy is thus part and parcel of possessing a critical research ethic. Being conscious of boundaries and relationships of power, as outlined by Ackerly and True above, requires that those sources of harm do not confine their effects to research participants alone. Gorard (2002), for example, notes that:

> most discussions of ethical considerations in research focus on possible harm to the research participants, to the exclusion of the possible harm done to future users of the evidence which researcher generates. [Those discussions] almost never consider the wasted resources, and worse, used in implementing policies that do not work.
>
> *(p. 2)*

For example, Godard's point has a clear relationship to the ethical problem of the Reinhart and Rogoff controversies, in which rigorous economic analysis about the connection between cutting government debt and increasing economic growth (Reinhart and Rogoff 2011) was later proved methodologically and statistically dubious (Coy 2013). Despite the fall out from those controversies, the support of Austerity-led growth (Reinhart and Rogoff 2013) and its policy applications in the UK, Europe and, most infamously, Greece has not diminished (Streeck and Schäfer 2013; Flassbeck, Lapavitsas and Lafontaine 2015). What should be stressed here is that the adoption of a pluralist methodology within political economy necessarily involves exposing the ethical transgressions of a supposedly rigorous positivism. Computational error is bad, but academic dishonesty is worse. Especially when the consequences of its implementation causes harm to people. In the case of Austerity, researchers with a critical ethic will seek not only to demonstrate that Austerity is logically, empirically and rationally wrong but also to expose the underlying power relations that cause Austerity-related harm.

By adopting a critical research ethic, we can arrive at new ways of connecting the practice of critical research with the critical theory of the Enlightenment tradition, which was dedicated to changing outmoded institutions and eliminating prejudiced and superstitious ideas. A fundamental claim of critical theory is that social science can and should contribute to the liberation of people from unnecessarily restrictive traditions, ideologies, assumptions, power relations and identity formations (Horkheimer, Adorno and Noeri 2002; Feyerabend 1993; Fay 1996; Jaggar 2015). The contributors to this volume support that claim in various ways. While some identify how feminist and post-colonial methodologies explicitly adopt and apply an emancipatory ethic, others provide in-depth qualitative analyses of forced labour and sexual labour or consider how the ethical framing of political economy is made explicit in the doing of research. Within the archive, the union, the network and the norm, a pluralist methodology reveals the clear ethical implications of reporting on overlooked or ignored power relations.

Expanding our understanding of ethics can significantly advance how we practise methodological pluralism. As most of us recognise, the Academy enjoys considerable cultural and political privilege; this is our 'situadeness'. Giving voice to harm in our academic research thus ensures that we use that privilege to provide a social good. In practice, giving voice to harm entails refusing to subordinate emotion to reason as a matter of routine during the research process. As Kjonstad and Willmott (1995) explain, '[E]motion is no less important for moral performance than reason' in informing our critical research ethic. Keeping in mind that political economy not only challenges hierarchy but also aims at its inversion or flattening, we need to adopt a pluralist methodology that fosters diversity by tempering the absolute knowledge claims, contributions and findings that underwrite dogma and tyranny (Willmott 2008). Indeed, acknowledging the limits of academic knowledge production is a necessary counterweight to positivism's assertion of its hegemony in terms of scientific knowledge production. Our critical pluralism involves combining inquisitiveness about and reflection upon methods and values with our knowledge claims relating to political economy.

Developing a reflexive methodology

The strength of our commitment to a pluralist methodology necessitates a reflexive dialogue that spells out the ways in which the emancipatory potential of reason can be used to critically examine and interact with the reality of the social world. In considering the construction of capitalism, for instance, we need to consider not only how it is socially produced and reproduced but also how it can be transformed. Within political economy, the aim of a pluralist methodology should be to combine critical theory with social science methods as a means of facilitating emancipatory change. Following Inayatullah and Blaney, we need to reframe the ethical question of critical political economy as follows: is capitalism a wound worth suffering? Exploring this question forces us to think about culture and history in ways that are normally foreclosed in structural and institutional accounts of the contemporary global political economy. Limiting ourselves solely to the ethic of 'do no harm' ignores the fact that harm is being done. For just this reason, Inayatullah and Blaney ask us to think about what purpose the harm of others serves and how it is culturally constituted and mediated.

Cultivating reflexivity in our pluralist methodology means paying 'serious attention … to the way different kinds of linguistic, social, political and theoretical elements are woven together in the process of knowledge development'; it also means recognising that 'empirical material is constructed, interpreted and written' during that process (Alvesson and Sköldberg 2009, p. 9). To put the matter a different way, reflexivity encourages us to understand how the research process influences objects of analysis, the field of research and situational power dynamics, and it compels us to confront the ethical challenges that call into question the established distinctions between object and subject, theory and reality and author and text. Acts of research breathe life into methods, which means that methods themselves are not static tools but rather dynamic processes. In contrast to positivism, which downplays the dynamism of methods in favour of rigour, parsimony, measurement, validity and causality; a reflexive, pluralist methodology requires a more direct engagement with the methods used in researching contemporary capitalism and formulating expert knowledge claims about it.

This is not to say that we need to reinvent the critical methodological wheel; there is, after all, ample literature on reflexive methods within politics and international relations. However, what we do need to do is to forge a common agenda for methodological advancement, an agenda that justifies the value of a pluralist methodology without specifying exactly what form it must take. More important, we should adopt a critical research ethic that invites those not working with human subjects to consider more closely how harm inflects their study of political and cultural economy.

Conclusion

This chapter has sought to cultivate a new language of methods to inform the development of pluralism within the study of political and cultural economy. Beginning by evaluating the social life of methods and the mutual constitutiveness of methods and the social world, we considered how methods are an object of analysis in their own right. Drawing together SLOM and the feminist research ethic, in practice, this means two things: first, we must be reflexive about how our methods are constituted by the social world that political economy seeks to understand; second, we must acknowledge that the object of our study, contemporary global capitalism, is constituted by our methods. For example, we should not only tacitly recognise but also openly and precisely explore how key benchmark measurements like Gross Domestic Product, inflation, exchange rates or the balance of payments actually constitute the twentieth-first-century growth regime in very political ways (Coyle 2015; Stiglitz, Sen and Fitoussi 2010; Waring 1989). The same goes for the many other quantitative and qualitative methods used to make visible global flows of credit, money, people and things across the planet: each of those measures correlates to a particular representation of the global economy, a representation that is not socially neutral.

Political economy as methodology opens up the connections between theory and practice that permits fluid transfers between the currently rigid categories of theory, concept, method, results and reporting. Such a fluid exchange breathes life into dry textbook understandings of methods and replaces those understandings with the idea that methods are a way of producing knowledge claims within the *craft* of research. Making decisions, and accounting for them, grounds pluralism in a 'set of questioning practices'. In using the phrase 'research ethic', I recognise that it has many different inflections within academia, including its use in the formal ethics approval process and in the entire tradition of philosophy dedicated to the study of systems of morals. In employing the phrase as I do, however, I mean for it to represent something akin to a work ethic – that is, a set of principles that guides our shared research agenda.

Rather than leading to the emergence of a new orthodoxy, cultivating a critical research ethic involves creating a reflexive space for evaluating how knowledge is created, re-created, enacted and embodied. For those who wish to practice critical research, the development of a critical research ethic must go hand in hand with an active engagement with the ethical dimensions of contemporary capitalism. What is perhaps most important to remember is that the direction of such an engagement is not pre-ordained; rather, each researcher has the ability to treat openly and independently the ethical concerns that arise throughout the research process.

Note

1 The University of Lancaster offers a comprehensive online repository – *The Research Ethics Guidebook: A Resource for Social Scientists* (www.ethicsguidebook.ac.uk/). It is a practical and incredibly useful guide to the different ethical dimensions of social scientific research.

Works cited

Abbott, Andrew. 2001. *Time Matters: On Theory and Method*. Chicago, IL: University of Chicago Press.
Ackerly, Brooke, and Jacqui True. 2008. 'Reflexivity in Practice: Power and Ethics in Feminist Research on International Relations'. *International Studies Review* 10 (4): 693–707. doi:10.1111/j.1468-2486.2008.00826.x.
Alvesson, Mats, and Kaj Sköldberg. 2009. *Reflexive Methodology: New Vistas for Qualitative Research*. London: Sage.
Amoore, Louise. 2014. 'Security and the Incalculable'. *Security Dialogue* 45 (5): 423–39.
Amoore, Louise, and Volha Piotukh. 2015. *Algorithmic Life: Calculative Devices in the Age of Big Data*. London: Routledge.
Amoureux, Jack L. 2015. *A Practice of Ethics for Global Politics: Ethical Reflexivity*. London: Routledge.
Bedford, Kate, and Shirin M. Rai. 2010. 'Feminists Theorize International Political Economy'. *Signs* 36 (1): 1–18. doi:10.1086/652910.

Coy, Peter. 2013. 'FAQ: Reinhart, Rogoff, and the Excel Error that Changed History'. Bloomberg com. www.bloomberg.com/news/articles/2013-04-18/faq-reinhart-rogoff-and-the-excel- error-that-changed-history.

Coyle, Diane. 2015. *GDP: A Brief but Affectionate History*. Revised and expanded edn. Princeton, NJ: Princeton University Press.

Denzin, Norman K. 1994. 'Evaluating Qualitative Research in the Poststructural Moment: The Lessons James Joyce Teaches Us'. *International Journal of Qualitative Studies in Education* 7 (4): 295–308. doi:10.1080/0951839940070401.

Douglas, Jack D. 1976. *Investigative Social Research: Individual and Team Field Research*. Beverly Hills, CA: Sage.

Erikson, Kai T. 1967. 'A Comment on Disguised Observation in Sociology'. *Social Problems* 14 (4): 366–73. doi:10.2307/798850.

Fay, Brian. 1996. *Contemporary Philosophy of Social Science: A Multicultural Approach*. London: Wiley.

Feyerabend, Paul. 1993. *Against Method*. London: Verso.

Flassbeck, Heiner, Costas Lapavitsas and Oskar Lafontaine. 2015. *Against the Troika: Crisis and Austerity in the Eurozone*. London: Verso.

Gatenby, Bev, and Maria Humphries. 2000. 'Feminist Participatory Action Research: Methodological and Ethical Issues'. *Women's Studies International Forum* 23 (1): 89–105. doi:10.1016/S0277-5395(99)00095-3.

Gewirtz, Paul. 1995. 'On "I Know It When I See It"'. *Yale Law Journal* 105: 1023–46.

Gorard, Stephen. 2002. 'Ethics and Equity: Pursuing the Perspective of Non-Participants'. *Social Research Update* 39: 1–4.

Horkheimer, Max, Theodor W. Adorno, and Gunzelin Noeri. 2002. *Dialectic of Enlightenment*. Palo Alto, CA: Stanford University Press.

Housley, William, Rob Procter, Adam Edwards, Peter Burnap, Matthew Williams, Luke Sloan, Omer Rana, Jeffrey Morgan, Alex Voss, and Anita Greenhill. 2014. 'Big and Broad Social Data and the Sociological Imagination: A Collaborative Response'. *Big Data & Society* 1 (2): 1–15. doi:10.1177/2053951714545135.

Israel, Mark, and Iain Hay. 2006. *Research Ethics for Social Scientists*. London: Sage.

Jaggar, Alison M. 2015. *Just Methods: An Interdisciplinary Feminist Reader*. London: Routledge.

Kjonstad, Bjørn, and Hugh Willmott. 1995. 'Business Ethics: Restrictive or Empowering?' *Journal of Business Ethics* 14 (6): 445–64.

Law, John, Evelyn Ruppert, and Mike Savage. 2011. 'The Double Social Life of Methods.' University of Manchester: Centre for Research on Socio-Cultural Change (CRESC). http://research.gold.ac.uk/7987/1/The%20Double%20Social%20Life%20of%20Methods%20CRESC%20Working%20Paper%2095.pdf.

Maiter, Sarah, Laura Simich, Nora Jacobson, and Julie Wise. 2008. 'Reciprocity An Ethic for Community-Based Participatory Action Research'. *Action Research* 6 (3): 305–25. doi:10.1177/1476750307083720.

Massey, Doreen. 1999. 'Imagining Globalization: Power-Geometries of Time-Space'. In *Global Futures*, edited by Avtar Brah, Mary J. Hickma, and Máirtín Mac an Ghaill, 27–44. Explorations in Sociology. Basingstoke: Palgrave Macmillan.

Miller, Tina, Melanie Mauthner, Maxine Birch and Julie Jessop. 2012. *Ethics in Qualitative Research*. London: Sage.

Reinhart, Carmen M., and Kenneth S. Rogoff. 2011. *This Time is Different: Eight Centuries of Financial Folly*. Reprint edn. Princeton, NJ: Princeton University Press.

Reinhart, Carmen M., and Kenneth S. Rogoff. 2013. 'Reinhart and Rogoff: Responding to Our Critics'. *The New York Times*, 25 April, sec. Opinion. www.nytimes.com/2013/04/26/opinion/reinhart-and-rogoff-responding-to-our-critics.html.

Ruppert, Evelyn, John Law, and Mike Savage. 2013. 'Reassembling Social Science Methods: The Challenge of Digital Devices'. *Theory, Culture & Society* 30 (4): 22–46. doi:10.1177/0263276413484941.

Salter, Mark B., and Can E. Mutlu. 2013. *Research Methods in Critical Security Studies: An Introduction*. London: Routledge.

Savage, Mike. 2010. *Identities and Social Change in Britain since 1940: The Politics of Method*. Oxford: Oxford UP.

Savage, Mike. 2013. 'The "Social Life of Methods": A Critical Introduction'. *Theory, Culture & Society* 30 (4): 3–21. doi:10.1177/0263276413486160.

Shepherd, Laura J. 2013. *Critical Approaches to Security: An Introduction to Theories and Methods*. London: Routledge.

SLOM:lab. 2016. Social Life of Methods Laboratory. www.slomlab.org/.

Social Research Council. 2016. 'Ethical Guidelines'. http://the-sra.org.uk/wp-content/uploads/ethics03.pdf.

Steinmetz, George. 2005. *The Politics of Method in the Human Sciences: Positivism and its Epistemological Others*. Durham, NC: Duke University Press.

Stiglitz, Joseph E., Amartya Sen and Jean-Paul Fitoussi. 2010. *Mismeasuring Our Lives: Why GDP Doesn't Add Up*. New York: The New Press.

Streeck, Wolfgang, and Armin Schäfer. 2013. *Politics in the Age of Austerity*. London: John Wiley & Sons.

Van Maanen, J. 1983. 'The Moral Fix: On the Ethics of Fieldwork'. In *Contemporary Field Research*, edited by Pollner Melvin and Robert M. Emerson. Boston, MA: Little, Brown.

Waring, Marilyn. 1989. *If Women Counted: A New Feminist Economics*. London: Macmillan.

Willmott, Hugh. 2008. 'For Informed Pluralism, Broad Relevance and Critical Reflexivity'. In *The Sage Handbook of New Approaches to Management and Organization*, edited by Daved Barry and Hans Hansen, 82–83. London: Sage.

AGILITY, INTERSECTIONALITY AND DELIBERATION

My path to an adaptive and transformative research process

Kia M. Q. Hall

It has been less than a year since I graduated from American University with a PhD in International Relations. My research examined women's bread-making in the matrifocal, Afro-indigenous Garifuna villages of Honduras. More specifically, I explored the making of cassava bread, known as *ereba* in the Garifuna language, as a form of community development. Despite institutional academic pressure to have a concise, linear research process – a process that can be planned out in a proposal and whose risks can be easily calculated by institutional review boards – my research process involved many twists and turns. This essay discusses the following components of my experience: the methodology that allowed me to be flexible and responsive in the field; the methods that enabled the forging of deep and intimate relationships with the community in which I conducted research; the deliberative moments at which my research direction shifted; the institutional factors that have the potential to facilitate or negate an adaptive research process; and the transformative power of personally meaningful research.

Entering the field with an open mind and an agile methodology

Entering the field, I knew that I wanted to research indigenous understandings of development, but I did not know precisely how I would do this. Wondering how I could say in advance of fieldwork what forms of development would be most important to my research community, I ultimately realized that doing so was impossible. Instead, I adopted a methodology that left room for me to respond to information and analysis uncovered during the research process. Grounded theory is an iterative, non-linear process of discovery that allows the researcher to shift the focus of data collection in response to analysis done in the field. More specifically, constructivist grounded theory allows for 'an analytic interpretation of participants' worlds and of the processes constituting how these worlds are constructed' (Charmaz 2006, p. 508).

Kathy Charmaz's *Constructing Grounded Theory* (2006) acted as a field manual that guided me through data collection, analysis and writing. When I arrived in the Garifuna villages, I first spent time getting to know the people. The decision to study development from the perspective of the *ereba* makers was not made until several weeks after I had been living in one of the villages. Only at that point did I realize that the long-standing culinary tradition of *ereba*-making provided an invaluable lens through which to understand community development. Not only recognizing that *ereba*-making would be a useful focal point for me as a researcher, I also came to understand that it would be culturally meaningful for the Garifuna community.

Intersectional knowledges

My study was based in the impoverished villages of Garifuna people, who are both indigenous and black in a *mestizo* (i.e., Spanish and indigenous) state; cultural norms in the villages are matrifocal in spite of their existence in a state that is patriarchal. The complexity of these interacting identities and social factors called for an *intersectional analysis* of the kind pioneered by black feminist scholars. In navigating this type of analysis, I was guided by Patricia Hill Collins's (2000) seminal text *Black Feminist Thought: Knowledge, Consciousness, and the Politics of Empowerment*. In that work, Collins explains that '[i]ntersectionality refers to particular forms of intersecting oppressions, for example, intersections of race and gender, or of sexuality and nation'; she also emphasizes that '[i]ntersectional paradigms remind us that oppression cannot be reduced to one fundamental type, and that oppressions work together in producing injustice' (p. 21).

In learning about the Garifuna community, I followed the path of black feminist anthropologists who engage in cultural immersion and participant observation. In addition to immersing myself in rural Garifuna community life, I also conducted semi-structured interviews to fill the gaps within my observations and experiences. In accordance with constructivist grounded theory methodology, the interviews I conducted were analyzed in the field in order that my subsequent data collection could respond to the circumstances of the research. Such in-the-field moments of analysis, moments when I had the opportunity to stop, reflect and determine my next steps, are what feminist International Relations scholars Brooke Ackerly and Jacqui True (2006) call 'deliberative moments.'

Deliberative moments

In their discussion of feminist methodologies, Ackerly and True (2006, p. 258) describe self-conscious deliberative moments in the following manner: 'Feminist critical scholars choose a point of self-conscious inclusion of some subjects and exclusion of others in setting their research agendas. This point is a *deliberative moment*, amid continual change, at which the research question can be adequately investigated.' In my research process, I had multiple deliberative moments, some of which were planned and some of which were spontaneous.

In the context of using constructivist grounded theory, every round of concentrated data analysis that I conducted was a deliberative moment, one at which I determined how to move forward with data collection. In terms of spontaneous deliberative moments, one of the best examples is the moment when I realized that the work in the cassava fields was differentiated according to sex. The gendered division of labor in the fields meant that I would have to cross the line of what was considered appropriate work for women if I wanted to observe and participate in men's work. Ultimately, I decided that I would continue to do 'women's work,' which would allow me to build a deeper rapport with the women who were the focal point of my study, rather than cause a distance to emerge between us as a result of the other behaviors in which I might participate.

Three factors that can make or break an adaptive research process

At this point, the strength of a highly adaptive approach should be clear: it allows the researcher to react and respond to circumstances in the field. Nevertheless, there are at least three institutional elements that can help or hinder an adaptive research process for doctoral students. First, a dissertation committee can either encourage or discourage re-framing and re-shaping of the research question and process. While many students are encouraged to select committee members based on shared regional focus or methods, I selected a committee chair with a similar feminist epistemology. This decision was critical to the support I received in engaging with feminist methods. My chair, Christine B. N. Chin, encouraged sensitivity to the research environment and the subsequent adaptation of the research project to that environment. A feminist and international political economist, Chin also mentored me in feminist research methods during a period when I was working as her research assistant. The book that she subsequently produced, *Cosmopolitan Sex Workers: Women and Migration in a Global City* (2013), stands as an example of international political economy research at its best.

Second, conducting research with human subjects requires the clearance of an institutional review board (IRB). Originally designed to protect research subjects from harm imposed by researchers, IRBs often require rigid and inflexible adherence to decisions made long before researchers have entered the field. In an ideal world, IRBs would create mechanisms by which students could make modifications in research design without having to bring research to a complete stop; among other things, this change in IRB practice would encourage flexibility and responsiveness to conditions encountered in the field. In my own research, the minimum standard of not harming 'research subjects' seemed insufficient to me. Instead, I embraced a more robust ethical standard that had previously been adopted by many black feminist anthropologists. As Irma McClaurin (2001, p. 57) notes:

> Black feminist anthropologists, whose primary research tool is *participant* observation, are faced with the task of fashioning a research paradigm that decolonizes and transforms – in other words, one that seeks to alleviate conditions of oppression through scholarship and activism rather than support them.

Following this standard of trying to leave the community better than I found it required a deeper level of engagement and more responsiveness to community needs and demands.

Finally, many academic departments have pre-defined dissertation formats that may or may not lend themselves to the diverse research projects undertaken by students. In constructivist grounded theory, writing is as much a part of analytical discovery as other parts of the research process. According to Kathy Charmaz (2006, p. 154):

> The discovery process in grounded theory extends into the writing and rewriting stages. You'll gain further insights and create more ideas about your data while you're writing. You'll see clearer connections between categories and draw implications from them. Thus writing and rewriting become crucial phases of the *analytic* process.

Because the writing process is so intimately liked to the analytic process, dissertations, and writing projects in general, should be formatted in ways that support and extend the broader research process and project. Charmaz (2006, p. 154) makes much this same point when she acknowledges that '[r]equired formats often presuppose a traditional logico-deductive organization' and argues that 'we need to rethink the [required] format and adapt it to our needs and goals rather than pour our work into standard categories.' More specifically, she advises that we should '[r]ethink and adapt a prescribed format in ways that work for [our] ideas rather than compromise [our] analysis' (p. 154). In my own case, I produced a nine-chapter dissertation that alternated between presenting theoretical frameworks, historical context and empirical findings; in constructing my final product, I was thus required to modify the university template significantly.

A research process that transforms

Being empowered by the right combination of methodology, methods, epistemology and committee members created a dynamic and transformative research process for me. My research was not a project detached from my 'real life.' Rather, it was the initiation of a relationship with my research community based on solidarity and a commitment to justice. In this context, completing my dissertation was only a small part of a much larger and more challenging solidarity-building effort.

In *Feminism Without Borders: Decolonizing Theory, Practising Solidarity* (2003, p. 7), Chandra Talpade Mohanty stresses three defining principles of solidarity:

> I define solidarity in terms of mutuality, accountability, and the recognition of common interests as the basis for relationships among diverse communities. Rather than assuming an enforced commonality of oppression, the practice of solidarity foregrounds communities of people who have chosen to work and fight together.

Guided by Mohanty's standards of mutuality, accountability and recognition of common interests, I have developed a website that has statements from villagers about the importance of *ereba* for community development. The website is a collaborative effort that embodies my gratitude to the *ereba*-making organizations that supported my ten months of field research. In creating the website, I aimed to fulfil Mohanty's standard of mutuality by giving support and exposure to the community members who had shared their lives and stories with me. The villagers featured on the site had the opportunity to review images and statements and make corrections before they were posted online. At all my research presentations, I share the website, which is a part of an awareness-raising and fundraising campaign. The site's content reflects a shared interest in Garifuna community development and is powered by the production and sale of *ereba*. I continue to maintain and update the website (www.erebairiona.org), which has generated more than $2,000 for local organizations. In January 2015, I will return to each of the villages where I conducted research in order to give a report on my activities since the conclusion of my fieldwork and to distribute the donated money to the groups. In doing this, I will continue to demonstrate my accountability to the community.

Conclusion

My research journey has been adaptive and responsive. Guided by constructivist grounded theory methodology, black feminist epistemology (i.e., intersectionality) and anthropological methods, I experienced a series of deliberative moments at which I was able to re-direct my research path as appropriate. Further, the mentorship of my dissertation chair, with whom I share a feminist epistemology, allowed me to navigate what could have been institutional barriers to an adaptive process. Finally, my dissertation was part of a larger personal project of advocating for social justice and thus depended on building solidarity with my research community. In *Feminist Theory: From Margin to Center* (1984, p. 64), bell hooks distinguishes between solidarity and support as follows: 'Support can be occasional. It can be given and just as easily withdrawn. Solidarity requires sustained, ongoing commitment.' Because I am committed to social justice and the elimination of poverty, I continue to interact with the Garifuna community of Honduras. My research project was only a small part of a larger social justice agenda influenced by ethical and personal commitments. In adopting such an agenda, I resemble many other feminists of color, indigenous scholars and groups who are marginalized in the mainstream IR canon. In solidarity with these scholars and communities, I engage my research community in ways that continue to enrich and transform my life.

Works cited

Ackerly, B & True, J 2006, 'Studying the struggles and wishes of the age: feminist theoretical methodology and feminist theoretical models,' in B Ackerly, M Stern and J True (eds.), *Feminist methodologies for international relations*, Cambridge UP, New York, pp. 241–60.

Charmaz, K 2006, *Constructing grounded theory: a practical guide through qualitative analysis*, Sage, Los Angeles.

Chin, CBN 2013, *Cosmopolitan sex workers: women and migration in a global city*, Oxford UP, New York.

Collins, PH 2000, *Black feminist thought: knowledge, consciousness, and the politics of empowerment*, 2nd edn, Routledge, New York.

hooks, b 1984, *Feminist theory: from margin to center*, South End Press, Boston, MA.

McClaurin, I 2001, 'Theorizing a black feminist self in anthropology: toward an autoethnographic approach,' in I McClauren (ed.), *Black feminist anthropology: theory, politics, praxis and poetics*, Rutgers UP, New Brunswick, NJ, pp. 49–76.

Mohanty, CT 2003, *Feminism without borders: decolonizing theory, practicing solidarity*, Duke UP, Durham, NC.

(DIS)EMBODIED METHODOLOGY IN INTERNATIONAL POLITICAL ECONOMY

Nicola Smith

There was a time when I understood International Political Economy (IPE) to mean 'bodies of thought' (realism, liberalism, Marxism, etc.), and so, not knowing which body to have, I tried each of them on for size. Realism didn't fit (too tight); liberalism felt wrong (unethically sourced materials); Marxism looked good (but I lacked the discipline to maintain it). Social constructivism suited my friends and felt pretty comfortable, and so that was the body I decided to have. As a social constructivist, I did a lot of work on ideas ('discourse') and thought a lot about other bodies of thought. But what I didn't do was engage in thought about bodies. Bodies didn't seem to happen in IPE; they appeared to exist somewhere else entirely, to be accessed only via metaphor (as in the above description) but always somewhere 'over there', never as the living, breathing stuff of the discipline. Bodies – or so I assumed – were off the cards.

In other contexts, though, I was thinking a lot about bodies: from the personal ('Will my body be able to produce another body, a child?') to the professional ('Do I under-perform in job interviews because I gesticulate wildly when nervous?') and the political ('The government should decriminalise the sale of sexual services.'). Indeed, while I was writing my PhD and then a monograph about states and markets – globalisation, economic development and social justice in the Irish Republic – it was bodies that I loved talking, reading and arguing about. I just didn't see them as 'IPE'.

In fact, bodies had been there all along; I hadn't seen them because I hadn't been looking in the right place. There was, of course, a long-standing 'body' of IPE scholarship – feminist scholarship – in which bodies not only mattered but were the very starting-point of political economic analysis. As I began to read (and take seriously) this scholarship, the international political economy shifted in front of me. Bodies started popping up everywhere. Globalisation? Bodies. Economic development? Bodies. Social justice? Bodies. They appeared in all these old spaces but, more than this, they pointed to vibrant new sites and terrains. Where once 'the economy' had represented the formal and monochromatic sphere of production and exchange, V. Spike Peterson's (2003) groundbreaking book, *A Critical Rewriting of Global Political Economy*, painted in rich colour the 'reproductive economy' – the informal, private sphere of domestic, emotional, erotic and caring labour. Gillian Youngs's (2000) *Political Economy, Power and the Body* allowed me to imagine the international political economy not as some abstract realm of 'states and markets' but rather as being produced by, and productive of, embodied human lives. And work on commercial sex by feminist scholars such as Anna Agathangelou (2005), Kamala Kempadoo (2004) and Julia O'Connell Davidson (2005) further helped me to think about the 'macro' level of global power relations and the 'micro' level of individual bodies as co-constituted, and intimately so.

Methodologically, too, feminists were calling for IPE to be more embodied for, as Jan Jindy Pettman (1997, p. 92) put it, 'body politics [are] not available for critique in disciplines practiced as dis-embodied, in the absence of bodies, both of the writers and of their subjects.' My work on queer sexual economies has sought to build upon and contribute to this agenda by considering how queer lives, bodies and identities might be rendered more visible in the study of globalisation and capitalism whilst also considering the place of queer theories and methodologies in/and IPE. In practice, this has involved talking a lot with other people about bodies – not just *the body* in some abstract, detached sense, but actual, material bodies, including my own. Queer scholarship – which I now find fits me best – encourages reflection not only on processes of knowledge production but also on the subject position of 'the academic', seeking (if not always succeeding) to radically disrupt the boundaries between *the researcher* and *the researched* and reminding us that if the international political economy is embodied then so, too, is the international political economist.

When embarking on my research on queer sex work in London and Amsterdam, I decided that a good starting point would be to try to trouble such boundaries – that is, I wanted to explicitly treat the body not only as an object of enquiry but also as a precondition for my status as an enquiring subject. For a whole variety of intersecting reasons – practical, ethical and personal – I did not take this to its logical extreme, although a number of other scholars have engaged directly in sex work for their research (see for instance Egan, Frank and Johnson 2006). Instead, my research primarily took the form of loosely structured interviews with sex workers in London and Amsterdam and, as part of that process, there were many times that I discussed and reflected upon my own corporeality. When it felt appropriate to do so – and this was by no means always the case – I talked about both specific bodily experiences (including profoundly visceral ones, such as having a child) and, more broadly, my own sense of, and relationship with, embodiment.

This was something of an experiment – I had certainly not learned to talk about fat thighs and hangovers during my research methods training – but I quickly found that this body-talk both helped to produce and was itself a product of those interviews that went 'well'. To put this into context, I had found it extremely difficult to secure interviews, in part because the legal, political and cultural oppression of sex workers means that many are simply not prepared to take the risk of speaking with someone else (particularly an academic) about their work and lives. I guaranteed all interviewees complete confidentiality and was careful to explain from the start the background, purpose, methodology and ethical approval processes of the research. But, for those people who did agree to speak with me, there was inevitably a sense of disconnect between the respective subject positions that we occupied (researcher/researched; academic/sex worker; etc.). This was in itself a consequence of the fact that interviews – like all modes of research – are structured by unequal power relations across multiple axes such as gender, race, class, dis/ability and sexuality. And yet interviews can also produce moments of relationality and connection. I found that, at times, such connections were made precisely in and through the language of 'being' and 'having' bodies. By recognising both of our existences as embodied subjects, the interviews therefore sometimes created possibilities to explore a whole variety of experiences, both different and shared, of embodiment (intimate, stigmatised, commodified, and so on).

Part of my motivation for this approach was political, for sex workers have all too often been constructed as bodies and bodies alone (objectified bodies, exploited bodies, commodified bodies, deviant bodies, diseased bodies – to 'sell one's body' is to 'sell oneself'). The last thing I wanted to do was to reproduce such objectifying and de-humanising discourses by subjecting only the interviewees' bodies to a feminist gaze. Instead, and drawing on the auto-ethnographic approach of scholars such as Elina Penttinen (2008), I wanted to challenge the perpetuation of the public/private dichotomy that underpins not only the content but also the methodology of so much contemporary IPE.

At least, that was my intention. What I hadn't bargained for – and I hadn't bargained for it at a personal, political or practical level – was that I might frequently want to be *dis*embodied. I hadn't anticipated that I might not want to be present as a 'body' or be feminised in this way; I certainly hadn't thought that I might want to retreat to the safety of being an honorary Enlightenment Man. But, on occasion, this is exactly what I sought to do. For example, although I was invited on a number of occasions to engage in participant observation (by attending a booking or watching a live webcam show), I hastily turned those offers down. Although I articulated this, and justified it to myself, in terms of ethical and legal issues (I did not have approval from the University to undertake such research), the simple fact was that I felt deeply uncomfortable with the idea of moving beyond the level of talk. This was not because I was worried about seeing bodies-in-action but rather because *I* did not want to become visible as a body, albeit an observing one. I realised that, for all of my desire to renegotiate a variety of substantive and methodological boundaries, the reality was that I wanted bodies (and especially my own) to remain hidden, after all. So much for political resistance through embodied research.

This desire to remain disembodied was further compounded by an issue that I had not really prepared myself for: that of plain old sexual harassment. The possibility that I might be verbally or physically harassed had been raised from the start by the University Ethics Committee, who were understandably concerned with my personal safety when undertaking interviews. I had developed a number of strategies for ensuring my safety (always meeting interviewees in a public location, always making sure someone knew where I was, etc.), and the reality was that the only time I felt in any way at risk was when I arrived back in my home town and would walk, in the dark, from the train to my car. However, what I hadn't anticipated or prepared myself for was that there might be ambiguity about the reason for and nature of the interviews. I had taken pains to clearly identify myself as a researcher and to specify in detail the aims and methodology of my research from the start, but a number of interviewees confessed that – even after all my disclaimers – they wondered whether I 'really' wanted to book them and whether all of this (including a brief feature on my research in the *Times Higher Education Supplement*) was part of some incredibly elaborate ruse.

Although such suspicions were, for the most part, quickly dispelled (using one's University email account would be an odd way to make a booking, for instance), there were still times when my interview requests were met with offers of 'free' bookings or demands for sexual 'payment', or else were taken as an invitation to send me sexually explicit images or texts. While I did not meet with anyone who propositioned me in this way, there were also times during the interviews themselves when I was explicitly sexualised and/or objectified. (For example, without any prompting or information about my sexual history or preferences, one bi, cis male escort decided that I was dearly in need of hands-on sexual counselling and that he was expertly qualified to provide this.) I found such encounters quite difficult to deal with, in large part because I appreciated that the culture of the sex industry is highly sexualised so that such propositions are an everyday part of it. But it was also because, when it came to it, I simply did not want to be constructed as 'a' body. So, I employed a number of strategies to achieve this, not just by saying 'Please don't send me any more explicit texts', but also by restating and reinforcing my own subject position as an academic (including in terms of being accountable to the University Ethics Committee).

Having completed the interviews – and now in the process of writing them up[1] – I am keenly aware of how my position as an academic involves further layers of disembodiment and of the power relations that are produced by, and productive of, this. As I listen back to the recordings of the interviews, I am intrigued and also somewhat embarrassed to hear the sounds of my own body captured on the tape: my voice, fast-paced and unevenly pitched, my stuttering, the coughs, the laughs … All of these are signs of my inability to perform authoritative masculinity and yet, as I go through the process of transforming speech into the written word, all of this can be erased. As writer, I get to decide which words get repeated (I can edit out all my own spoken words if I choose to), and in so doing, I can remove any traces of my own body (including my very presence at the interview – I can literally write myself out of the text).

Indeed, it is customary for the author to remark upon the physical appearance of an interviewee (albeit in a 'non-identifying' way), but it is rare to find detailed descriptions of the author herself. And so, even as we take pains to reflect upon matters of reflexivity and positionality (including through discussions of our own gender, race, class, dis/ablity, sexuality, etc.), academics still do not quite manage to make ourselves visible *as bodies*. To bring it back to 'my' body: the reality was that, when I did the interviews, I was a new mother who had scarcely slept for months. How did that shape 'my' knowledge? How did that shape 'the' research? Yet, while it felt appropriate, on occasion, to discuss my own embodiment during the interviews themselves, to *write* about all of that is another matter entirely. Simply put, I don't think I have the courage to immortalise my own body in the written word (and in the 'academic voice', no less). As a feminist scholar, then, I actively seek to *theorise*, *research* and *write* the body, and yet it is my own disembodiment that remains a precondition for precisely this endeavour.

Note

1 At the time of writing (May 2013).

Acknowledgements

I am grateful to the Leverhulme Trust for funding the research upon which this chapter is based (Project Grant F/007 094/BJ).

Works cited

Agathangelou, A 2005, *The global political economy of sex: desire, violence, and insecurity in Mediterranean nation states*, Palgrave Macmillan, London.
Egan, RD, Frank, K & Johnson, ML 2006, *Flesh for fantasy: producing and consuming exotic dance*, Seal Press, New York.
Kempadoo, K 2004, *Sexing the Caribbean: gender, race, and sexual labor*, Psychology Press, Hove.
O'Connell Davidson, J 2005, *Children in the global sex trade*, Polity, Cambridge.
Penttinen, E 2008, *Globalization, prostitution and sex-trafficking: corporeal politics*, Routledge, London.
Peterson, VS 2003, *A critical rewriting of global political economy: integrating reproductive, productive and virtual economies*, Routledge, London.
Pettman, JJ 1997, 'Body politics: international sex tourism', *Third World Quarterly*, vol. 18, no. 1, pp. 93–108.
Youngs, G 2000, *Political economy, power and the body: global perspectives*, Palgrave MacMillan, London.

CRITICAL METHODOLOGY AND THE PROBLEM OF HISTORY

Samuel Knafo

The question of method, for me, came relatively late and in an unexpected way. When I was pursuing my graduate studies, debates over the nature of knowledge (epistemology) occupied a great place in IR, as they were seen as pivotal for challenging a hegemonic model of science that left little room for critical and interpretive approaches (Cox 1981; Lapid 1989). In this context, methodology was usually considered with suspicion. Seen as the preserve of positivists, methodological debates were, to the minds of many critical scholars, misleading attempts to specify a practice that could capture 'the world as it really is'. Questions of method were often treated as secondary and mostly relevant for people who did fieldwork or worked with data sets. Those two issues remained peripheral for someone like me, who was working primarily on theoretical matters and large-scale history. Like many others at the time, I did not see methodology as a defining feature of critical enquiry or as a practice that would demarcate a particular approach as critical.

It was eventually a dissatisfaction with theory that brought me to issues of methodology. More specifically, I had become concerned about the difficult relationship of theory to history, a relationship that seemed to involve an inevitable trade-off (Wood 1995). For the more one seeks to develop abstract theories which speak to multiple cases, the more it is necessary to generalise and neglect historical specificities. Inversely, the attempt to bring history back into the picture often seems to require the abandonment of grand narratives that leave little room for contingency and specificity. With these observations in mind, I made it my central objective to develop a method that would allow me to make general claims that were attuned to, or more precisely based on, historical specificity. But how to reconcile both? The key for me was to develop comparative methods and to use them as tools for historicisation. Although these methods are usually employed to find common patterns in different cases and thus to abstract once more from context, I was interested in drawing productive comparisons that would help me contrast and specify my ideas. Later on, I came to refer to this approach as a radical historicism. As I show below, the ambition of this approach was to find methodological principles based on this comparative thinking that would maximise the use and significance of history in the very way we theorise and conceptualise issues of global political economy.

My concern with navigating the history/theory trade-off profoundly influenced my work on the rise of liberal financial governance in nineteenth-century Britain and its main institution, the gold standard (Knafo 2013). First, it changed how I approached the object of my research. My intention was to frame my problematic in fully historical terms. This meant, among other things, discarding as much as possible any form of deductive reasoning about liberal governance. As I began researching, I was struck by how the practices of liberal governance were commonly defined in theoretical terms as general claims about the nature of this practice without (or with very limited) references to its concrete historical settings. Scholars, of course, had clear ideas about where to locate the practices of liberal governance, but their conceptualisations of such governance did not explicitly include contextual material. In fact, they were usually intentionally devoid of contextual references in order for these concepts to work across a variety of contexts where liberal governance was said to have been implemented. As a result the focus was placed on general points such as the idea that liberalism limits state intervention or that it promotes a market or capitalist logic.

Ultimately, it became clear to me that many problematic assumptions were entrenched in such general and abstract 'starting points'. Those points of departure tended to yield axiomatic approaches that foregrounded pre-existing understandings of liberal governance by stating in advance what was the object of research, and only then working to reconcile any incongruities that emerged from looking at history. Historical evidence thus came after theoretical framing, which meant that history always had to be reconciled to theory and not vice versa. In the case of my own research, I noticed that scholars recognised that the state had intervened more than was traditionally assumed, but found ways of showing either that these interventions were relatively unimportant or that liberalism had not been fully implemented (Polanyi 1957). The incongruity between history and existing models was too often read as a sign that history did not fully play out as the models would have suggested (Eichengreen 1992), rather than as a sign compelling us to rethink the gold standard in the first place.

To move away from abstract, deductive reasoning, I decided to rely systematically on comparative work. This involved me comparing the nineteenth-century gold standard to what existed previously in Britain, in particular, and in Europe, more generally. Problematising my object of research through comparisons with other regimes of governance allowed me to use history to re-set the puzzle of the gold standard in historical terms. For if one society organised its practices of governance differently than others, that difference represented an obvious case of something socially constructed which required an explanation. This is how I came to move away from the idea that liberal financial governance was characterised by its supposedly limited level of intervention, a feature which simply cannot be established on the basis of historical facts about nineteenth-century financial governance. Instead I pointed to three more concrete historical features which were drawn from my comparisons: the striking stability of the pound, the fact that Britain relied solely on gold to anchor its currency contrary to other states which used bimetallism with a predilection for silver, and the creation of a central bank. The challenge then was to develop an explanation for these three features of liberal financial governance.

This brings me to the second aspect of my methodology, which involves considering how we use history to *explain* social developments. The question here is one of historicisation, or more specifically how we use history in order to *explain* social developments, and it involves what space we give to social construction and agency. Like many others, I was attracted to Marx's famous dictum that people make their own history even if they do not do so under conditions of their own making. What struck me, however, was that most people who accepted that dictum usually focused only on its second part. By contrast, the leitmotif of much of my work has been to make good on the first part of the dictum and emphasise agency. For it is not enough to claim that agency matters. The real challenge is to grasp what is significant about this agency and what difference it makes to our narratives. Indeed, agency is difficult to perceive because of the asymmetry which exists between structural conditions (such as the structures of financial markets) and the impact that a single agent can make on society. It is easy to see what difference an individual can make to their immediate surroundings, but much more difficult to specify what difference people make to the broader social processes we are interested in when doing global political economy. This is why, I argued, scholars continue to fetishise the structures that govern social life assuming that they are imbued with a life of their own, as if they impose their own logic on society (Knafo 2002, 2010). Due to inherent imbalance between structures and agency, it is futile to ascertain their respective influence. This type of exercise will always necessarily yield structural accounts that reify social reality.

Instead of such accounts, we need a rigorous practice that counterbalances this problem of perspective. I thus came to see it as a *corrective lens required for pursuing a critical project which is based precisely on the idea that social dynamics are not transparent*. Employing such a methodology in my research meant systematically tracing the agencies involved in the making of liberal financial governance as a means of better appreciating *what differences people make*. For the challenge is to show, against the overwhelming impression that individuals are simply governed by transcendental structural laws, that it is still people through their agency who make history, *even* if they do not do so under the conditions of their own making.

This led me to construct my historical narrative of the rise of liberal financial governance around a series of commitments which were aimed to place in perspective, usually through some form of comparison, the agencies involved in the construction of liberal financial governance. This work of tracing involved three different aspects.

1. Characterise the concrete agencies in terms of their specific features

I decided to systematically look into what marked out the key actors who played a role in political struggles over financial governance or who made key social, regulatory or financial innovations, with an eye to focus on the *specific* features of their position and the distinctive nature of their relationships to other agents. Instead of turning to generic characterisations, for example the fact that these actors were bankers, capitalists or workers, all terms which were already imbued with strong associations, I looked for what distinguished these actors from the generic characterisations we use. Looking at bankers, for example, I would focus on what distinctive features would differentiate these bankers from other bankers. The purpose of doing this was to avoid falling back on the kind of assumptions that usually stem from deductive reasoning rather than historical enquiry. Why, I asked myself, did Birmingham bankers oppose the gold standard while dominant bankers in Manchester did not? For me this was not a simple detail. It offered a key insight into the politics of the time, which were particularly valuable because they disrupted the classic stereotypes which had come to cast the gold standard as favourable to financiers in general.

This form of rigour had a big impact on my analysis which is difficult to capture in a paragraph. The example of the Bank of England, however, may help to convey what difference such a method can make. As I mentioned, most analysis of liberal financial governance started from the idea that the gold standard was an institution that imposed constraints on central banks like the Bank of England by forcing them to guarantee the convertibility of banknotes at a fixed rate. Neglected in most studies of the gold standard, however, was the fact that the Bank of England was a private institution at the time of the gold standard's adoption, an institution that explicitly operated in the interests of its shareholders. Scholars, of course, knew this, but they usually felt comfortable ignoring it in their conceptualisations. And yet, this changed everything, because re-including that fact meant that the gold standard now appeared as an attempt by the state to discipline a market actor (i.e. the Bank of England), rather than a liberal attempt to limit the intervention of the state itself.

2. Build a narrative based on what difference the innovations of agents make

The second aspect of this focus on agency was to emphasise the creativity of agents and their ability to make a difference. It was important for me not to simply describe what people have done, as many scholars often do in covering history. The reason for this is simply that this type of historical work often fails to properly establish the agencies involved and is fully amenable to a highly structural account where history merely illustrates the theory. Although we may know that a certain government has adopted a policy or that a financier has developed a new financial instrument, it remains to be determined what difference these facts really make to our accounts. Do these developments simply reflect the broader context in which they took place, or do they inflect the narrative in significant ways?

In order to break this functionalist thinking which always normalises innovations as the 'normal' response that one might expect from a given actor under specific types of pressure, I systematically tried to establish what was counterintuitive about innovations. I did this first by showing why this innovation was surprising at the time, something which can be established through comparisons, for example with how similar agents operated or simply with what these innovators used to do previously so as to specify what was new. This could also be captured by showing the reaction, surprise or resistance of others to these innovations. In short, the challenge was to find an interesting angle to convey this. My assumption was that if a practice stands out at a particular juncture, it is probably because there is something surprising about it, otherwise others would have done the same thing. But emphasising the counterintuitive nature of a development was also a way to challenge how we retrospectively come to normalise developments we now take for granted because we are used to them. By establishing through comparisons why these developments were not what should be expected, I was interested in establishing what difference agencies make in history and forcing myself to systematically reflect on the significance of their social innovations.

3. Analyse social developments largely as unintended effects of social struggles

Finally, such an account can only become truly historicist if we detach agency from intentions. For what agents produce through their strategies or actions rarely conforms to their expectations or intentions. A crucial component of any historicist analysis is thus to account for the effects of agency in terms of unintended effects. In this way, one can move away from functionalist approaches which explain developments in terms of what was needed (e.g. for the reproduction of neoliberalism or for solving a financial crisis). By separating agency from intentions, I wanted to recapture what is counterintuitive about this history by demonstrating, for example, that central banking required a massive leap of imagination that no agent in the nineteenth century was able to make. By recognising this, we can problematise what agents were actually trying to do, and grasp how their motivations were very different from what we now assume, because these agents never foresaw what they ended up constructing. One of the central ideas of my book *The Making of Modern Finance* (Knafo 2013) was precisely that the interventions of Liberal governance were constructed through a series of institutions aimed at disciplining market activity partly because repeated failures to achieve certain policy goals led state officials to look for increasingly disciplinary tools to achieve their goals. In that respect, the ideas of liberalism may have been geared towards liberalising the market, but the means that were put in place in its name were usually intended to empower the state in relation to market activity so as to make sure the latter would behave as state officials intended. While this never managed to fully stabilise financial markets as intended, it ended up setting the foundations for Central Banking, the most important institution of modern economic governance.

As I have suggested throughout this piece, radical historicism is a practice based on a series of commitments that systematically place emphasis on history. Too often, critical scholars have evaded methodological questions by suggesting that an awareness of the socially constructed dynamics they study is sufficient. It has always seemed to me ironic that critical scholars who have criticised mainstream scholars for relying on common sense can themselves place an inordinate amount of faith in their *own* ability to make judgements without getting trapped in their own common sense (Knafo 2015). In that respect, radical historicism constitutes precisely a lens to force us to go in places we would not go otherwise, to destabilise through rigorous methodological means our biases and make it difficult to project these on what we study. The goal is to make historicisation, through the systematic use of historical comparisons, the very process by which we theorise, rather than a practice aimed simply at adding details to a narrative already set at a theoretical level.

Works cited

Cox, RW 1981, 'Social forces, states and world orders: beyond international relations theory', *Millenium: Journal of International Studies*, vol. 10, no. 2, pp. 126–55.

Eichengreen, B 1992, *Golden fetters: the gold standard and the Great Depression 1919–1939*, Oxford UP, New York.

Knafo, S 2002, 'The fetishizing subject of Marx's *Capital*', *Capital and Class*, vol. 76, pp. 183–213.

Knafo, S 2010, 'Critical approaches and the legacy of the agent/structure debate in international relations', *Cambridge Review of International Affairs*, vol. 23, no. 3, pp. 493–516.

Knafo, S 2013, *The making of modern finance: liberal governance and the gold standard*, Routledge, London.

Knafo, S 2015, 'Bourdieu and the dead end of reflexivity: on the impossible task of locating the subject', *Review of International Studies*, FirstView Article, pp. 1–23.

Lapid, Y 1989, 'The third debate: on the prospects of international theory in a post-positivist era', *International Studies Quarterly*, vol. 33, no. 3, pp. 235–54.

Polanyi, K 1957, *The great transformation: the political and economic origins of our time*, Beacon, Boston, MA.

Wood, EM 1995, *Democracy against capitalism: renewing historical materialism*, Cambridge UP, Cambridge.

4

ITERATIVE REFLEXIVE RESEARCH STRATEGY

Johnna Montgomerie

This chapter further develops the idea of a pluralist methodology of political economy by suggesting how it can be pragmatic about sources, strategic about methods and informed by the critical research ethic (outlined in chapter three). Developing on from Ackerly and True (2010), I put forward an iterative reflexive research strategy that involves being willing and able to recognise and take advantage of 'deliberative moments', moments that shed light on the rationale of one's research and enable that research's narration. Explicitly narrating the key deliberative moments that inform one's final argument requires a new way of articulating how knowledge claims emerge from research practice.

In establishing a pluralist methodology, we should remind ourselves that critical epistemology is always conscious of boundaries. Because that epistemology concerns what is 'counted' as evidence or knowledge and what is not, we must never assume that methods are neutral tools of analysis. With this in mind, the current chapter treats research as a craft and underscores the importance of establishing a rationale for one's choices, accounting for one's judgements and explaining the key trade-offs of critical social research.

Although pluralism offers many opportunities to develop methodologies within the study of political economy, those opportunities also come with real challenges to research design and practice. As I suggested in the previous chapter and as the vignettes in this volume make clear, pluralism in action requires reflexivity to be effective. For just this reason, I suggest that we cultivate a shared language of professional judgement, decision-making and credibility that informs our understanding of methodological rigour.

For any given research project, the methods one uses are driven by the research puzzle at hand. At the same time, the development of a research strategy involves cultivating a critical research ethic, an ethic that, among other things, strives to uncover what is hidden, to give voice to the voiceless and to cast light into the shadows of the global economy. By characterising research as a craft that depends on the constant evaluation of what certain methodologies do and how they do it, we place much-needed emphasis on the personal and professional contexts that inform how we negotiate choices, trade-offs and judgements.

Political economy as pluralism in practice

A key strength of pluralism is that it promotes a broader conception of what 'counts' as relevant evidence within political economy (Hveem 2009; Phillips 2009). Yet a pluralist methodology will remain undeveloped unless we cultivate a critical reflexivity about how methods inform our knowledge claims (Bohman 1999). In practice, cultivating critical reflexivity entails working with existing critical epistemologies while also finding new collective meanings and practices in materialist and postmodern ontologies (Coleman and Ringrose 2013; Milonakis and Fine 2009). This is no small task, but it is worth the effort, as it will give new credibility to a pluralist methodology by focusing on the challenges and puzzles of studying the contemporary global economy. By engaging in a collaborative dialogue, we can begin to initiate a shift away from concerns about the theoretical 'correctness' of methods to questions about their evidentiary validity or merit. As the vignettes in this volume suggest, individual interests, ethical commitments, hard work and institutional environments all contribute to our very broad field of research. Moreover, those vignettes underscore how researchers' professional journeys and the work-based practices of academic research disrupt the public/private divide that traditionally confines our understanding of what methods do. Such ruptures encourage a more in-depth discussion of pluralist methodology (Willmott 2008) and require us to be more informed about and engaged with the ways that methods, evidence and analysis coalesce to produce novel knowledge claims.

One benefit of participating in such discussions is that we can move away from the academic hierarchies that determine what does or does not belong to the established canon or what does or does not have relevance for the latest iteration of the state-of-the-art debate. To bypass such hierarchies, we need to shift our focus from notions of discipline, inclusion and exclusion to considerations of how the practice of pluralism moves, innovates and adapts. Putting emphasis on action, movement and transformation helps us to understand what doing research looks like and means, whether we are talking in terms of the collection of evidence or the writing-up of results.

Including the social life of methods suggests we also begin to consider how methods can be objects of analysis in their own right. Although textbooks and other sources offer much information on the practicalities of using different methods, they often fail to discuss how those same methods lead to the production of different kinds of expert knowledge claim. To put the matter in another fashion, the tendency to view methods as tools leads us to ignore how the employment of methodology is a form of academic craftsmanship.

The craft of research is typically presented as stages of completing a dissertation or steps in a research design (Booth, Colomb and Williams 2009; Shively 2013). In contrast, scholars such as Robert Alford (1998) suggest that the academic craft of inquiry begins with an understanding of how to translate elements of the researcher's own history, personal experience and issues into research questions. Following Alford, the current volume examines the process of craftsmanship through professional journeys, placing particular emphasis on how critical researchers face strategic challenges when they move off the well-trodden path of methodological individualism and opt to forego prescribed methods for making causal claims. Although avoiding methodological individualism and causal prescriptions opens up the possibility of taking rich methodological routes, it also forces the researcher to make his or her own way. It is important to note that entering uncharted methodological territory does not usually depend on some abstract process of reasoning; rather, researchers who decide to go against the traditional methodological grain face hard work that takes place over long periods of time, within (changing) institutions and through processes of identity-making. One virtue of the current project is that it makes very 'real' and legitimate some of the struggles that researchers deal with but that textbooks do not talk about; at the same time, it offers some strategies for how to tackle issues and dilemmas.

Viewing research as a craft pushes us to think about how we negotiate the choices, trade-offs and judgements that pluralism encourages. As many of the contributors to this volume note, their current methodologies sprang from an interest in critical theory. The task before them was thus to grapple with big questions – structure versus agency, generality versus specificity, or the relation between the material, discursive, ideational and cultural – while simultaneously addressing specific concerns and finding evidence about concrete social phenomena. The difficulty of balancing these two registers should not be underestimated, especially because there is no clear path for incorporating theoretical and political insights into practical research. At the same time that we recognise the difficulty of balancing those registers, however, we should also remember that a great deal of purpose and agency stems from relying on a critical research ethic that seeks out the tensions, puzzles, orthodoxies, silences and mundane routines of contemporary capitalism.

Iterative reflexive research strategy

An iterative research strategy emphasises the *movement* of research. Doing political economy is not straightforward but rather contested, fluid and open to serendipity. The goal of an iterative research strategy is thus to find problems, to give answers to questions, to uncover the hidden and to hear the voiceless while also dealing with research problems pragmatically and in accordance with one's critical research ethic (Ackerly and True 2008). Although research design is usually presented as a series of steps or categories (e.g., literature review, research question, hypothesis, methods, ethics, etc.), researchers at all levels of academic scholarship acknowledge that one's research design will most likely change when conducting actual research.

For precisely this reason, the iterative, reflexive research strategy I put forward seeks to illustrate critical processes that inform the doing of research, not a series of steps that must be taken.

In using the word 'strategy', I mean to include all stages of the research process: defining the problem; establishing the object of analysis; developing a methodology; choosing methods; analysing evidence; and writing about the research. Each of these stages is iterative and constitutive, which means that each informs the others in ways that only the person doing the research can account for. Referring to a 'research strategy' instead of a 'research design' allows us to place emphasis on the decision-making that is at the very core of critical social research. The proposed schema is therefore an invitation to the researcher to acknowledge up front the reality of facing key choices and the need to develop a strategy to deal with them. Those choices and strategies may relate to the basic questions of any research project (e.g., the who, what, when, where, how and why), or they may involve the researcher reflecting on practices and explaining key decisions for the reader's benefit. Whatever the case, accounting for how we craft our research informs the knowledge claims that emanate from it. Indeed, part of developing a richer methodological practice involves extending our conception of research into the writing and publishing phases, mostly because writing and publishing are intricately linked to our larger professional journey.

Pragmatism in research means making trade-offs. Drawing upon a critical research ethic thus requires the researcher to articulate key judgements, perceptions and decisions. As noted previously, Ackerly and True (2010) describe these key judgements as 'deliberative moments' within the research process; such moments can be anticipated as part of the larger research puzzle or can occur at unforeseen times during the research process. Sometimes, deliberative moments involve taking decisions that make the research project more manageable; at other times, a deliberative moment may involve a researcher refining an object of analysis. Accounting for these deliberative moments foregrounds the ethical implications of using methods not just as tools but as constitutive processes of knowledge creation. Moreover, cultivating deliberative moments reinforces pluralist rigour by compelling the researcher to take into consideration questions of integrity, accountability and privilege. By crafting an account of the mundane aspects of doing research and by making the most of deliberative moments, we shape the kinds of evidence being produced and prepare ourselves for honest discussions of evidentiary weight within specific forms of inquiry.

As the process map in Figure 4.1 moves from left to right, each double-sided arrow signals a deliberative moment a researcher anticipates or encounters. A researcher's choice of a topic shapes his or her research problem(s) – that is, whether something needs to be better understood or whether a problem needs to be solved – and that problem, in turn, guides the researcher's questions and engagement with evidence. When the object of analysis finally emerges, the researcher will be required to choose methods that are capable of answering the organising research questions.

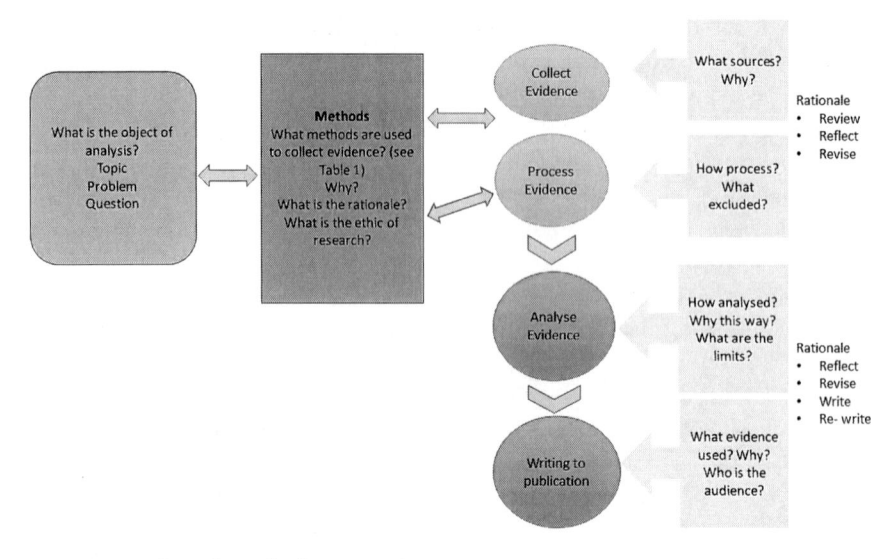

FIGURE 4.1 Iterative reflexive research strategy

Forging a new methodological path involves openly acknowledging the messiness of the research process, which is often overlooked in discussions of research results. Accounting for the choices or deliberative moments that shape our conclusions is essential to advancing a pluralist methodology. By explaining why we have done what we have done, we enact the ethic that guides our research. The autobiographical vignettes in the current volume illustrate just this point. Each of these vignettes shows in a different way how choices and deliberative moments shape methodological practices. Whether a particular researcher experiences conflicts, wishes to give a description of real-world activities, seeks to make a contribution or strives to develop new ideas within our discipline, the actions he or she takes (and the reactions that stem from those actions) lead to a dynamic research process. Instead of believing that we must move from asking a research question to gathering and testing evidence and then to reporting findings, we can adopt a more fluid procedure that allows us to demonstrate our commitment to an ethical, reflexive and adaptive form of pluralist research.

What is the object of analysis?

The first stage in an iterative, reflexive research strategy is defining the object of analysis. As Figure 4.1 indicates, the object of analysis is determined by considering three interrelated variables: the topic, the problem and the question(s) that define an individual's research agenda. The topic relates to the 'key words' that define what the research is about and that, to a large extent, indicate the researcher's areas of expertise. The 'question' and the 'problem' are what bring a reader to one's book or article; they are the building blocks of making expert claims. Together, the topic, question and problem form the object of analysis, or the substance of what is being researched.

Bob Jessop (2004) has outlined how cultural political economy is a form of critical semiotics. On his account, the field's focus on meaning-making activities and processes provides a way of moving past the subject/object dichotomy and of concentrating on the constitution and co-evolution of the object of analysis within wider ensembles of social relations (p. 162). Following Jessop, I suggest that researchers zero in on a subject of analysis (or topic) and then consider how their problems and questions condition or place constraints on that subject (or topic). Before articulating the object of analysis, in other words, researchers must set out the parameters of what is being researched.

In practical terms, choosing a research topic is about making key choices that allow the researcher to narrow down a topic into a manageable segment or piece. The global political economy is a big system, and it gets even bigger when researchers strive to account for history, change and inequality. The purpose or motivator of any critical research is to identify gaps between norms and practice, theory and evidence, model and outcome and/or structure and agency. Establishing a topic therefore involves refining the subject of analysis in a way that adequately captures the blind-spots in, or the outposts of, the global political economy.

We see from this volume's contributors that narrowing one's topic can be the most painstaking part of research, as it involves evaluating the wider structure and institutional context of a topic and then unpacking key tensions, silences and omissions. In many cases, researchers wish to account for the history of a topic and to discover how it fits into a larger developmental context (i.e., What came before the thing I am studying? Why is what I am studying relevant?). Sam Knafo, for example, describes how he researched the emergence of liberal governance in the Central Bank by focusing on what is not told in historical accounts or established theory. Providing context and clear parameters for one's topic is thus an important opening move when developing a research strategy.

Asking questions is also a well-established aspect of critical research. Yet figuring out how to ask relevant questions to advance one's research strategy is not a straightforward process. The set of questioning practices that defines a critical research ethic compels us to ask not just why a subject or topic matters but *for whom* it matters. We must also ask the basic 'So what?' question, which requires us to consider the relevance of pursing a particular line of inquiry.

The question and problem driving a research strategy are not identical, although they are related. Critical research questions articulate a problem – a silence, frictions, a gap, an omission – in such a way that *not* answering the question keeps us from knowing something more important. In everyday language, a problem is something to avoid; in academic research, however, a problem is what we are trying to find. I make this distinction between question and problem in order to re-shape how we understand problem-solving as part of critical research. This relates specifically to how Robert Cox (Cox and Sinclair 1996) has mapped out the difference between 'problem-solving' and 'critical' theory in order to underscore the constraints that the creation of instrumental knowledge puts on understanding the global economy:

> [W]hereas the problem-solving approach leads to further analytical subdivision and limitation of the issue to be dealt with, the critical approach leads toward the construction of a larger picture of the whole of which the initially contemplated part is just one component, and seeks to understand the processes of change in which both parts and whole are involved.
>
> *(p. 89)*

In this excerpt, Cox directly echoes Habermas's (1989) distinction between instrumental, hermeneutic and critical modes of knowledge. On Cox's account, problem-solving theory involves the creation of instrumental knowledge – that is, it seeks to smooth out, and in a depoliticised way, the relationships and institutions that are particular sources of trouble. To put the matter differently, problem-solving theory aims to solve problems in a way that does not call into question existing social power relations.

Since Cox originally made the distinction between problem-solving and critical research, there is greater consensus that positivist methodology enables an instrumentalist logic wherein methodological expertise is tied up with forms of classfication and modes of arraying difference (Pickstone 2000). In my advocacy of the social life of methods, I wish to move past just that methodological complex that constrains us to separate theory, substance and method into three separate spheres (Law, Ruppert and Savage 2011). Clinging to the familiar critique of positivism reinforces the general tendency to believe that research questions (hypotheses) are derived from theory, while methods provide the tools that allow such questions to be answered (or 'tested'). However, there is nothing inherently positivist about problem-solving theories. If we consider for a moment the scale of the ecological, economic and humanitarian crises that plague the contemporary global economy, we should certainly not discount the potential usefulness of theories that could solve these problems (Fraser 2014; Brown et al. 2013; Bryan et al. 2012). Any theory or method that enables us to identify problems and work toward solutions need not be dismissed beforehand as solely an instrumentalist knowledge claim.

To avoid this, I suggest that we consider how *practical* problems are indicative of a wider *research* problem. Practical problems are caused by some condition in the world (e.g., income or gender inequality) that makes us unhappy or outraged. These problems are solved by *doing* something, whether that be designing a research study or contributing to policy or institutional process as forms of action-research (Whyte 1991; Khanlou and Peter 2005). From the perspective of a critical research ethic, researchers seek to locate a problem and find a solution that either eliminates or ameliorates its social costs. In contrast to practical problems, research problems indicate there is a lack of understanding or knowledge about the world; in identifying such problems, we either implicitly or explicitly believe we should or could understand them if we tried. We solve research problems by understanding social phenomena better.

In making a distinction between practical and research problems, I do not mean to suggest that the two kinds of problem are unrelated; quite the contrary, practical problems stem from research problems, and research problems relate to real-world conditions that need solutions. As a result, we need to consider how our understanding of the meaning of the word 'problem' is informed by our critical research ethic, which should always be attuned to the limits and privileges of academic research. Although we should be wary of creating instrumentalist knowledge for its own sake, we should still recognise the value of problem-solving as a motivating force within a critical research ethic.

Accounting for methods

The second movement of the iterative, reflexive research strategy is accounting for the methods used to examine the object of analysis. Refining the object of analysis involves selecting a particular method, the use of which may demonstrate the necessity or virtue of reconceptualising the object of analysis itself. When we account for our methods, we must therefore accept that they are not neutral or free of agency. Moreover, we must evaluate our methods in terms of the kinds of evidence they produce. To put the matter differently, we might say that the methods we use constitute the evidence our research creates (Law and Ruppert 2013). In recognising that our methods can be both subjects and objects of analysis, we also come to understand that they are not simple tools but rather constitutive processes that produce particular kinds or types of evidence. Being reflexive about how methods create evidence enables us to bridge the divides that are frequently said to obtain between facts and ideas and rational and emotional logics. In addition, evaluating the choices, judgements and trade-offs of using different methods in the collection, processing, sorting, analysis and interpretation of evidence helps us to understand accurately the truly transformative dynamics of social research.

The number of available methods for conducting social research is practically endless. In most cases, however, those methods are presented as tools of analysis that offer an array of approaches based on the specific needs of one's research design (see Table 4.1). Navigating between methods is part of a pluralist methodology, but it can also be very frustrating for the researcher. As the contributors to this volume explain, they often moved from a suspicion of methods – or, in Runyan's terms, a suspicion of disciplining apparatuses – before developing their own critical methodologies. How those authors overcame their suspicions and arrived at the methodologies that now guide their research reflects a personal process of (self-) examination, a process that is tied to each individual's identity, body, history and academic experience.

Looking now to the bottom half of Figure 4.1, it outlines the movement from evidence collection and processing to analysing and writing about our research findings. As was the case in other parts of the research process, these latter stages also

TABLE 4.1 Methods for social research

Name	Description	Key Contributions
Action Research	A type of applied social research that includes the researcher's direct involvement in problem solving. The researcher is 'situated' in the field and uses participative methods for data collection, analysis and diagnosis of the problem. Information is fed-back to those who originated it in order to understand the functioning of the system, or to solve the problem.	Costello (2003) Hult & Lennung (1980) Reason & Bradbury(2001) Stringer (2013)
Archival Research	An archive is a store of information that has already been gathered for some reason aside from the research project at hand. Archival research involves primary research that seeks out and extracts evidence from original archival records. Typically a text-based analysis, but with the rise of the digital archive it can include visual analysis.	Cozby (1977) Goodwin (2009) Welch (2000)
Case Study	A research strategy focused on understanding the dynamics present within a single 'setting' with a strong focus on real-life context, uses multiple sources of evidence of meaningful characteristics to offer a credible and holistic picture of social phenomenon.	Eisenhardt & Graebner (2007) Merriam(1991) Yin (2014)
Comparative Case Study	Adapts the case study method to include multiple cases in order to make comparisons between them. There are different research designs to collect and use data: content analysis, survey data, archival data, descriptive statistical analysis, focus groups and interviews are all compatible, not competitive, with comparative case study research because they are used to validate the knowledge claims derived from it.	George & Bennett (2005) Kaarbo & Beasley (1999) Ragin (2014) Yin (2011)
Content Analysis	Content analysis is not a single method, but an approach to interpreting meaning from text. Methods can be computer-assisted coding, summation of typology derived from text (counting and comparison of keywords), or directed approach that starts with a theory or relevant research findings as guidance for initial codes.	Hsieh & Shannon (2005) Krippendorf (2012) Neuendorf (2016)
Cultural Artefacts	Artefacts are human creations that give information about the culture of its creator and users. Current and ancient artefacts offer a material way to engage technological processes, economic development, social structure and aesthetic.	Du Gay et al. (2013) Hicks & Beaudry (2010) Harvey (1992) Watts (1981)

TABLE 4.1 (*cont.*)

Name	Description	Key Contributions
Descriptive Statistics	Uses statistical sources to elucidate trends by describing the features of the data and providing summaries about the sample and the measures. The results can be presented as graphical analysis, and usually form the basis of virtually every quantitative analysis of datasets.	Winkler (2009) Runyon (1977) Loether & McTavish (1974)
Document Analysis	Document analysis is a systematic procedure for reviewing or evaluating documents – both printed and digital material. There are different types of research design, but they have the shared requirement that data be examined and interpreted in order to elicit meaning, gain understanding and develop empirical knowledge.	Bowen (2009) Rapley (2008) Corbin & Strauss (2008)
Ethnographic Methods	Ethnographic methods investigate the actions of people in everyday contexts and relies on data gathered from a range of sources, including: documentary evidence, participant observation, informal conversations; and context from the 'field' of research. The researcher is situated within the field and is guided by ethical considerations for his or her object of study.	Hammersley & Atkinson(2007) Brewer (2000) Wolcott (1999) Bryman (2001)
Focus Group	A technique of qualitative data collection that embeds individual response within group interaction. Research design determines the size of the group and the strategy to engage them in responses that then become the evidence to be analysed.	Berg & Lune (2012), Krueger & Casey (2014) Ritchie et al. (2013) Morgan (1996)
Interviews	A technique of qualitative research that interprets human voice and experience based on responses to questions, either open-ended dialogue or a structured format. Research design varies, but a key element is the relationship between the interviewer and the interviewee, in terms of building trust and contextualising the responses given.	Kahn & Cannell (1957) King & Horrocks (2010) Seidman (2015)
Participant Observation	A method in which the researcher is situated in the daily activities, rituals, interactions and events of a group of people as a means of learning explicit and tacit aspects of life, routines and culture. Research design varies; there is a focus on ethics and contextualising findings.	Dewalt & Dewalt (2011) Jorgensen (1989) Spradley (2016)
Regression Analysis	A form of statistical modelling, that estimates the degrees of relationship among variables. There is a plethora of modelling techniques based on assumptions; most seek to estimate the conditional expectation of the dependent variable given the independent variables.	Freund et al. (2006) Gordon (2015) Rawlings et al. (2006) Armstrong (2012)

TABLE 4.1 (*cont.*)

Name	Description	Key Contributions
Survey	A technique focused on human responses to questions, which can vary in terms of the population engaged, the sampling technique and the quantity and style of questions asked. The research design sets out the question tree. The procedures used to collect the answers all have the potential to affect how well the survey is able to answer the research question.	Fowler (2013) Rossi et al. (2013) De Vaus (2013)
Visual Artefacts	Opens up the artefact method to a wider range of 'media' that is not just text or speech. Visual data can be images from the production of films, photographs, social media content, archival pictures, media images, websites or maps. Analysing this data involves looking beyond the surface appearances of an image to uncover the image's multiple layers of culturally informed meanings that represent socio-cultural phenomena.	Rose (2016) Clarke (2007) Banks and Zeitlyn (2015)

involve anticipating and cultivating deliberative moments. What should be stressed is that writing is not separate from the research process but integral to it. The choices we make when analysing evidence effect not only the final results we arrive at but also the ways in which we narrate those results in prose. Because researchers continue to revise their work until they send off the final proofs of their journal articles or monographs, it is important that we concentrate as much on how we articulate our findings as we do on determining which results we choose to include in our publications. By focusing reflexively and deliberatively on our research as we write about it, we work against the positivist insistence that only dispassionate research faithfully attends to evidence and accurately presents results.

Kia Hall's chapter in particular offers an honest accounting of the deliberative moments that shaped her doctoral project and, in doing so, provides a good example of how to integrate reflexive methods into our research and writing. Framing critical social research as an iterative strategy acknowledges the reality of shuttling back and forth between concepts and data, structure and specificity, past and present, theory and practice, involving a continual process of reconceptualisation, reflexive ethical considerations, judgement, rationale and argument. The work is never done, only abandoned when the final proofs are due. Political economy as methodology involves the whole process of inquiry – from the conceptualisation of the problem, theoretical debate, specification of research practices, analytic frameworks and epistemological presuppositions – evidence collection is not a self-contained phase in a linear process. Rather, all aspects of the research process are interrelated and all bear on each other. Of course this takes us into unfamiliar territory because it demands we are personally accountable for our knowledge claims by tracing how the decisions made within the 'doing' of research ultimately affected the outcome. Providing a justification or rationale for these choices invites new avenues of developing the craft of critical research.

Conclusion

This chapter developed a highly stylised map of an iterative and reflexive research strategy. That strategy has three key movements: determining how the object of analysis is formed, accounting for method and developing evidence to make knowledge claims. In delimiting these movements, I do not mean to offer a rigid guide but rather to point to key reflexive moments in the research process. Incorporating the social life of methods means we account for our choices in order to maintain our critical research ethic. This does not require a fundamental re-invention of methods; we do not need to start at the beginning but rather forge a new path. Therefore, any choice of methods should deal directly with how they are constituted by the social world but also how they constitute it.

An iterative reflexive strategy carves a new space dedicated to narrating key choices and the rationale behind them in order to contribute to the collective advancement of a political economy methodology. In practice this means making space within our research process, conference papers, journal articles and monographs to account for the decisions, judgements and choices by explaining our rationale as well as their perceived consequences on the final results. In no way will engaging in reflexive methodological practices be easy, nor will accounting for key decisions made in the research process be simple. It might mean highlighting how external and/or internal institutional processes intervene within research to shape its course and, ultimately, its outcomes. For example, whether a doctoral researcher is funded to conduct research or not will influence the types of choice available for how the research is done. Another example could be detailing how the lack of access to a community, organisation or network changed the focus of research, or what the lack of quality quantitative data means to the scope for using statistical trends to describe social change. The intent is to open a dialogue about how political economy would benefit from researchers' adoption of an iterative, reflexive methodology.

Bibliography

Ackerly, Brooke, and Jacqui True. 2008. 'Reflexivity in Practice: Power and Ethics in Feminist Research on International Relations'. *International Studies Review* 10 (4): 693–707. doi:10.1111/j.1468-2486.2008.00826.x.

Ackerly, Brooke, and Jacqui True. 2010, *Doing Feminist Research in Political and Social Science*. New York: Palgrave Macmillan.

Alford, Robert R. 1998. *The Craft of Inquiry: Theories, Methods, Evidence*. Oxford: Oxford University Press.

Armstrong, J. Scott. 2012. 'Illusions in Regression Analysis'. *International Journal of Forecasting* 28 (3): 689–94. doi:10.1016/j.ijforecast.2012.02.001.

Banks, Marcus, and David Zeitlyn. 2015. *Visual Methods in Social Research*. London: Sage.

Berg, Bruce Lawrence, and Howard Lune. 2012. *Qualitative Research Methods for the Social Sciences*. Boston, MA: Pearson.

Bohman, James. 1999. 'Theories, Practices, and Pluralism: A Pragmatic Interpretation of Critical Social Science'. *Philosophy of the Social Sciences* 29 (4): 459–80.

Booth, Wayne C., Gregory G. Colomb, and Joseph M. Williams. 2009. *The Craft of Research*. 3rd edn. Chicago, IL: University of Chicago Press.

Bowen, Glenn A. 2009. 'Document Analysis as a Qualitative Research Method'. *Qualitative Research Journal* 9 (2): 27–40.

Brewer, John. 2000. *Ethnography*. London: McGraw-Hill Education.

Brown, Gareth, Emma Dowling, David Harvie, and Keir Milburn. 2013. 'Careless Talk: Social Reproduction and Fault Lines of the Crisis in the United Kingdom'. *Social Justice* 39 (1): 78–98.

Bryan, D., R. Martin, J. Montgomerie, and K. Williams. 2012. 'An Important Failure: Knowledge Limits and the Financial Crisis'. *Economy and Society* 41 (3): 299–315.

Bryman, Alan. 2001. *Ethnography*. London: Sage.

Clarke, Michael. 2007. *Verbalising the Visual: Translating Art and Design Into Words*. Worthing: AVA Publishing.

Coleman, Rebecca, and Jessica Ringrose. 2013. *Deleuze and Research Methodologies*. Edinburgh: Edinburgh University Press.

Corbin, Juliet, and Anselm L. Strauss. 2008. *Basics of Qualitative Research: Techniques and Procedures for Developing Grounded Theory*. London: Sage.

Costello, Patrick J. M. 2003. *Action Research*. London: A&C Black.

Cox, Robert W., and Timothy Sinclair. 1996. *Approaches to World Order*. Cambridge Studies in International Relations. Cambridge: Cambridge University Press.

Cozby, Paul C. 1977. *Methods in Behavioral Research*. Houston, TX: Mayfield Publishing Company.

De Vaus, David. 2013. *Surveys in Social Research*. London: Routledge.

DeWalt, Kathleen M., and Billie R. DeWalt. 2011. *Participant Observation: A Guide for Fieldworkers*. Lanham, MD: Rowman Altamira.

Du Gay, Paul, Stuart Hall, Linda Janes, Anders Koed Madsen, Hugh Mackay, and Keith Negus. 2013. *Doing Cultural Studies: The Story of the Sony Walkman*. London: Sage.

Eisenhardt, Kathleen M., and Melissa E. Graebner. 2007. 'Theory Building from Cases – Opportunities and Challenges'. *Academy of Management Journal* 50 (1): 25–32.

Fowler, Floyd J. Jr. 2013. *Survey Research Methods*. London: Sage.

Fraser, Nancy. 2014. 'Can Society Be Commodities All the Way Down? Post-Polanyian Reflections on Capitalist Crisis'. *Economy and Society* 43 (4): 541–58. doi:10.1080/03085147.2014.898822.

Freund, Rudolf J., William J. Wilson, and Ping Sa. 2006. *Regression Analysis*. Cambridge, MA: Academic Press.

George, Alexander L., and Andrew Bennett. 2005. *Case Studies and Theory Development in the Social Sciences*. Cambridge, MA: MIT Press.

Goodwin, James C. 2009. *Research in Psychology: Methods and Design*, 6th edition, Hoboken, NJ: John Wiley and Sons.

Gordon, Rachel A. 2015. *Regression Analysis for the Social Sciences*. London: Routledge.

Habermas, Jurgen. 1989. *Theory of Communicative Action, Volume 2: Critique of Functionalist Reason*. Cambridge: Polity Press.

Hammersley, Martyn, and Paul Atkinson. 2007. *Ethnography: Principles in Practice*. London: Routledge.

Harvey, David. 1992. *The Condition of Postmodernity: An Enquiry into the Origins of Cultural Change*. Cambridge, MA: Blackwell.

Hicks, Dan, and Mary C. Beaudry. 2010. *The Oxford Handbook of Material Culture Studies*. Oxford: Oxford UP.

Hsieh, Hsiu-Fang, and Sarah E. Shannon. 2005. 'Three Approaches to Qualitative Content Analysis'. *Qualitative Health Research* 15 (9): 1277–88.

Hult, Margareta, and Sven-Åke Lennung. 1980. 'Towards a Definition of Action Research: A Note and Bibliography'. *Journal of Management Studies* 17 (2): 241–50. doi:10.1111/j.1467-6486.1980.tb00087.x.

Hveem, Helge. 2009. 'Pluralist IPE: A View from Outside the "Schools"'. *New Political Economy* 14 (3): 367–76. doi:10.1080/13563460903087516.

Jessop, Bob. 2004. 'Critical Semiotic Analysis and Cultural Political Economy'. *Critical Discourse Studies* 1 (2): 159–74. doi:10.1080/17405900410001674506.

Jorgensen, Danny L. 1989. *Participant Observation: A Methodology for Human Studies*. London: Sage.

Kaarbo, Juliet, and Ryan K. Beasley. 1999. 'A Practical Guide to the Comparative Case Study Method in Political Psychology'. *Political Psychology* 20 (2): 369–91.

Kahn, Robert Louis, and Charles F. Cannell. 1957. *The Dynamics of Interviewing: Theory, Technique, and Cases*. New York: John Wiley and Sons.

Khanlou, N., and E. Peter. 2005. 'Participatory Action Research: Considerations for Ethical Review'. *Social Science & Medicine* 60 (10): 2333–40. doi:10.1016/j.socscimed.2004.10.004.

King, Nigel, and Christine Horrocks. 2010. *Interviews in Qualitative Research*. London: Sage.

Krippendorff, Klaus. 2012. *Content Analysis: An Introduction to its Methodology*. London: Sage.

Krueger, Richard A., and Mary Anne Casey. 2014. *Focus Groups: A Practical Guide for Applied Research*. Los Angeles: Sage.

Law, John, and Evelyn Ruppert. 2013. 'The Social Life of Methods: Devices'. *Journal of Cultural Economy* 6 (3): 229–40. doi:10.1080/17530350.2013.812042.

Law, John, Evelyn Ruppert, and Mike Savage. 2011. 'The Double Social Life of Methods'. University of Manchester: Centre for Research on Socio-Cultural Change (CRESC). http://research.gold.ac.uk/7987/1/The%20Double%20Social%20Life%20of%20Methods%20CRESC%20Working%20Paper%2095.pdf.

Loether, Herman J., and Donald G. McTavish. 1974. *Descriptive Statistics for Sociologists: An Introduction*. Boston, MA: Allyn and Bacon.

Merriam, Sharan B. 1991. *Case Study Research in Education: A Qualitative Approach*. Stoughton, WI: Books on Demand.

Milonakis, Dimitris, and Ben Fine. 2009. *From Political Economy to Economics: Method, the Social and the Historical in the Evolution of Economic Theory*. London: Routledge.

Morgan, David L. 1996. *Focus Groups as Qualitative Research*. London: Sage.

Neuendorf, Kimberly A. 2016. *The Content Analysis Guidebook*. London: Sage.

Phillips, Nicola. 2009. 'The Slow Death of Pluralism'. *Review of International Political Economy* 16 (1): 85–94. doi:10.1080/09692290802524125.

Pickstone, John V. 2000. *Ways of Knowing: A New History of Science, Technology and Medicine*. Manchester: Manchester University Press.

Ragin, Charles C. 2014. *The Comparative Method: Moving Beyond Qualitative and Quantitative Strategies*. Berkeley: University of California Press.

Rapley, Tim. 2008. *Doing Conversation, Discourse and Document Analysis*. London: Sage.

Rawlings, John O., Sastry G. Pantula and David A. Dickey. 2006. *Applied Regression Analysis: A Research Tool*. Berlin: Springer Science & Business Media.

Reason, Peter, and Hilary Bradbury. 2001. *Handbook of Action Research: Participative Inquiry and Practice*. London: Sage.

Ritchie, Jane, Jane Lewis, Carol McNaughton Nicholls, and Rachel Ormston. 2013. *Qualitative Research Practice: A Guide for Social Science Students and Researchers*. London: Sage.

Rose, Gillian. 2016. *Visual Methodologies: An Introduction to Researching with Visual Materials*. London: Sage.

Rossi, Peter H., James D. Wright and Andy B. Anderson. 2013. *Handbook of Survey Research*. Cambridge, MA: Academic Press.

Runyon, Richard P. 1977. *Descriptive Statistics: A Contemporary Approach*. Boston, MA: Addison-Wesley.

Seidman, Irving. 2015. *Interviewing as Qualitative Research: A Guide for Researchers in Education and the Social Sciences*. 4th edn. New York: Teachers College Press.

Shively, W. Phillips. 2013. *The Craft of Political Research*. London: Pearson.

Spradley, James P. 2016. *Participant Observation*. Long Grove, IL: Waveland Press.

Stringer, Ernest T. 2013. *Action Research*. London: Sage.

Watts, Richard J. 1981. *The Pragmalinguistics Analysis of Narrative Texts: Narrative Co-operation in Charles Dickens's 'Hard Times'*. Tubingen, Germany: Gunter Narr Verlag.

Welch, Catherine. 2000. 'The Archaeology of Business Networks: The Use of Archival Records in Case Study Research'. *Journal of Strategic Marketing* 8 (2): 197–208. doi:10.1080/0965254X.2000.10815560.

Whyte, William Foote. 1991. *Participatory Action Research*. Sage Focus Editions, Vol. 123. Thousand Oaks, CA: Sage.

Willmott, Hugh. 2008. 'For Informed Pluralism, Broad Relevance and Critical Reflexivity'. In *The Sage Handbook of New Approaches to Management and Organization*, edited by Daved Barry and Hans Hansen, 82–83. London: Sage.

Winkler, Othmar W. 2009. *Interpreting Economic and Social Data: A Foundation of Descriptive Statistics*. Berlin: Springer Science & Business Media.

Wolcott, Harry F. 1999. *Ethnography: A Way of Seeing*. Lanham, MD: Rowman Altamira.

Yin, Robert K. 2011. *Applications of Case Study Research*. 3rd edn. Thousand Oaks, CA: Sage.

Yin, Robert K. 2014. *Case Study Research: Design and Methods*. 5th edn. Thousand Oaks, CA: Sage.

DOING RESEARCH IN THE SHADOWS OF THE GLOBAL POLITICAL ECONOMY

Nicola Phillips

In the late 2000s, I embarked on a new line of research focusing on the worst forms of exploitation in the global economy. More specifically, I began to consider what is usually termed 'unfree' or 'forced' labour, as well as child labour and human trafficking for labour exploitation (e.g. Barrientos et al. 2013; Bhaskaran et al. 2010, 2014; Phillips 2013a, b, c; Phillips & Sakamoto 2012; Phillips et al. 2014). This project built on my long-standing interests in the global political economy of production and trade, development, labour, migration, inequality and informality. It took me into uncharted waters in terms of new and distinctive methodological demands and challenges while also offering me interesting insights into some of the problems of 'doing' political economy research, especially on issues encapsulated in what has been called the 'illicit international political economy' (IIPE) (Andreas 2004; also Friman & Andreas 1999). Processes associated with forced labour, child labour and trafficking occur in the shadows of the global economy, are associated with global and local crime and affect some of the most vulnerable people in the world. Doing research in this area posed considerable challenges, especially in terms of how one 'does' the necessary empirical work in logistical terms and how, methodologically speaking, one can approach the study of these issues empirically, analytically and theoretically.

Opening up a range of questions about how methods influence the shape of our field, research on IPE offers a very stark illustration of the ways in which increasingly rigid assumptions about 'proper' methods and evidence in social science act in some contexts to set and police the parameters of what is and can be studied (Phillips 2009; Phillips & Weaver 2010). Indeed, one of the reasons that issues of forced labour, child labour and human trafficking may have received so little attention is that they inevitably defy systematic qualitative and quantitative study and thus stand outside the research parameters favoured or considered sufficiently 'rigorous' or 'scientific' by particular constituencies within our discipline. This is lamentable not simply in intellectual terms but also in that it closes down incentives for work on problems of such immediate importance in the contemporary world. After all, a better understanding of what we are dealing with is critical to the elaboration of effective strategies for addressing the most extreme forms of human exploitation.

The question that I have faced is thus one of navigation. Both intellectually and logistically, how do I conduct research on the global problems of labour exploitation when many of the usual sources of data and information are not available and when empirical research, despite its value as the basis for understanding, argumentation and theorisation, is fraught with difficulty (and sometimes danger)?

Meeting the challenges

My efforts have been organised around two related research grants. The first sought to explore the complex relationship between chronic poverty and unfree labour and involved a comparative study of child labour in the Indian garments sector and what is usually called 'slave labour' in Brazilian agriculture. The second project, funded by a Fellowship grant over three years, focused on how we can both understand the global problems of unfree labour and trafficking and account for their resilience in the global economy.

My research questions, which have been concerned with the 'big picture' of labour exploitation, have shaped my choice of methodological approach. Among other things, I ask myself the following questions: What is it about the global economy – about how networks of global production and trade are organised and function – that generates the conditions in which exploitative practices emerge and persist? What is it about the wider social and developmental context that gives rise to vulnerabilities (of individuals, communities and particular social groups) to these kinds of exploitation? How do particular forms of public and private governance shape problems of exploitation and their incidence at the same time that they seek to respond to them? As these questions suggest, my primary objective is to develop an understanding of the political economy of exploitative processes, not to develop statistical estimates or to engage in detailed quantitative analysis. In this sense, my work is theoretically driven, even as it relies on – and prioritises – empirical research as a means of richly substantiating the 'why' and 'how' of forced labour, trafficking and child labour.

I use a range of primary methods to these ends, including household surveys (to develop a sense of the profile of households with child labour, which are integrated into the Delhi garments sector), basic statistical analysis of existing data (in countries like the UK and Brazil, to capture what we know of the incidence of problems of exploitation and the profile of the people who are vulnerable to them), elite and non-elite interviews (with a wide range of informants, including workers and people who have experienced forms of exploitation) and general forms of participant observation (such as following labour inspection teams). Having had to accept the impossibility of pursuing a single method of collecting data or understanding exploitative practices, I have sought to embrace what might best be described as a 'magpie' approach, which involves pursuing a wide variety of methods for collecting information, taking insights from wherever they are to be found and relying on the cumulative results of research as the basis for building my account of the political economy of forced labour and trafficking.

The strength of my magpie approach is that it permits a breadth of insight through the deployment of multiple methods. This is extremely valuable in the particular areas I study and others like them in IIPE, a field that presents significant methodological barriers and hurdles. The drawback is that it invites objections from methodological 'purists' about rigour and the status of data. Without question, it necessitates a certain degree of circumspection in making claims when, given the nature of the subject matter, 'hard' quantitative data are unavailable and the possibilities for systematic qualitative research are circumscribed. Nevertheless, I remain convinced that such methodological constraints cannot be allowed to determine what can be studied; nor should they close off research on issues that are of pressing importance and centrality to the global political economy and the people who live and work in it.

Unavailability of data

There are no systematic datasets on the problems of forced labour and trafficking. We now have a range of estimates from some national governments and international organisations, such as the International Labour Organization (ILO), but these vary substantially as a result of divergent methodologies for estimation. The pools of data we have are valuable and useful, but they can only reveal what has previously been investigated, reported or identified and do not offer accurate accounts of the scale or profile of the problem. As with all datasets, much depends on a series of decisions – often political – about what is to be measured and where the focus of responses is to lie. For instance, in Europe and America, anti-trafficking efforts focus largely on sexual exploitation, while labour exploitation has only recently started to receive more attention. Similarly, in Brazil, the high incidence of 'slave labour' identified in the sugar cane sector stems from the Brazilian government's decision to concentrate labour inspection resources in that sector as part of the effort to promote ethanol production as a means of economic development.

The unavailability or patchiness of data is a problem in two senses. First, because there is a huge demand for numbers in the policy world and the media, the absence of reliable figures permits arguments that downplay the importance of the problem or seek to delay action to deal with it for political or other motives. Second, without reliable data, the resulting research can fall foul of dominant disciplinary preferences for methods based on the collation and analysis of large datasets. My response to this latter problem has been to be careful about the claims that I make for the data that exist or I have compiled; I also openly acknowledge my data's limitations and supplement the use of existing data with other methods. Some of the methods I use, such as household surveys, have sought to assemble new quantitative data. Mostly, however, I have prioritised qualitative methods based on interviews and participant observation.

The problems of 'sampling'

Directly related to these data problems is the fact that many of the methodological approaches that have been deemed 'proper' for conducting quantitative and qualitative research are simply impossible to deploy in the study of issues such as forced labour, child labour or human trafficking. For instance, I frequently hear that my own and others' research has a sample size of workers that is too small to form the basis for conclusions. Such reactions are frustrating for a number of reasons, chief among which is that it takes an enormous amount of time and effort to find the people who are the most invisible members of the global labour force. When such people are located, one faces myriad issues, including the ethical dilemmas associated with asking them to participate in research, the difficulties of working with those who often have very limited or no literacy and the problem of overcoming exploited individuals' entirely understandable reluctance to speak openly about their experience. In response to critiques of my data, I suggest that while they may not be comprehensive, they do offer us unique insights and add to what we know about the problems in question. Though we clearly *need* to know much more, each new piece of careful research is a step along the way and helps to illuminate where we should focus our future energies.

A similar difficulty relates to sampling techniques. It is simply not possible to construct the same kind of random samples when investigating human trafficking or money laundering as it is when, say, studying electoral behaviour in an advanced democracy. In our research in Brazil (2012), Leonardo Sakamoto and I relied on the Brazilian government's databank to identify workers, and the field research team then attempted to make contact with them. Once the team managed to contact such workers, they asked them whether they knew of others who might be willing to speak about their experiences. While clearly not textbook sampling, this approach was the only route available and involved painstaking work. Similarly, in the research I conducted with collaborators on child labour in India (Bhaskaran et al. 2010, 2014; Phillips et al. 2014), our household survey was constructed on the basis of a snowballing sampling technique, which was constrained by both the problem of inducing people to speak openly about matters of exploitation and the ethical considerations associated with such conversations.

Logistical difficulties

Conducting research in the darkest shadows of the global economy – and not infrequently in its most inaccessible geographical or social locations, such as in the remotest parts of the Amazon basin or in the slum areas of Delhi – presents a range of logistical difficulties. The dangers for researchers and other parties involved cannot be underestimated, particularly where organised criminal groups have extensive control and power. In contexts that might initially seem less extreme, such as in Europe or North America, the difficulties are no less enormous, as people who have been trafficked might often disappear rather than engage with authorities, may be deported by immigration authorities or may be subject to criminal prosecutions if they choose to speak about their experiences. Some of the 'elite' groups that one might wish to consult tend to be equally nervous about issues of exploitation. Firms, for instance, are often concerned about image and reputation and can be reluctant to discuss such issues. Meanwhile, immigration and other political authorities tend to be wary of talking about such problems because of the political consequences of greater exposure. In short, matters of exploitation are not always characterised by open debate and cooperation between agencies and individuals working on them. Logistical difficulties also extend to basic problems such as language and cultural knowledge, both of which are essential when interacting with vulnerable people or those who have endured traumatic experiences.

Depending on the context in which I have been working, my approach to dealing with some of the aforementioned problems has been to take one or more of three routes. First, and as was the case in my comparative research on Brazil and India, I have chosen to work in collaboration with research partners. My collaborators have been experienced in dealing with these logistical problems, have been able to mobilise a rich network of connections in order to gain access to people and organisations and have possessed a wide range of skills that I personally do not possess. Second, I have been willing and eager to learn from others – particularly those in non-governmental or international organisations – who have been able to command resources (logistical and otherwise) that would have been unavailable to me as a lone researcher. More specifically, by consulting and learning from others, I have been able to use the outputs of that research as secondary sources and have benefited from interviewing or speaking informally to those people about their work and its findings. Third, I have chosen to persevere regardless of the obstacles. Establishing relationships of trust takes time and a great deal of effort, but those relationships are essential both to gaining access to information and data and to learning from interviews and conversations with people who are willing to share their perspectives.

Works cited

Andreas, P 2004, 'Illicit international political economy: the clandestine side of globalization', *Review of International Political Economy*, vol. 11, no. 3, pp. 641–52.

Barrientos, S, Kothari, U & Phillips, N 2013, 'Dynamics of unfree labour in the contemporary global economy', introduction to a symposium edited by the authors, *Journal of Development Studies*. doi:10.1080/00220388.2013.780043.

Bhaskaran, R, Nathan, D, Phillips N & Upendranadh, C 2010, 'Home-based child labour in Delhi's garment sector: contemporary forms of unfree labour in global production', *Indian Journal of Labour Economics*, vol 53, no. 4, pp. 607–24.

Bhaskaran, R, Nathan, D, Phillips, N & Upendranadh, C 2014, 'Vulnerable workers and labour standards (non-) compliance in global production networks: home-based child labour in Delhi's garment sector', in A Luinstra, A Rossi & J Pickles (eds), *Toward better work: understanding labour in apparel global value chains*, International Labour Organization and Palgrave Macmillan, London, pp. 172–90.

Friman, H, Andreas, R & Andreas, P (eds) 1999, *The illicit global economy and state power*, Rowman and Littlefield, Oxford.

Phillips, N 2009, 'The slow death of pluralism', *Review of International Political Economy*, vol. 16, no. 1, pp. 85–94.

Phillips, N 2013a, 'Adverse incorporation and unfree labour in the global economy: comparative perspectives from Brazil and India', *Economy and Society*, vol. 42, no. 2, pp. 171–96.

Phillips, N 2013b, 'Human trafficking, slavery and the governance of global supply chains', presented at the Annual Convention of the International Studies Association, San Francisco, CA, USA, 3–6 April.

Phillips, N 2013c, 'The failures and failings of governance: slavery and human trafficking in global production networks', paper presented at the workshop on 'Governance in a "GVC" World', Duke University, Durham, NC, USA, 11–13 April.

Phillips, N & Sakamoto, L 2012, 'Global production networks, chronic poverty and "slave labor" in Brazil', *Studies in Comparative International Development*, vol. 47, no. 3, pp. 287–315.

Phillips, N & Weaver, CE (eds) 2010, *International political economy: debating the past, present and future*, Routledge, London.

Phillips, N, Bhaskaran, R, Nathan, D and Upendranadh, C 2014, 'The social foundations of global production networks: towards a global political economy of child labour', *Third World Quarterly*, vol. 35, no. 3, pp. 428–46.

REFLECTIONS ON THE ARCHIVE AS A CRITICAL RESOURCE

Chris Rogers

The task of reflecting on how I chose my research methods has required a consideration of my transition from an undergraduate student to a doctoral candidate, as well as a reflection on what a judicious use of archival documents can tell us beyond a historical account of particular political decisions made by civil servants and the core executive. I have been particularly interested in the ways that the archive can inform us about contests over different kinds of economic programme and economic policy, what such contests suggest about the nature of the state in the abstract, and the ways in which particular states use domestic statecraft in an attempt to mediate such contests. Increasingly, I have also been reflecting on the extent to which the archive itself might be considered a site of contest. This chapter provides a brief account of the way in which I have used the archive before offering some reflections on how the archive fits within a 'toolbox' of methodologies that might be useful as part of a 'critical' political economy project. The chapter also considers the challenges the archive poses to such a project.

The archive as a critical resource

I first visited the National Archives in Kew, South West London, to fulfil a requirement for my undergraduate degree. Visiting the Archives, my peers and I were asked to find references for and documents on a topic that interested us in relation to issues of British economic management. The nature of the assignment we were asked to complete suggested that the archive's methodological potential related to its status as a repository of historical facts that might be useful in providing historical context for contemporary matters within political economy. While accessing such facts is certainly an important part of archival work, my undergraduate and post-graduate studies showed me that the archive could do much more than provide historical contextualisation.

Studying British economic management as an undergraduate influenced my thinking about the archive in two ways. First, as I read archive-influenced texts like Peter Burnham's *The Political Economy of Economy of Post-War Reconstruction* (1990) and *Remaking the Post-War World Economy* (2003), I realised that using archival material could represent a useful empirical contribution to academic literature on the politics of economic policy-making. This realisation led me to believe that a research project drawing heavily on newly released or unused archival material might be a direction for my doctoral studies. Second, I came to understand that the archive can shed light on the ways in which prevailing forms of social relationship change or are recreated through political action. As regards this second point, I was particularly influenced by Burnham's (1990) use of the archive to illustrate how state managers acted strategically to manage tensions in the relationship between labour and capital.

My own archival research focused on the politics of economic policy-making in Britain between 1974 and 1976. In particular, I concentrated on Britain's loan from the International Monetary Fund in December 1976. Where earlier work on the period suggested that leaks from official sources had diminished the significance of archival material related to this episode (Hickson 2005, p. 227), I felt that referring to archival material would add something to the existing literature, even if the archive's contribution was primarily to confirm existing accounts. At the same time, the potential contribution of the archive was set off by prominent debates in critical political economy about the extent to which political elites used various rules, institutions and discourses (see, for example, Burnham 2001; Watson & Hay 2003) in order to depoliticise aspects of policy. As well as demonstrating 'not only the complete range of influences to which government was subject at any given time but also what did not change' (Lowe 1997, pp. 240–41), the archive allowed me to examine both the extent to which policy-makers' preferences were not publicly revealed and the degree to which public statements or leaks diverged from the line taken in confidential discussions as part of a strategy to depoliticise contentious aspects of policy.

Preparation for my archival work involved considering the authenticity, credibility, representativeness and meaning of documents as part of a judicious use of archival material. Much methodological literature (see, for example, Scott 1990; May 1997; Bryman 2001; Burnham et al. 2004) discusses these issues, each of which raises difficult philosophical questions about meaning and truth. While the archive reveals objective facts about who said what, where they said it and when they said it, explaining these facts is a highly contingent process that yields a subjective understanding of political processes. From a purely historical perspective, then, the archive may be able to produce an authoritative account of certain events, but from a critical political economy perspective, which is intrinsically linked to a problematisation and assessment of the process of change in social, economic and political relations, the archive is more likely to yield an interpretation that is itself subject to contest.

Coming to understand that research outputs based on the archive are fundamentally contestable interpretations of facts, I have increasingly reflected on how the archive itself can be understood not only as a resource that provides insight into struggles over social, economic and political processes but also as a site of struggle. Key to this line of thought has been a consideration of the different ways archival material can be accessed. The majority of my own archival research was conducted at the National Archives in Kew, where access to records is ostensibly free to anybody. Most researchers, however, are constrained by their research budgets and by the amount of time they have available to travel to and from required archives. The understandably broad nature of catalogue descriptions can also mean that some time is spent reading documents not directly relevant to the research at hand, even with the help of extremely knowledgeable staff.

Although expanding digitisation programs have also helped researchers effectively access archival material, the digitisation process is not unproblematic. Indeed, that process might itself be considered indicative of a struggle over the archive. Seeing that some documents, but not others, have been digitised, one might assume that the digitised records are more important than other non-digitised ones. This issue is further complicated, at least at the National Archives, by shortened operating hours. As digitisation increases at that facility, reading rooms have been less frequently open and target times for document delivery have been extended. To put the matter a different way, the opening of the archive represented by digitisation has also been accompanied by the archive's closure in other respects.

While Cabinet Papers and Memoranda are now available online, other records are arguably more difficult to access in the reading rooms themselves. It is therefore necessary for users of the archive to reflect carefully on the principal actor designations they employ instead of simply drawing on the resources that are easiest to access. Such problems may ultimately be resolved as 'born-digital' records become the norm; yet records created in roughly the last thirty years continue to occupy a peculiar space between the physical and digital archives and may be concealed despite attempts to provide more material digitally.

If the digitisation of the archive has contributed to its status as a site of contest, Freedom of Information has presented a similar obstacle. Although Freedom of Information would appear to open the archive to greater scrutiny, Tony Blair (cited in Kettle 2010) has argued that it stifles political debate. Noting that government involves frank conversation, Blair explains, 'If those conversations are put out in a published form that afterwards are liable to be highlighted in particular ways, you are going to be cautious.' In this remark, Blair implies that opening the archive may prohibit good government. His comment also suggests that government officials view the archive as a ground of struggle. In the face of such struggle, it is important that we continue to reflect on the nature of the archive and its use as a methodological tool in critical enquiry. The significance of such reflections for critical political economy cannot be understated.

Conclusions

This short chapter has considered the archive's ability to play a role in critical political economy's methodological 'toolbox'. Highlighting how the archive allows for the contextualisation of political processes, the chapter has also demonstrated the kinds of struggle that the archive unleashes for political and economic decision-making. The larger purpose of this chapter has been to suggest that the archive can shed light on the processes through which prevailing forms of social relationship are changed or recreated through political action. As a research method, the archive can not only help to confirm facts and existing interpretations of political events; it can also reveal dissonance between private and public discourses, a dissonance that illustrates the ways in which political strategies are used to mediate contradictions faced by state managers. While this chapter has been concerned to demonstrate that the archive, in combination with other methods, can illuminate contests or struggles over policy, it has also aimed to underscore that the interpretations produced through archival research are likely to be subjective. What's more, the chapter has strived to elucidate how the evolution of physical and digital spaces, as well as the existence of Freedom of Information, has shaped the role the archive plays.

Works cited

Bryman, A 2001, *Social research methods*, Oxford UP, Oxford.
Burnham, P 1990, *The political economy of post-war reconstruction*, Macmillan, London.
Burnham, P 2001, 'New labour and the politics of depoliticisation', *British Journal of Politics and International Relations*, vol. 3, no. 2, pp. 127–49.
Burnham, P 2003, *Remaking the post-war world economy: robot and British policy in the 1950s*, Palgrave Macmillan, London.
Burnham, P, Gilland, K, Grant W & Layton-Henry, Z 2004, *Research methods in politics*, Palgrave Macmillan, Basingstoke.
Hickson, K 2005, *The IMF crisis of 1976 and British politics*, IB Tauris, London.
Kettle, M 2010, 'World exclusive Tony Blair interview', *The Guardian*, 1 September, viewed 17 June 2016, www.guardian.co.uk/politics/2010/sep/01/tony-blair-a-journey-interview.
Lowe, R 1997, 'Plumbing new depths: contemporary historians and the public record office', *Contemporary British History*, vol. 8, no. 2, pp. 239–65.
May, T 1997, *Social research: issues, methods and processes*, 2nd edn, Open UP, Buckingham.
Scott, J 1990, *A matter of record*, Polity, Cambridge.
Watson, M & Hay, C 2003, 'Rendering the contingent necessary: the discourse of globalization and the logic of no alternative in the political economy of new labour', *Policy & Politics*, vol. 31, no. 1, pp. 289–305.

QUALITATIVE RESEARCH PRACTICES AND CRITICAL POLITICAL ECONOMY

Ian Bruff

My 2008 monograph *Culture and Consensus in European Varieties of Capitalism: A 'Common Sense' Analysis* (Bruff 2008) was based on my doctoral thesis, for which I studied from 2000 to 2005. Obtaining my PhD took me longer than the norm (4.5 years compared to an average of 3–4 years in the UK) largely because of my profound sense of insecurity about what I was doing. Intuitively, I quickly formed opinions about my topic, which related principally to the integral role of culture in the evolution of national political economies, especially during times of crisis. However, I was confronted by two key challenges: first, how to conceptualise culture in a manner that retained an emphasis on the material conditions of our existence without reducing culture to something akin to, or entirely separate from, 'the economy'; and second, how to demonstrate the viability of this conceptualisation through empirical research. In many respects it was only in my PhD viva – Colin Hay and Hugo Radice were my examiners – that I finally gained an understanding of how to overcome these challenges. As a result, my monograph is considerably better than my PhD thesis, as it represents a settled, confident approach to the topic.

Aside from helping me to get a better grasp on my topic, the process of 'doing' my PhD profoundly shaped how I viewed the art of engaging in political economy research. I sought to defend my intuitive sense that 'culture matters' in a range of hostile 'political science' forums, and I wished to follow up on those intuitions via qualitative interviews in my case study countries, the Netherlands and Germany. In the first year of my doctoral studies, I had a searing experience at the 2001 European Consortium for Political Research conference in Canterbury, when I was told that I would fail my viva on account of not producing hypotheses that could lead to generalisable propositions through quantitative and scientific testing. What I would give to go back to that presentation armed with what I know now about these issues! In contrast to my positivist friends, I felt I needed to arrive at a reasonably watertight conceptualisation of the role of culture in the evolution of national political economies *before* I got my feet dirty in the Netherlands and Germany. Otherwise, I feared, I would fall into the empiricist trap. As I already recognised, most grounded theory and action research approaches – not to mention positivist social science more broadly, which adheres to the fiction that theory and 'data' can somehow be separate – end up with the scholar being little more than a disinterested, atheoretical observer of 'stuff' (see also my paper with Bastiaan van Apeldoorn and Magnus Ryner 2010).

At times, I found it difficult to work out how to translate the relatively abstract notions I was considering into a concrete research strategy. I knew that qualitative interviews with the tripartite 'social partners' (trade unions, political parties, employers' associations) were likely to be the most appropriate method, as I wanted to carry out an in-depth, qualitative exploration of elite 'common sense' in the context of my specific conceptual understanding of the state in capitalist political economies. But how I should manage the intermediate issues – especially with regard to the questions I asked, the strategy I adopted during the interviews themselves and the method I used to write up the interviews after their conclusion – remained unclear. Thankfully, I enrolled in two courses at the University of Essex Summer School in Social Science Data Analysis and Collection. Over four weeks, those courses – 'Ethnographic and Qualitative Methodologies' and 'Qualitative Interviewing and Focus Groups' – helped me to answer many of the questions with which I was struggling. Both courses were run by sociologists, and my exposure to their discipline opened my eyes to how far behind other fields political science lagged when it came to qualitative research practices rooted in post-positivist approaches.

These crucial insights have informed much of my subsequent work. For instance, my chapter in *Critical International Political Economy* (2011), a volume I co-edited with Stuart Shields and Huw Macartney, made the case for going outside International Political Economy in order to return to it enriched by an engagement with broader currents in critical social theory. More generally, the insights I gathered during my doctoral studies pushed me to investigate literatures and debates on qualitative research practices. Nowadays, I frequently recommend the works I consulted to PhD students in IPE and other areas of political science who are facing issues similar to those I confronted over a decade ago. Three books, in particular, stand out from my time as a doctoral student: Steinar Kvale's *InterViews* (1996), Fiona Devine and Sue Heath's *Sociological Research Methods in Context* (1999) and Jane Ritchie and Jane Lewis's *Qualitative Research Practice* volume (2003). In my view, these texts are utterly essential for IPE scholars who wish to produce innovative work based on qualitative research rooted in post-positivist approaches. And they say nothing about political economy, which is probably a good thing!

InterViews is in some ways a philosophical text, but Kvale combines his philosophical bent with a very practical approach to arranging, conducting and analysing interviews. I found his advice particularly useful when it came to making the best use of the interview transcript. The entire monograph is worth reading, but I especially recommend the final chapters. The Devine/Heath and Ritchie/Lewis books are more focused but for just that reason reveal much about the messy, compromise-driven, pragmatic nature of empirical, and especially qualitative, research. More specifically, those works underscore that no project or specific interview situation will *ever* be ideal. While such a recognition may seem frightening, it should also be viewed as liberating. As Devine, Heath, Ritchie and Lewis so clearly demonstrate, one's research strategy can be systematic and rigorous even in an unideal world *and* can provide valuable contributions to existing literatures. Accepting that the navigation of the research process is rooted in *your* judgements, *your* intuitions and *your* decisions leads to a heightened sense of both responsibility and empowerment.

When I finally arrived in the Netherlands and Germany, the interviews I conducted were not structured (as in surveys) or unstructured (as in ethnography). Neither, however, were they 'semi-structured' in the way that the term is commonly used. In contrast to the usual approach of asking a similar range of questions in each interview, I devised a 'topic guide' that listed all the different aspects of the case study I was interested in and that included a sample question (or questions) below each aspect. I was fully aware that it would be impossible to ask questions linked to each and every aspect of a topic, especially as there were over 20 topics for both the Netherlands and Germany. Although certain key points were present in every interview, I used the topic guide as a menu that allowed me to choose a certain number of necessary and/or desirable 'courses' for the interview I was conducting. Doing this enabled me to respond to opinions and comments made in earlier interviews and thus to build an inter-subjective narrative that took into account the evolving journey of the interview process and its key themes. For example, one of my Dutch interviewees waxed lyrical about the potato starch industry in the eastern Netherlands for over half an hour. While this had no relevance for the project, I later ended up with some priceless comments from him as a result of having earlier shown respect for his perspective.

Of course, *no* piece of research – no matter how thorough, comprehensive and wide-ranging – covers all bases. Key to an effective strategy is thus a navigation of the research process that is rooted in *your* judgements, *your* intuitions and *your* decisions. I am fully aware that my study could, for example, have drawn upon Eurobarometer survey data or could have been rooted in an approach that, taking culture as a Williams-esque 'whole way of life', privileged non-elite sources; indeed, there are excellent studies of the Netherlands and Germany based on one or the other of these strategies. However, my research questions, combined with my prior conceptualisation of culture and how I wanted to study it, pointed me in a different direction. While a further 10 years' experience and accumulation of expertise have made me think that I would now do some things differently than I did then, the approach I took during my doctoral studies – and especially my explicit reliance on non-Political Science literatures – is still central to how I engage in political economy research today.

Works cited

Bruff, I 2008, *Culture and consensus in European varieties of capitalism: a 'common sense' analysis*, Palgrave Macmillan, Basingstroke.

Bruff, I 2011, 'Overcoming the state/market dichotomy', in S Shields, I Bruff & H Macartney (eds), *Critical international political economy: dialogue, debate and dissensus*, Palgrave Macmillan, Basingstoke, pp. 80–98.

Devine, F & Heath, S 1999, *Sociological research methods in context*, Macmillan, Basingstoke.

Kvale, S 1996, *InterViews: an introduction to qualitative research interviewing*, Sage, London.

Ritchie, J & Lewis, J (eds) 2003, *Qualitative research practice: a guide for social science students and researchers*, Sage, London.

van Apeldoorn, B, Bruff, I & Ryner, M 2010, 'The richness and diversity of critical IPE perspectives: moving beyond the debate on the "British School"', in N Phillips & C Weaver (eds), *International political economy: debating the past, present and future*, Routledge, London, pp. 215–22.

5
ON EVIDENCE AND CORROBORATION

Johnna Montgomerie

This chapter makes an explicit effort to consider how meaning is produced within a political economy methodology. Jessop and Sum (2010) use semiosis to interpret and, in part, explain events, processes, tendencies and emergent structures in the field of political economy. They explain: 'Semiosis involves the social production of inter-subjective meaning and, as such, is a foundational moment of all social practises and relations' (p. 447). In consequence, political economy makes a methodological and, more importantly, ontological turn (also see: Jessop 2004). Incorporating this insight into the existing reflections on the lexicon of social science methods, we can begin to see a new path for engaging in empirical research, a path that is not reducible to a single methodological commitment or theoretical understanding of truth. Although we are building upon the longstanding tradition of using human experience as an empirical source of evidence, we should also recognise the obligation to account for how that evidence is collected, sorted, organised, analysed and reported without endorsing a singular way of determining what counts (and does not count) as empirical evidence. More specifically, the pluralist methodology advocated here involves acknowledging that human experience is worth considering or evaluating as evidence, even as it insists that the value of the expert knowledge claims derived from such evidence should not be conflated with the value of the evidence itself.

With this conception of evidence in mind, we can understand methods as ways of collecting empirical evidence; those ways may include, but are not limited to, asking questions, reading documents, and observing both controlled and uncontrolled situations. Although some methods lend themselves more readily to certain epistemological perspectives, it is worth noting that no method of data collection is inherently positivist, phenomenological or critical. For just this reason, the pluralist methodology I propose examines empirical evidence while simultaneously making explicit the presuppositions that inform the knowledge claims that are generated through researchers' acts of enquiry. The previous chapter outlined the iterative and reflexive practices underlying our methodology and pushed us to think strategically about how we 'do' research. Here, we consider how evidence claims shape our crafting of knowledge claims. To this end, we build upon our earlier discussion of the critical research ethic and the importance of accounting for deliberative movements or key choices, and we do so with the aim of contextualising the evidence that results from conducting research.

The remainder of this chapter is guided by three reflexive questions, each of which is designed to cultivate a way of articulating critical researchers' evidentiary judgements. The first of these questions is, '*What kind of evidence is being presented?*' This question seeks to draw attention to how methods produce specific representations of evidence that inform knowledge claims. Too often in research, the qualities and character of different types of evidence are not adequately considered or addressed. For example, an in-depth document analysis of World Bank reports would no doubt produce a different kind of evidence than would interviews of those reports' authors or World Bank stakeholders. Because document analysis and qualitative interviews create different types of evidence, we need to consider how they are used singly and how they could be used together to create various knowledge claims.

The second reflexive question guiding this chapter is, '*What are the limits of the evidence under examination?*' This question is intended to highlight evidentiary context and to address *how* and *why* collected evidence matters to the study of political economy. In asking this question, we work against the universalising and essentialising nature of positivist epistemology by openly and freely acknowledging the explicit context and limits of the evidence we develop and examine within our pluralist methodology. The third question we must ask ourselves – '*What is our evidence, evidence of?*' – picks up where the second question leaves off by prompting us to address wider theoretical concerns and to articulate the causality that informs our resulting knowledge claims. Taken together, the three questions orientating this chapter thus represent a set of questioning practices that transform how we 'do' political economy. Rather than simply offering another account of the discipline's formation, this chapter seeks to demonstrate that the study of political economy can be thought of as a form of pluralism-in-action, one that grounds itself in dialogue in order to unpack how we create meaning from evidence.

This is an initial attempt to reflexively consider what kind of evidence methods make when using political economy as a pluralist methodology. In particular, by making direct reference to the contributions to this volume, but also being conscious of how these practices are indicative of the types of critical research problem many of the readers of this book would want to cultivate. Using the autobiographical accounts as indicative of practice, I try to unpack the ways in which being reflexive about evidence can innovate methodological practice. First, by putting evidence in its context – professional as well as existential.

At its conclusion, the current chapter reflects on how corroboration serves as an organising concept for constructing critical-ethical knowledge claims. As will become clear, the conceptual strength of pluralism depends on our ability to mobilise independent sources of evidence to support the existence of a crucial fact, relationship, trend, idea or norm; by putting emphasis on the evidentiary basis of knowledge claims, corroboration allows us to support the critical research ethic in a meaningful way.

What is evidence of cultural political economy?

Politics, economics, culture and society are not totalities; nor do they operate in logical fashions. Rather, they are overlapping social spheres that are bound by time and space and that have both material and discursive manifestations (Fraser 2014; Barad 2001). Developing a critical research ethic allows us to engage with those overlapping social spheres in a way that is attuned to the transformative dynamics of academic research. Using an iterative reflexive strategy involves explicitly moving against the tendency to consider methods as no more than sets of predefined tools used to find 'truth'. As previous chapters have noted, conceiving of methods as a set of unchanging tools confuses those tools with the process of 'doing' research work and ignores the mutual constitutiveness of methods and the social world (Law, Ruppert and Savage 2011). In practice, the act of going out into the world to collect empirical evidence often disrupts or undermines the original research question and design. Because it is imperative to acknowledge that representations of truth exist in specific historical, political, economic and cultural contexts, critical research should involve articulating how methods make evidence.

In an earlier chapter, we considered the value of embracing and discussing the deliberative moments that propel acts of research. The current chapter builds upon the previous one by underscoring how choices and judgements shape not only the processing and analysing of evidence but also the communicating or writing-up of knowledge claims derived from evidence. Using pluralist methods involves exploring and expressing our strategies of bringing together multiple kinds of evidence to make knowledge claims. As many of the autobiographical vignettes in this volume suggest, engaging with complex research puzzles requires an openness to accumulating evidence from a wide range of sources, including archives, interviews, text, media, observations or focus groups; the vignettes also illustrate that the relationship between those sources and the evidence they provide needs to be accounted for within the research process (see: Cunliffe 2011). Being attentive to how evidence comes into being enables us to focus on how it is accumulated, sorted and processed. Moreover, by considering how we move from empirical sources to evidentiary claims, we come to understand that the sources we select and the evidence we collect produce the meaning that underlies our resulting knowledge claims. Opening up this process to critical reflection involves acknowledging the messiness and selectivity involved in using evidence to support an argument or to publish a journal article or monograph (Neal 2013). Traditional accounts of methodologies ignore such messiness and selectivity and instead imply the linearity of applying a method, getting results and publishing findings. In contrast, foregrounding choice during the research process entails accepting ethical accountability for the evidentiary basis of one's knowledge claims and revealing the rationale behind one's decision to trust certain pieces or kinds of evidence.

In practical terms, adopting a pluralist methodology involves being reflexive, not hierarchical, in our understanding of how sources of evidence are mobilised to support expert claims. More specifically, it involves doing away with familiar rankings of evidence (i.e., primary, secondary and tertiary) that effectively limit the types of analysis that are possible. Rather than curtailing what we research and how we research, a pragmatic approach to evidence eschews evidentiary hierarchies and the established quantitative-qualitative research binary (Bohman 1999; Thies 2002). Through the lens of a pluralist methodology, 'doing' political economy means being attentive to the research process and the plurality of sources from which we derive evidence. As we reflexively capitalise on the deliberative moments that occur during the research process, we ultimately come to understand that judgement and context, not generalisability and universalisation, underlie our selection of evidence and the knowledge claims that result from it.

Reflexivity and evidence

Of late, the concept of the Anthropocene has become important outside political science and international relations as a means of explaining how human interaction with the natural world manifests in geological time (for further discussion see: Weber 2013, p. 232; Dalby 2011). To be more precise, the Anthropocene represents a new geological period that has arisen as a result of human actions, actions that have, in many ways, been determined or influenced by the march of global capitalism (Yusoff 2013). Confronting humans' transformation of the physical world, social scientists of all stripes have felt compelled to reflect methodologically on the ways in which we can disentangle facts from ideas across time and space. Within political economy, such reflection involves examining the human social contexts that directly relate to and reveal information about the non-human forces that shape social phenomena. By introducing the concept of the Anthropocene into our work, we enable ourselves to reconsider the meaning of discovery within the social sciences and equip ourselves to devise new ways of understanding the cultural movement of human civilisation.

In the spirit of embracing the notion of the Anthropocene in our pluralist methodology, the following sections draw on this volume's autobiographical vignettes to consider the relationship between reflexivity and evidence. Although the vignettes present much material for discussion, I wish to concentrate here on how the contributors mobilise three kinds of evidence in their research practices: human subjects, texts and institutions. These categories are not meant to represent an exhaustive list of the types of evidence generated by humans. Rather, my aim is to emphasise the social embeddedness of evidence, whether it is collected from national statistical databases, interviews, documents or observations. Each of these sources of evidence is part of the human civilisation inhabited by researchers and from which they cannot dissociate themselves.

Human subjects

Many vignettes in this volume draw evidence from 'human subjects' – that is, from actual people who provide information about ideas, relationships, histories, communities, networks and norms. In his contribution, for instance, Matthew Paterson provides evidence of the professional and political networks that emerged out of the global environmental crisis, while John Hultgren discusses his use of texts and human-focused methods to understand the connection between environmental phenomena and political and social change. By asking actual people how they work or understand political problems, such as 'environmental crisis', Paterson and Hultgren rely on a mix of sources and qualitative methods that offer different perspectives on the imbrication of local politics and global issues. The contexts in which such methods are anchored have different and significant ramifications for researchers' management of the insider/outsider distinction (Dwyer and Buckle 2009). Whether a researcher chooses to use observation, surveys, focus groups or ethnography, his or her research ultimately produces evidence that is inflected by his or her choice of method.

One limitation of drawing evidence from actual people is that the specific contexts in which those people exist directly affects whether they act, how they act and how they make meaning out of their actions, reactions and inactions. We can see how specific contexts impose constraints most clearly in Liam Stanley's vignette, which relies on focus groups to collect evidence about how people make meaning out of economic crisis and political change. Although Stanley identifies ways in which the elite-centred understandings of Austerity have been disrupted in modern society, he also remains attuned to the limits of small-group meaning-making and its ability to challenge established political consensus. In Stanley's case, demographic categories and sample bias continue to have value in showing the limits of evidence produced by focus groups. Yet in stipulating that his focus groups were held after the United Kingdom 2010 elections of the coalition Conservative and Liberal Democrat government, Stanley also suggests that his evidence may be limited by time. To be more precise, his evidence, having been collected in 2010, necessarily concentrates on the inception of Austerity as a national policy rhetoric and not on the continuing effects of its entrenchment in British society (also see: Stanley 2014). What should be stressed, however, is that such a limitation of evidence does not mean that that evidence has no use or cannot form the basis for future innovation. On the contrary, the limitations of evidence collected at one point in time can directly inform how evidence is collected and used in later research.

The importance of reflexivity becomes clear in other vignettes that consider the transformation of bodies into things during the academic research process. Robbie Shilliam makes this point explicitly when she highlights the 'thingification of labouring persons' as a central ethical challenge to European narratives of political economy and offers in those narratives' stead a redemptive ethic of research (also see: Louis 2007). In much the same way, Nicola Phillips sheds light on the labouring persons in the shadows of the contemporary global political economy and, in doing so, challenges the ethical soundness of simply counting the number of exploited workers as a means of generalising about the 'new slavery'. Finally, Nicola Smith's examination of labouring bodies in the sex industry exposes the awkward intimacies of academic research and reminds us of our shared corporeality with the people whom we research.

In reading Shilliam's, Phillips's and Smith's vignettes, we can understand that contextualising the limits of human-focused evidence involves accepting that the object of inquiry is not separate from the person providing evidence of it. Regardless of the research site, we must remain conscious of the types of evidence produced from our selected methods. Where evidence gathered from human subjects is concerned, such consciousness necessarily entails being attuned to the humanness of the evidence itself.

Texts

No less than evidence gathered from human subjects, evidence gathered from texts benefits from reflexivity. There are many different types of text-based method, including document analysis, content analysis and literature reviews, that produce evidence of institutional practices, political movements and the intellectual history of ideas or disciplines. In their vignette, Inayatullah and Blaney discuss their text-based 'reading as method' approach. Using texts as a key source of evidence requires treating contradictions as necessary, which involves critically engaging with the canon of economic thought in order to identify and problematise the assumptions that obscure capitalism's social-constructedness and contingency.

The archive also offers a rich, if sometimes contradictory, source of evidence (Geiger, Moore and Savage 2010). It is worth emphasising here that the authority of the archive cannot be assumed but must rather be articulated and contextualised. Indeed, one paradox of the archive is that its destabilisation through, among other things, digitalisation has revealed new possibilities for the production of knowledge (Beer and Burrows 2013). Within his autobiographical vignette, Chris Rogers treats the archive as a highly politicised text that provides evidence about the political processes of government. Concentrating on how decision-making by political parties, core executives and civil servants constitutes the archive, Rogers examines the contests and struggles over economics within the elite policy-making circles of the 1980s and calls into question established understandings of a coherent Thatcherite agenda. One limitation of relying on the archive in this fashion is, of course, that the archive itself is composed of only those texts that the political elite deemed worthy of preservation. Such a recognition, however, does not undermine the archive's value but rather encourages us once more to place emphasis on the context of the evidence we collect and examine.

Because the current volume overwhelmingly focuses on qualitative methods, it gives little attention to critical researchers' reliance on quantitative methods. Yet many of the contributors to this volume, myself included, do make use of an array of quantitative methods when conducting research. Those methods include, but are not limited to, statistical analysis of national accounts and survey data and examinations of international statistical databases and benchmark indicators (see, for example: Brenner 1998; Engelen et al. 2011; Piketty 2014; Dorling 2015). Like other methods already discussed, quantitative methods serve as a form of textual analysis, even though the texts in question consist of numbers rather than words. For example, Gross Domestic Product (GDP) is a foundational variable for any quantitative analysis of the international political economy, and by critically assessing the GDP, we are able to see its limitations as a numerical/textual representation of the value-added produced by a national economy (Stiglitz, Sen and Fitoussi 2010; Waring 2015). At present critical forms of quantitative analysis are at the margins of both critical social theory and positivist social science; hopefully a new focus on methods within the critical school will forge a new path towards more direct engagement with quantitative methods.

Institutions

The final kind of evidence highlighted in this volume relates to institutions, which can be understood as regularised patterns of human interaction that are informed by ideas, norms and cultural practices. These patterns are recognisable both in amorphous sociological institutions, such as the family, and in formal legal entities, such as the nation state and international organisations. On the whole, contributors to this volume have placed particular emphasis on the normative power of institutions. Focusing his research in the Netherlands and Germany, for instance, Ian Bruff uses in-depth interviews and text-based methods to study the relationships between governments, businesses and unions and the commonsense norms that govern both those relationships and the wider political economy. In a related fashion, Dimitris Stevis concentrates on how organised labour effects social change. Relying on a range of evidentiary sources from within the union movement, Stevis develops a typology for sorting and ordering the overlapping sources of evidence that point to the changing cultural norms of unionism as it encounters the material realities of the contemporary global economy. In both Bruff's and Stevis's vignettes, we can see how interaction within and across institutional forms organises and gives relevance to the evidence presented. By drawing out the relationships and social patterns that influence states, unions and firms, Bruff and Stevis shed light on institutional behaviours, processes and power structures within contemporary capitalism.

Despite the skill with which contributors to this volume discuss their research on institutions, we should emphasise that providing evidence of the emergence or maintenance of institutions is not a straightforward task. As was the case with evidence gleaned from human subjects and texts, evidence related to institutions has value only when its context is taken into account. One limitation of studying institutions concerns the nature of institutions themselves, which change over time and thus often foil efforts to identify continuities. Chris May's contribution to this volume is particularly valuable in examining the changing character of institutions. Concentrating his current research into the Rule of Law on how institutional norms change against the backdrop of history, May demonstrates the need for accessing and relying on multiple evidentiary sources in one's attempt to capture how norms shape, justify and legitimate cultural practices. In a related vein, Sam Knafo uses primary archival texts, history and Marxist theory to study the institutional creation of liberal financial governance. By tracing how the Treasury, the Bank and the bond market have developed the institutional practices of liberal financial governance, Knafo's work allows us to understand what differences people make to institutional formation. Therefore, providing evidence of institutions presents a balance act between accounting for the social dynamics of making institutions and assuming too much stability in that dynamic over time. This tension is partially eased by clearly articulating material and cultural limits, this boundary is where resistance and countervailing social forces mediate power.

What is our evidence, evidence of?

No less than in determining the kinds of evidence we accept, we need to be reflexive in using our evidence to advance expert knowledge claims. By asking ourselves what our evidence is evidence of, we engage in a set of questioning practices that tie back to the concerns of the previous chapter: namely, the formation of the object of analysis, the relevance of our evidence to the topic at hand and the problem and question that motivated our research in the first place.

The value of our evidence can be multifold. On the one hand, evidence can inform theoretical abstraction; on the other hand, it can support claims about the unfolding of social phenomena or highlight a specific problem. For some time, critical theories of society have tended to be dominated by theoretical abstraction, which means that empirical evidence has often been taken for granted or viewed as an encumbrance to abstract theoretical reasoning. On one level, suspicion of empirical material is understandable, as 'facts' about surface appearances may seem to reify common sense and run counter to critical-dialectical thinking. However, a theoretical analysis that fails to address the material world through empirical evidence is itself limited because it usually overlooks historically specific social processes and thus fails to bridge the gap between theory and praxis. At worst, such theoretical analyses are purely speculative, which makes their failings remarkably similar to those levelled against methodological individualism.

The fundamental challenge of doing critical social research is thus negotiating how evidence is presented as fact – or 'things as they really are' – while still keeping in mind that facts are socially constructed. As we advance our expert knowledge claims, we need to address this tension openly. One way of doing this, I believe, is to consider corroboration as a way of conceptualising the authority of pluralist expert claims. On the most basic level, corroboration refers to how independent sources of evidence support the same critical fact or relationship. Yet the understanding of corroboration I am advocating here is more than a simple restatement of traditional notions of objectivity and the representativeness of findings. In contrast, a pluralist methodology requires both an open admission that no social research is without bias and an acknowledgement that particular acts of research are based on the judgements of the author, who decides what does and does not count as evidence. Within this framework, corroboration is a way of building up critical knowledge claims by offering authoritative and credible evidence to support them. At the same time, effective corroboration involves explicitly describing how claims are validated and applying an iterative, reflexive strategy during the analysing and writing phases of academic research. When academic expertise is informed by a critical research ethic, it does not take social structures, social processes, history or norms for granted; instead, it tries to dig beneath the surface of appearances, to seek out the unseen and the unheard and to discover new ways of understanding social transformation.

If part of the challenge of a pluralist methodology is accounting for the differences between evidence and data, idea and fact, another part is being explicit about how evidence either disrupts or confirms assumptions, hypotheses or beliefs; and, the ways in which causality is emergent not universal. Positivism frames causality in terms of the degree and direction of relationships between an independent and (up to several) dependent variables, and the conditions of making knowledge claims about causality are conditioned by the (mainly statistical) validity of the findings and ability to reproduce them. This notion of causality is particularly tailored to positivist methodology because it allows little scope for epistemology – causal relationships are supposedly universal, existing across time and space, and are therefore expressions of actual truth not social understandings of what constitutes truth. Salter suggests rather than starting from scratch when developing critical methods, we instead consider what critical epistemology brings to bear on claims to causality, most significantly that causality emerges from research (Salter and Mutlu 2013, pp. 16–17). Therefore, rather than imagining there is a truth about global capitalism that, through the use of methods, we can uncover, emergent causality recognises how the most significant relationships we find come from research; it does not exist independently of it. This concept is particularly useful when accounting for how evidence becomes a knowledge claim.

Here again, an emphasis on context is all important, as context provides a basis for interpreting the relevance of critical empirical findings. In speaking of context, I mean to underscore not only the historical, cultural or social context of what is researched but also the context of the researcher and his or her research practice. Because a critical research ethic involves the researcher's consciousness of his or her situatedness and the situatedness of his or her claims, a pluralist methodology that depends on such an ethic underscores that critical research claims cannot be dissociated from their institutional context. To echo Salter and Mutlu (2013, p. 23), what ultimately will unite the broader community of critical scholars who adopt a pluralist methodology will be both their insistence on reflexivity and the clarity of their stance regarding their research.

Conclusion

This chapter outlined the different reflexive practices that can be used to turn evidence into critical knowledge claims. By adopting a set of questioning practices, we can provide meaningful context for the evidence we present in our research. As the autobiographical vignettes in this volume demonstrate and as this chapter has tried to suggest, doing critical research under the umbrella of a pluralist methodology involves negotiating between theory and practice, data and fact, and idea and norm.

Reflexivity embeds the evidence within the research practice in order to foreground the craft of making professional judgements and decisions; therefore, credibility becomes a key factor in making knowledge claims. Conducting a 'conversation with the self' about the credibility of the evidence presented to support expert claims is a guidepost for unpacking how the situatedness of the researcher shapes the evidence created by acts of research. Interpretive research accounts for all the aspects of how the object of analysis is studied, including the researcher's own presence (Gasson 2004). Because it is in the 'doing' of research that all the relevant choices are made about what sources are used, methods deployed, findings selected and is the author of the text. Critical research ethics seeks to make reflexive research internally consistent by ensuring in practice the situated and embodied researcher has accounted for his/her influences on the final outcome. Being dispassionate means not having a stake in a particular outcome from the research, or accepting that you can be wrong in your interpretation of the facts; this is an ethical practice not an existential state. This is a decisive advantage for those doing pluralist research because being wrong and going down blind-alleys is integral to this style of research, but this largely remains unarticulated. Accounting for how evidence is produced emphasises the interpretive dynamics of academic research that does not assume there is some generalisable law governing human behaviour or civilisation. Instead, the focus is on the authenticity or credibility of the evidence used to support knowledge claims.

When we make such negotiations in the light of a critical research ethic, we open ourselves up to finding new and unexpected sources of evidence and to advancing critical knowledge claims that have strong and lasting value.

Works cited

Barad, Karen. 2001. 'Reconfiguring Space, Time and Matter'. In *Feminist Locations: Global and Local, Theory and Practice*, edited by Marianne DeKoven, 75–109. New Brunswick, NJ: Rutgers University Press.

Beer, David, and Roger Burrows. 2013. 'Popular Culture, Digital Archives and the New Social Life of Data'. *Theory, Culture & Society* 30 (4): 47–71. doi:10.1177/0263276413476542.

Bohman, James. 1999. 'Theories, Practices, and Pluralism: A Pragmatic Interpretation of Critical Social Science'. *Philosophy of the Social Sciences* 29 (4): 459–80.

Brenner, R. 1998. 'The Economics of Global Turbulence'. *New Left Review* 229: 1–258.

Cunliffe, Ann L. 2011. 'Crafting Qualitative Research Morgan and Smircich 30 Years On'. *Organizational Research Methods* 14 (4): 647–73. doi:10.1177/1094428110373658.

Dalby, Simon. 2011. 'Geographies of the International System: Globalization, Empire and the Anthropocene'. *In International Studies: Interdisciplinary Approaches*, edited by P. Aalto, V. Harle and S. Moisio, 125–48. Dordrecht: Springer.

Dorling, Danny. 2015. *Inequality and the 1%*. London: Verso.

Dwyer, Sonya Corbin, and Jennifer L. Buckle. 2009. 'The Space Between: On Being an Insider-Outsider in Qualitative Research'. *International Journal of Qualitative Methods* 8 (1): 54–63. doi:10.1177/160940690900800105.

Engelen, Ewald, Ismail Ertürk, Julie Froud, Sukhdev Johal, Adam Leaver, Mick Moran, Adriana Nilsson and Karel Williams. 2011. *After the Great Complacence: Financial Crisis and the Politics of Reform*. Oxford: Oxford University Press.

Fraser, Nancy. 2014. 'Can Society Be Commodities All the Way Down? Post-Polanyian Reflections on Capitalist Crisis'. *Economy and Society* 43 (4): 541–58. doi:10.1080/03085147.2014.898822.

Gasson, Susan. 2004. 'Rigor in Grounded Theory Research: An Interpretive Perspective on Generating Theory from Qualitative Field Studies'. In *The Handbook of Information Systems Research*, edited by Michael E. Whitman and Amy B. Woszczynski, 79–102. Calgary, AB: Idea Group Inc (IGI).

Geiger, Till, Niamh Moore, and Mike Savage. 2010. 'The Archive in Question'. Working Paper. NCRM. http://eprints.ncrm.ac.uk/921/.

Jessop, Bob. 2004. 'Critical Semiotic Analysis and Cultural Political Economy'. *Critical Discourse Studies* 1 (2): 159–74. doi:10.1080/17405900410001674506.

Jessop, Bob, and Ngai-Ling Sum. 2010. 'Cultural Political Economy: Logics of Discovery, Epistemic Fallacies, the Complexity of Emergence, and the Potential of the Cultural Turn'. *New Political Economy* 15 (3): 445–51. doi:10.1080/13563461003802051.

Law, John, Evelyn Ruppert, and Mike Savage. 2011. 'The Double Social Life of Methods'. University of Manchester: Centre for Research on Socio-Cultural Change (CRESC). http://research.gold.ac.uk/7987/1/The%20Double%20Social%20Life%20of%20Methods%20CRESC%20Working%20Paper%2095.pdf.

Louis, Renee Pualani. 2007. 'Can You Hear Us Now? Voices from the Margin: Using Indigenous Methodologies in Geographic Research'. *Geographical Research* 45 (2): 130–39. doi:10.1111/j.1745-5871.2007.00443.x.

Neal, Andrew. 2013. 'Empiricism without Positivism'. In *Research Methods in Critical Security Studies: An Introduction*, edited by MB Salter & CE Mutlu, 42–45. London: Routledge.

Piketty, Thomas. 2014. *Capital in the Twenty-First Century*. Cambridge, MA: Harvard University Press.

Salter, MB, and Mutlu, CE. (eds.) 2013. *Research Methods in Critical Security Studies: An Introduction*. London: Routledge.

Stanley, Liam. 2014. '"We're Reaping What We Sowed": Everyday Crisis Narratives and Acquiescence to the Age of Austerity'. *New Political Economy* 19 (6): 895–917. doi:10.1080/13563467.2013.861412.

Stiglitz, Joseph E., Amartya Sen, and Jean-Paul Fitoussi. 2010. *Mismeasuring Our Lives: Why GDP Doesn't Add Up*. New York: The New Press.

Thies, Cameron G. 2002. 'A Pragmatic Guide to Qualitative Historical Analysis in the Study of International Relations'. *International Studies Perspectives* 3 (4): 351–72. doi:10.1111/1528-3577.t01-1-00099.

Waring, Marilyn. 2015. *Counting for Nothing: What Men Value and What Women are Worth*. Toronto: University of Toronto Press.

Weber, Cynthia. 2013. *International Relations Theory: A Critical Introduction*. London: Routledge.

Yusoff, Kathryn. 2013. 'Geologic Life: Prehistory, Climate, Futures in the Anthropocene'. *Environment and Planning D: Society and Space* 31 (5): 779–95. doi:10.1068/d11512.

EVERYDAY ECONOMIC NARRATIVES

Liam Stanley

In July 2012, the British Prime Minister announced that the 'age of austerity' – a period of unprecedentedly large spending cuts in the name of fiscal deficit reduction – would probably last at least ten more years. In many ways, this was unsurprising. The Coalition government were struggling to meet their deficit-reduction targets, a process made all the more difficult by the Eurozone crisis. Some were predicting a triple-dip recession. Beyond the difficulties of enacting fiscal consolidation during an economic downturn, the projected continuation of austerity was in many ways unremarkable. However, if we take a step back, the sheer novelty of this situation becomes clear. As some perceptive journalists were quick to note, Great Britain, a liberal democratic nation, saw its elected leader all but *promising* ten years of hardship. And no one really seemed to care.

I thought it would be interesting to talk to people to see how and why the British public seemed to consent to these promises of austerity. Within this short piece, I elaborate and reflect upon the methods I have used in addressing this puzzle. More specifically, I concentrate on how I use focus group interviews with members of the public to understand consent to austerity in particular and the justification of economic ideas in general. This discussion takes place within wider methodological debates about emerging constructivist, everyday and 'analytical eclectic' approaches to political economy research. Analysing everyday economic narratives, I argue, can help craft responses to both specific research questions and the wider puzzles that make studying political economy so interesting.

As a student, I became fascinated and convinced by accounts that analysed the politics of economic ideas (e.g., Blyth 2002, Hay & Rosamond 2002). In an influential application of this approach, scholars often argued that the transformation of the British Labour Party into New Labour – an ideological move to the centre ground that presumably upset the more left-leaning grassroots – was dependent upon a discursive construction of globalisation in which old social democracy had no place (Watson & Hay 2003). This specific 'business school' idea of globalisation was crucial to imbuing an otherwise contestable shift with a logic of 'no alternative'. To put the matter a different way, people may have been prompted to protest or seek alternatives to this ideological shift if party elites had not consistently reproduced a discourse that in effect closed down debate and legitimated their own position.

Although it is important to appreciate the potentially anti-democratic slant of these strategies, I also wondered to what extent they worked through politicians tricking the public into obedience through rhetoric. Perhaps politicians were seeking to maximise their legitimacy by communicating their ideas in ways that chimed with what people know from shared expectations, experiences and norms about how an economy should work.

The concept of crisis is central in understanding the politics of austerity. Constructivist scholarship tells us that the process of crisis management involves more than different actors or factions rationally responding to economic failure because failure is itself established through a highly contingent interpretive battle (Hay 1999; Blyth 2002). No economic actor has access to the workings of the economy if only because their beliefs and actions stem from ideas about how the economy should work. These ideas about the economy are intersubjective – that is, they are reproduced and reinforced through the practices of groups of people – and thus open to change. For precisely that reason, the way in which a crisis is narrated matters. If one blames, say, the unions for holding back economic progress, then the solution to that problem will logically involve doing something about the unions. Yet, as constructivists argue, the narratives that follow the identification of a problem do not necessarily emerge because of their inherent validity; instead, they often arise because of their simplicity, and their ability to bring together a whole series of events and unambiguously blame a set of people in a convincing manner.

The idea of fiscal consolidation in the UK was based on a crisis, to the extent that a crisis narrative and the fiscal consolidation plan are in a sense mutually constitutive. The prominent narrative of 'Labour's Debt Crisis' was almost sublime in its simplicity. According to Conservative politicians, the previous Labour government had overspent on expanding the size of the state, and in the presence of a recession, the state, much like a prudent household, needed to cut back on spending in order to preserve the UK's international credibility. By invoking 'crisis' as part of this narrative, the Conservatives succeeded in arguing that the need for intervention was an immediate one if the UK was to be saved.

Many scholars and commentators were critical of this narrative, whether because they believed it was wrong, disingenuous or ideologically motivated. Yet even if we agree that that narrative is problematic, we still have to reckon with the fact that much of the British public reluctantly accepted it and its implications. However, it is difficult to make sense of this acquiescence from a constructivist perspective. Implicit in much constructivist scholarship is the notion that the ideas and narratives espoused by elites hold sway because the elites themselves hold power. As proponents of 'everyday IPE' (Hobson & Seabrooke 2007) have made clear, some constructivist work assumes that elite actors receive legitimacy by proclamation

(Seabrooke 2006). This assumption is precisely what needs to be challenged. In my research I have recognised that crisis is more than what elites make of it, which means that IPE needs to develop research methods that go beyond elites.

I discovered the potential of the ethnographic methods favoured by cultural anthropologists when I was studying interdisciplinary research methods for my master's degree. By the time I began pursuing doctoral research, I intuitively felt that implicit assumptions within shared everyday narratives of crisis would highlight the reasons behind the public's acquiescence to austerity. I was therefore committed early on to the notion that the best way to research how the narrative of 'Labour's Debt Crisis' resonated with the mood of the times was to talk to people. Other options – such as a public-choice societal interests framework, surveys or the use of proxies, including the media – would not provide the depth required to understand the complex cultural politics of acquiescence. At the same time, however, I realised that methodologies used in constructivist and everyday IPE literature did not emphasise intersubjectivity and non-elites in the way that I believed would be most valuable.

This is where Rudra Sil and Peter Katzenstein's *Beyond Paradigms* (2010) proved useful. The starting point of their argument is admitting the limits of meta-theoretical debate – in terms of both relevance and intellectual progress – and the need for a complementary 'analytical eclectic' approach that rejects the supposed incommensurability of paradigms. Making the case for a problem- or puzzle-driven approach that draws on any number of insights from different paradigms, Sil and Katzenstein argue (and illuminate with convincing examples) that concepts and methods should not be selected because they belong to a particular theoretical camp but rather because they are appropriate to the task at hand. This is a potentially fruitful path for discovering new things about political economy. What I took away from Sil and Kazenstein's book was the paradoxical notion that while concepts and paradigms do help us to 'see' or focus on the objects of analysis, the vision they present can often be tunnelled and can thus lead to the creation of a multitude of unacknowledged blind spots. More than anything, then, 'analytical eclecticism' helped me to justify making bold methodological choices.

My starting assumption was that crises must resonate with a public mood in order to be effective and to be legitimated. With this in mind, I determined that focus groups would be a suitable method for pursuing my research. Not only does that method encourage the kind of in-depth conversation ideally suited to interpretive analysis; in addition, the conversation that springs from the method represents a sort of public performance in which participants tend to act as if they are 'speaking to a gallery' governed by the norms of public discourse. Focus groups thus differ from individual interviews in important and theoretically relevant ways.

William Gamson's *Talking Politics* (1992) proved to be an inspiration as regards my use of focus groups. Gamson's project essentially involved talking with groups of citizens as a means of witnessing and analysing the ways in which they discussed political issues. Finding that media narratives worked alongside everyday experience and popular wisdom in informing discussions of political issues, Gamson advanced a relatively simple argument: 'People are not so passive [and] [p]eople are not so dumb … [as they] frequently appear in social science portraits' (p. 4). Throughout my research, I have found no reason to disagree with this basic claim.

The sort of qualitative research I conducted can, however, come at a cost in terms of both labour and resources. In addition, one must deal with the fact that the philosophical foundation for generating knowledge claims through qualitative research is perceived to diverge from the epistemological rules of the game that are usually said to underpin the discipline. For these reasons I think it is particularly important to think of political economy research as a kind of craft. Within my own research, I did my utmost to use other data and sources to corroborate the arguments that came from my analysis of focus group discussions. Doing so helped me to craft an argument that looked at the bigger picture and to ensure that my analysis remained political economy research, not just a focus group study about economic issues.

My argument may seem an obvious one: people reluctantly accepted austerity because they believed deficit reduction was necessary to avert the deepening of the financial crisis. Yet if the argument was simple, what my research revealed about the way in which austerity was narrated was not. Rather than merely accepting elite rhetoric at face value, many of the participants I interviewed rejected the terms of the elite crisis narrative. Yet many participants still justified spending cuts in the name of deficit reduction. I found that austerity was typically legitimated through reference to popular wisdom (e.g., 'one pays one's debts' and 'one only buys what one can afford') and everyday experiences (of the credit crunch, for instance).

This finding raises the possibility of a curious tension in the everyday politics of post-2008 reform. The experience of a financialised boom and bust, in which the over-extension of (consumer and housing) credit played such an important part in many stories, helped to forge a 'mood' that was receptive to a further – and this time moralised – story of a (state) crisis of over-spending. Both the mood and narrative produced in the wake of the 2008 crisis came into being by virtue of the sense-making process itself, a process in which rules and experiences were extrapolated from the personal level to navigate the intangibility and complexity of state finances.

While these findings tell us something new about the politics of economic ideas, they also open up the possibility of exploring wider puzzles about the slow resurging interest in the 'justification' of capitalism (Boltanski & Thévenot 2006; Morgan & du Gay 2013). In the wake of the 2008 financial crisis, such questions have, of course, become increasingly important as political economy researchers work to understand why that crisis did not produce a collective mood of 'things must change'. While the solution to this puzzle still remains hazy, I believe that analysing everyday economic narratives is not only a useful method for addressing specific research questions in political economy but also a crucial part of crafting responses to questions of how capitalism is justified.

Bibliography

Blyth, M 2002, *Great transformations: economic ideas and institutional change in the twentieth century*, Cambridge UP, Cambridge.

Boltanski, L & Thévenot, L 2006, *On justification: economies of worth*, Princeton UP, Princeton, NJ.

Gamson, WA 1992, *Talking politics*, Cambridge UP, Cambridege.

Hay, C 1999, 'Crisis and the structural transformation of the state: interrogating the process of change', *British Journal of Politics and International Relations*, vol. 1, no. 3, pp. 317–44.

Hay, C & Rosamond, B 2002, 'Globalization, European integration and the discursive construction of economic imperatives', *Journal of European Public Policy*, vol. 9, no. 2, pp. 147–67.

Hobson, JM & Seabrooke, L 2007, *Everyday politics of the world economy*, Cambridge UP, Cambridge.

Morgan, G & du Gay, P (eds) 2013, *New spirits of capitalism? Crises, justifications, and dynamics*, Oxford UP, Oxford.

Seabrooke, L 2006, *The social sources of financial power: domestic legitimacy and international financial orders*, Cornell UP, Ithaca, NY.

Sil, R & Katzenstein, P 2010, *Beyond paradigms: analytical eclecticism in the study of world politics*, Palgrave Macmillan, Houndmills, Basingstoke.

Watson, M & Hay, C 2003, 'The discourse of globalisation and the logic of no alternative: rendering the contingent necessary in the political economy of New Labour', *Policy & Politics,* vol. 30, no. 4, pp. 289–305.

Widmaier, WW, Blyth, M & Seabrook, L 2007, 'Exogenous shocks or endogenous constructions? The meanings of wars and crises', *International Studies Quarterly*, vol. 51, no. 4, pp. 747–59.

SOCIAL NETWORK ANALYSIS AND CRITICAL POLITICAL ECONOMY

Matthew Paterson

I suspect I am not alone in finding it more or less impossible to reconstruct a narrative about what drives my methodological approach. I share many of the assumptions about research that Chris May outlines in his contribution to this book, although I doubt I could express it so eloquently. In particular, I think it important to remain open to the diversity of the methods we may use in our research and to keep in mind that the use of any given method should be driven by the questions we ask of the world, not by some notion that particular methods are inherently superior to others.

Over the course of my career, I have engaged in research using a variety of methods, including documentary analysis, discourse analysis of advertising and media articles, direct observation of various types of event (e.g., UN climate change conferences and carbon market business fairs) and social network analysis. When I have made use of semi-structured interviews, I have tended to allow them to veer toward the un-structured end of the semi-structured spectrum because I believe interviewees are more likely to say interesting things if I let them go in the directions they want. Recently, I have even published an article involving regression analysis (Lachapelle & Paterson 2013). That article stands as a testimony to the beauty of collaboration, which does not necessitate that a single researcher possess skill in all available methods, but that they understand the underlying issue and the context in which certain methods may be useful.

My view would be that good research in any tradition should be capable of deploying different methods and bringing them to bear on different aspects of the tradition's focal problems. This seems to me particularly important for critical political economy. At some times, we may want to explore in detail the character of the production of broad economic inequalities. At other times, we may wish to consider the character of justificatory discourse for particular sorts of political-economic projects. Or we may be interested in the long history of theoretical reflection that has characterised capitalist degradations as 'normal'. In still other moments, we may be interested in the strategies of critical social movements and their possibilities for transformative action. To be researched effectively, each of these subjects requires a different combination of methods.

I have recently been inspired by two books about methodology, which I read in preparation for teaching a PhD research methodology course – which is essentially a research design course – at the University of Ottawa. One of those books is Bent Flyvbjerg's *Making Social Science Matter* (2001), and the other is Jason Glynos and David Howarth's *Logics of Critical Explanation in Social and Political Theory* (2007). Flyvbjerg's book was greeted by a response in US political science that strikes me as based on a basic misunderstanding of his argument. It was viciously attacked by orthodox political scientists for its demolition job on the pretensions of positivism, which Flyvbjerg achieved not by critiquing positivism's epistemological underpinnings but rather by showing that positivism had failed on its own terms. That is, he demonstrates that positivism, in its search for covering laws, has failed to demonstrate the sorts of 'growth of knowledge' that the natural sciences (are presumed to) exhibit. However, far from leading to an undermining of the importance of research methods, as positivists imply, Flyvbjerg argues that research focused on concrete and specific problems is benefited, not weakened, by the use of a wide range of methods and their embedding in an overall 'phronetic' methodological approach. For instance, when statistical research insists that only a good R^2 with a solid p-value counts as evidence, it reveals itself as the one-dimensional argument it is. But conversely, statistical research becomes recuperated as an important aspect of research activity, but only when situated in relation to other methods and clear objects and important questions, not as a fetish object and end in itself.

In my own research, I have become attracted to learning about and using research methods that go beyond my comfort zone and skill set. To this end, I have found collaboration to be extremely valuable. Indeed, taken to its logical conclusion, Flyvbjerg's argument about relying on a variety of methods lends support to collaborative projects, as the effective use of many methods requires a mastery that very few individuals possess on their own. Whether or nor Flyvbjerg would agree with that last point, his book does suggest that researchers should have a reasonably diverse set of methodological skills and that they should combine them in creative and interesting ways. In addition, his work suggests that PhD training should enable early-career researchers to develop these diverse methodological skill sets.

One method I have particularly enjoyed using over the last couple years is social network analysis (SNA) (see, for example, Scott 1991; Ward, Stovel & Sacks 2011; Hafner-Burton, Kahler & Montgomery 2009; Cao 2010). SNA is a method for formally analysing the pattern of connections between things. Those things, which are referred to as 'nodes' in SNA, can, in principle, be anything: individuals, organisations, events or even ideas or technologies. And the ways that those things can be connected ('edges' in SNA) are similarly diverse. Nodes can be connected to each other for example via co-participation in the same meeting, appearing in the same publication, having attended the same educational establishment and so on. I have a colleague, for instance, who is a political theorist who uses SNA to trace the character of debates in critical social and political thought, as well as public space (e.g. Couture et al. 2011). The point is that specifying links between nodes is a conceptual question depending on the aims of the research and these links can take many forms. There are, however, often data availability problems which impose practical limits on the ability to operationalise the links and thus carry out the research effectively.

I started pursuing SNA in a project on the politics of carbon markets, in collaboration with Steven Bernstein, Michele Betsill and Matthew Hoffmann (see Paterson et al. 2014).[1] More recently, I have learned to use the SNA software myself (UCINET, see Borgatti et al. 2002, 2013) and have employed it in work on the sociology of the UN Intergovernmental Panel on Climate Change (Corbera et al. 2015) and in work on the character of global carbon/sustainability accounting networks (Thistlethwaite & Paterson 2015). For the purpose of this chapter, however, I will discuss the article on emissions trading systems (ETS) that I co-authored with Bernstein, Betsill and Hoffmann.

In the ETS article, we envisaged our network analysis as a way of thinking about how different places that use emissions trading as a policy response to climate change are connected to each other. My co-authors and I considered the participants in policy processes at these places and explored the nature of the transnational network that links these participants and the places with which they are affiliated. While we recognised that those places could be connected in other ways (e.g., through diplomatic pressure or a more fluid flow of ideas), we saw the value of investigating direct connections between individuals and organisations.

Figure 5.1 illustrates these connections in the context of our project.

This figure describes the network of actors involved at various venues where emissions trading has been developed as a policy in relation to climate change. The meaning of 'venues' varies somewhat. Most of the venues are sites where ET is operational or will become so in the near future. The principal sites of this kind are the EU ETS, the Regional Greenhouse Gas Initiative (northeastern USA), the UK (pilot ETS 2003–5) and the Western Climate Initiative (western US states plus various Canadian provinces, of which California and Québec implemented an ETS in 2013, and Ontario is due to join them in 2017). Figure 5.1 also features a number of sites (e.g., the US, the OECD and UNCTAD) at which ET was discussed in the early stages of the politicisation of climate change. For each venue, we had to decide what sorts of data source to use. Our focus was on who was participating in high level meetings where ET policies were being designed. These meetings vary significantly according to venue both in terms of the different processes at each venue and the availability of data.

All actors in Figure 5.1 participated in policy design meetings at at least two venues. Our goal was to focus on the specific character of the trans-national links between the venues, links that we charted by way of individual actors. Because we collected the data for each individual regarding the organisations for which they worked, we were also able to analyse a transnational network of organisations. In Figure 5.1, each link between two actors signifies that those actors participated together at at least one specific venue (a 'one-degree network').

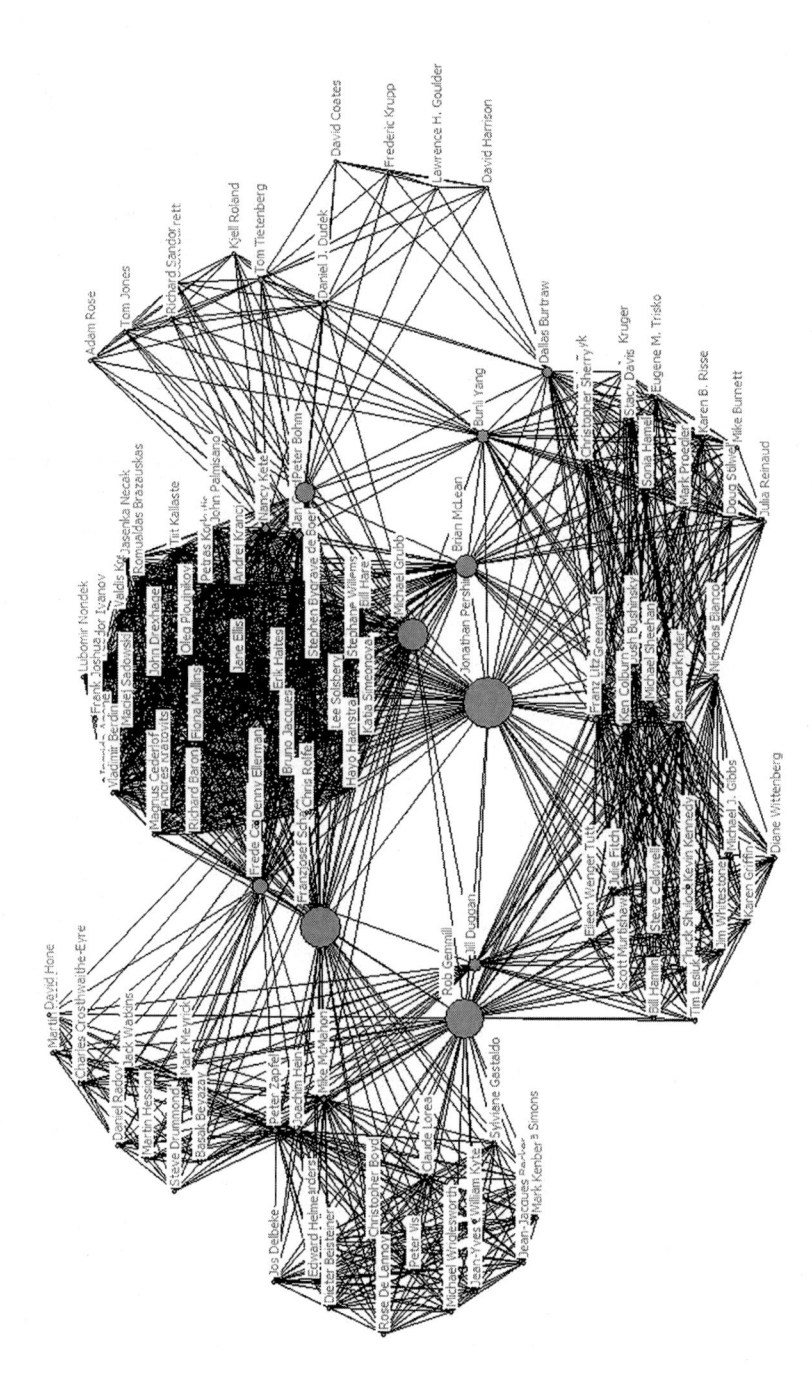

FIGURE 5.1 Emissions trading trans-national networks. Ties indicate that two connected nodes participated in at least one emissions trading policy venue together. Some nodes are moved slightly from their mathematically determined position for ease of reading.

Source: redrawn in UCINET based on data from Paterson et al. (2014).

The other significant feature of Figure 5.1 relates to the larger-than-normal blue squares attached to the names of some individuals. These squares signify individuals with a high 'betweenness score' – that is, individuals who may play a particularly significant role in the network as a whole. Specifically, this particular measure means that if these individuals were removed from the network, the network itself would become significantly less connected. While Figure 5.1 does not show the character of the work done by individuals with high betweenness scores (i.e., whether they act as gatekeepers for information flows or whether they have particular kinds of authority), it remains suggestive of their importance to the network as a whole.

The clusters in Figure 5.1 might be understood as representing specific venues, as UNICET software groups together most closely the individuals who participate at the same venue; the individuals who link the different venues thus appear reasonably clearly. The dense cluster in the middle of the figure, for example, represents the group of actors involved in the development of ET for the Kyoto Protocol.

The use of SNA has enabled us to infer a number of things about the character of trans-national ET networks:

- The network is surprisingly sparse; just a few individuals are the connecting actors among the venues.
- The US venues (the two at the bottom of the image) are largely disconnected from the rest of the network, while the EU and UK (the two on the left) are much more closely connected both to the Kyoto network (the blob in the middle) and to the early venues (the smaller clusters on the right).
- The network is mostly a trans-national rather than a trans-governmental one (see Slaughter 2004 for the distinction between these terms). The organisational network demonstrated this (see Paterson et al. 2014, pp. 19–22, for the visualisations and fuller analysis). Most of the network connections in this organisational network are made by actors from private corporations, think-tanks or NGOs, and relatively few were government officials.
- The trans-national connections are almost all made up by actors from the USA or the UK. Indeed, the only exception in Figure 5.1 is Schaffhausen.

In terms of critical political economy, these observations would have potential use as part of a research project designed to explore the character of contemporary capitalist politics. There are a few ways we might think about this.

First (and most obvious), these observations might be valuable in work on the trans-national capitalist class. William Carroll and various colleagues (see especially Carroll 2010) have deployed SNA extensively to extend Kees van der Pijl's (1998) simpler analysis of interlocking directorships (i.e., how corporations are connected to each other by directors sitting on multiple boards). Van der Pijl used the notion of interlocking directorships to show how different firms and sectors shift in centrality and power within the organisation of global capital. While his analysis had the virtue of demonstrating that global political-economic transitions are reproduced at the level of firms, Carroll (2010) uses SNA to explore much more complex dynamics. In particular, he considers the relations between interlocking directorships and members of key trans-national corporate policy organisations, such as the Trilateral Commission and the World Economic Forum; he also concentrates on the centrality of different cities and regions in the global political economy, the particular power of billionaire investors and the distinctions between different types of corporate elite.

Second, the observations uncovered through our ETS research could be extended further. In van der Pijl's terms (1998), the network that Figure 5.1 illustrates represents a 'cadre class' – that is, it is a network of professionals whose direct interests are only contingently connected to capital. Although there are obvious exceptions to this characterisation, the network outlined in Figure 5.1 could be productively pursued in terms of class, gender, race/ethnicity, national origin, educational background and so on.

Third, the findings of our SNA-based research might be applicable to debates about changing relations between the public and private sectors. As noted previously, links in the network are primarily achieved through corporate actors or thinktanks. This might lead us to wonder whether some sort of privatisation of governance is occurring. To answer such a question, we would need to take account of the fact that individuals are frequently employed by different but related organisations at different times. We would also need to consider whether private actors who later assume public office pursue private interests while in office.

Fourth, the observations of our ETS article could complicate the standard narrative that sees ET as a neo-liberalisation of climate governance driven by the USA. Although it is commonly asserted that the USA imposed ET on others during the Kyoto Protocol negotiations, network analysis suggests a more subtle process is going on. Certainly, the USA bargained hard for ET in the diplomatic forums prior to Kyoto; yet our findings show that a network of experts favouring ET within Europe was already in existence. Further work on the dynamics of ET adoption is thus needed.

Up until this point, I have been attempting to emphasise the usefulness of SNA in interrogating critically the sorts of assumption that scholars in critical political economy routinely make about the main features of contemporary capitalism. At this point, though, it might be worthwhile to consider some of the limits of network analysis.

SNA is highly dependent on the availability and reliability of certain sorts of data. As a result, one might inadvertently privilege certain aspects of political networks solely because data related to those aspects are easily collected. In this connection, we might reflect on the frequent use of SNA in work on social media, especially Twitter, which allows for the automation of data collection.

In using SNA, we must be careful whether the inferences we draw from the network patterns that we see are legitimate ones. It is not clear, for example, how we should interpret the centrality of particular people or organisations in a given network, and also why particular people or organisations come to play those key roles once they have been identified. Do certain actors play a larger role because of background structural power? Or do they become central to a network because of their own agency? Alternatively, perhaps they become central for largely arbitrary reasons – that is, by being 'in the right place at the right time' or by having random interpersonal connections. Answering these questions requires additional research that SNA itself cannot provide. However, even if we cannot agree how particular individuals become central within a network, that network centrality can be seen as a source of power for that individual – their ability to be the key person you need to go to if for example you want to learn about how ET worked in one jurisdiction to help you work out how to develop it in another that they are working in. SNA may not, therefore, tell us much about the structural sources of actors' power, but it can help us to work out the *effects* of the network structure on their power.

Researchers who use SNA may too easily get drawn in by the visual imagery that such analysis produces. Because that imagery is a sort of reification of how politics work, we must always keep in mind that it is an artefact of the technique itself and a reflection of the data collection with all of its limits.

Finally – and this is where we come full circle – SNA, though useful in its own right, becomes much more so when it is combined with other sorts of method. For example, our analysis of ETS politics might be usefully combined with discourse analysis as a means of determining how the network's organisational form and the relation of its venues to the trans-national network shape (and are shaped by) each venue's local politics. In other contexts, SNA and discourse analysis could be combined to explore how particular discourses circulate within particular groups or how networks and discourses can be understood in relation to hegemony and counter-hegemony.

Note

1 The project itself is not explicitly couched in terms of critical political economy (CPE), although the methods and material are certainly capable of being used in that discipline. I certainly envisage connecting the project to my existing CPE work on climate change, which is mostly focused on a critique of commodification. Steven, Michele and Matthew are not in any way responsible for the comments in this chapter, although they did assist with the work that went into the image reproduced in this piece and for some of the empirical interpretations advanced here. For the ETS project, Matthew Hoffmann completed the formal parts of the network analysis.

Works cited

Borgatti, SP, & Everett, MG 2013, *Analyzing social networks*. Sage, Los Angeles.
Borgatti, S, Everett, M & Freeman, L 2002, *Ucinet for Windows: software for social network analysis*, Analytic Technologies, Harvard, Cambridge, MA.
Cao, X 2010, 'Networks as channels of policy diffusion: explaining worldwide changes in capital taxation, 1998–2006', *International Studies Quarterly*, vol. 54, no. 3, pp. 823–54.
Carroll, WK 2010, *The making of a transnational capitalist class*, Zed Books, London.
Corbera, E, Calvet-Mir, L, Hughes, H, & Paterson, M 2016, 'Patterns of authorship in the IPCC Working Group III report', *Nature Climate Change*, vol. 6, January, pp. 94–99.

Couture, JP, Bernier-Renaud, L & St-Louis, JC 2011, 'Le réseau des revues d'idées au Québec: esquisse d'une problématique en cours', *Globe: Revue internationale d'études québécoises*, vol. 14, no. 2, pp. 59–83.

Flyvbjerg, B 2001, *Making social science matter: why social inquiry fails and how it can succeed again*, Cambridge UP, Cambridge.

Glynos, J & Howarth, D 2007, *Logics of critical explanation in social and political theory*, Routledge, London.

Hafner-Burton, E, Kahler, M, & Montgomery, A 2009, 'Network analysis for International Relations', *International Organization*, vol. 63, no. 3, pp. 559–92.

Lachapelle, E, & Paterson, M 2013, 'Drivers of national climate policy', *Climate Policy*, vol. 13, no. 5, pp. 547–71.

Paterson, M, Hoffmann, M, Betsill, M & Bernstein, S 2014, 'The micro foundations of policy diffusion towards complex global governance: an analysis of the transnational carbon emission trading network', *Comparative Political Studies* vol. 47, no. 4, pp. 420–49.

Scott, J 1991, *Social network analysis*, Sage, London.

Slaughter, AM 2004, *A new world order*, Princeton UP, Princeton, NJ.

Thistlethwaite, J & Paterson, M 2015, 'Private governance and accounting for sustainability networks', *Environment and Planning C: Government and Policy*, online first version, doi:10.1177/0263774X15604841.

van der Pijl, K 1998, *Transnational classes and International Relations*, Routledge, London.

Ward, M, Stovel, K, & Sacks, A 2011, 'Network analysis and political science', *Annual Review of Political Science*, vol. 14, pp. 245–64.

CONCLUSION

Johnna Montgomerie

There is a present-day parable that tells the story of the owner of a goldfish. As she cleans the fishbowl she places the fish in a bathtub and remarks that the goldfish continues to swim in its usual small circle because it cannot see beyond the horizon of the fishbowl it is accustomed to. The lesson is that self-imposed habits of thought and action limit the possibilities for growth. The pessimist in me immediately jumps to the reality that, most likely, the goldfish ends up back in the fish bowl regardless of its sojourn to the bathtub; but still, the hopeful narrative of the parable suggests the value of being on the lookout for new horizons to appear. Therefore, this book concludes by looking outward to new possibilities, by first starting a conversation with fellow intrepid travellers on their professional journey to look beyond the well-worn path of critiquing positivism to new, potentially more rewarding, horizons.

The first two substantive chapters made the case for reimagining critical research by forging a new path away from the familiar small circles of disciplinary and sub-disciplinary debates. Endlessly critiquing the fanciful nature of the social scientific method claims to neutrality is arguably as fruitless as the blind envy of positivists, who seek to simply paper over the ethical cracks in the epistemological commitment to the neutral observation of facts. The acknowledgement of confirmation bias and false positives in 'hard' scientific research is already long standing, it shows that even the natural sciences are opening up the reflexive acknowledgement of the social and political processes of their own academic knowledge creation. For example, there is an open and very political dialogue about the 'publication bias' within scientific research, where only the positive results – confirming the existence of a relationship – are successful in peer-review (Rothstein, Sutton and Borenstein 2006). This institutional practice shapes what is deemed a failed experiment, because without generalisability there is no claim to knowledge, which signals to every instrumental researcher that only these types of result are worth pursuing because they will not be published. Over time, this practice prompted a backlash in the form of a growing call to publish all negative findings (Elsevier 2016). Principally because scientific knowledge is not just formed of the relationships deemed statistically significant but also those that are not; this has informed calls for the creation of an open database of failed drug trials in medical research, or the *New Negatives of Plant Science* peer review journal that aims to improve scientific knowledge by accounting for what is known *not* to be true.

Closer to our social scientific home, the positivist bastions of Psychology and Economics have similarly, although much more reluctantly, been called out on their own scientific failings. Recent reviews found that over half of published psychology studies and just under half of economics studies published in leading disciplinary journals cannot be replicated (Hamermesh 2007; Baker 2015) – calling into question the very positivist epistemological principles that define rigour: if your findings cannot be replicated then they have failed to make a generalisable claim. This is just one aspect of the intensifying crisis pervading positivist social science that is entirely of its own making, which having gone unacknowledged expostulates the relevance of positivist analysis as a method for making meaningful claims about social phenomena. Little will come from further engagement with a methodology besieged on all sides trying to maintain its dominance in the face of real failings of accuracy and relevance to which there is no simple fix at the level of method or theory. Acknowledging the failings of positivism requires us to forge our own methodological path in a different direction and not just a victory march celebrating the fall of orthodoxy.

A small effort is made here to forge a new terrain of engagement by starting a discussion with others willing to move beyond the familiar (and tired) critique of positivism. We need to move beyond the familiar impulse to engage in disciplining practices that seek to name and rename various sub-disciplines – for example: political economy, critical political economy, cultural economy, cultural political economy and many other combinations of these terms – because they only mark the relevant differences not the important commonalities of these cognate forms of social inquiry. Instead the focus is on the diversity and richness of critical social research as a field of inquiry with ample methodological innovations that are simply overlooked when always set against the positivist aesthetic register. Breaking this self-inflicted silence over methods means speaking out by developing a language and dialogue about methods, including detailed evidence within the autobiographies about how methods shape the everyday practices of academic research. In practical terms it could mean keeping 'field notes' of our research journey in order to inscribe methods into the grammar of our research practice; or, it could mean making a reflexive space to engage in the iterative process of questioning and justifying key choices about the evidence, the analysis and the conclusions that drive the everyday logics of academic research.

The alternative offered is to integrate a new language of methods into our discussions and debates within the study of cultural political economy. Throughout, the autobiographical vignettes showed how methods are not allied with any specific theoretical approach; instead, when evidence is mobilised even the aesthetic or rule-of-thumb methods matter in shaping knowledge claims. The academics that participated in the workshops, conference panels and roundtables, especially the authors of the autobiographical chapters, offer evidentiary texts articulating how methods shape the 'doing' of critical research. Their testimony offers a new opportunity to consider what the critical school 'does' rather than just redefining what exactly it 'is'.

In doing so, light was cast on how methods shape the type of critical research done in the critical school, but also carve out a new terrain of inquiry. Namely, that cultural political economy is not a discipline but a *de facto* pluralist methodology with a nascent research ethic. From the autobiographical vignettes we see, in action, how the pluralist methodology of the critical school is used to explore, for instance, how the institution emerged historically, how norms change over time, how the economy is mediated through people's lives. Unpacking the 'how' of cultural political economy analysis means addressing the real trade-offs of interrogating something as complex as capitalism. It involves a dual movement of being reflexive about who 'does' methods and what methods 'do'. This means nurturing a critical research ethic that is attuned to the social life of methods (SLOM) within academic knowledge production.

To put it more simply, examining who does methods reveals how methods are an embodied process deeply implicated in the professional practice of the academic researcher. For example, to doctoral candidates, methods are as closely tied to the opinions of their committee of supervisors (and, ultimately, their internal and external examiners) as to the subject/object of analysis. Similarly, established academics claim that the methodological preferences of research councils or peer-reviewed journals shape how and what they research. Methods are embodied as 'the work' of research and shaped by the academic environment. From the autobiographical vignettes we can detect the implicit pluralist methodology already used in cultural political economy and by integrating this with Ackerly and True's (2008) feminist research ethic, we can advance the professional accounting for choices and practices. My insistence on such an ethic tallies with the central theme of this volume – that is, with its focus on both the act of 'doing' research and our desire to improve the quality of our scholarship's knowledge claims.

Looking more closely at what researchers 'do' reveals how knowledge practices are shaped through multiple social iterations of the research and writing-up processes. Chapter four introduced the iterative research strategy to emphasise the movement of research because doing political economy is not straightforward but rather contested, fluid and open to serendipity. The goal of an iterative research strategy is thus to find problems, to uncover the hidden and to hear the voiceless, to give answers to questions, and at the same time to deal with the ethical concerns that regularly inflect the process of doing research, analysing results and then publishing within academic outlets. From this perspective, the ethical rigour of scholarship on political economy stems in no small part from researchers' ability and willingness to account for their decisions and judgements in a clear and convincing manner. When researchers fail to offer sound accounts of their research processes, they reveal their limited understanding of their own 'situatedness' (Ackerly and True 2008). To some degree, the Academy – as a site of privilege, knowledge creation and professionalisation – encourages a blindness to one's position within it. Yet it is important to keep in mind that the Academy is a site that hosts every kind of politics, including those most relevant to our study of political economy.

For just this reason, we must constantly remind ourselves that our priorities and commitments should be balanced during the research process and that our methods are more than static instruments that we use in the advancement of knowledge claims. Instead, we should understand our methods as part of a more intricate research ethic that must be openly accounted for and acknowledged, and we must evaluate the usefulness of any particular method based on the types of evidence it creates; a recognition of which is key to a transformative pluralist methodology.

Accounting for these choices is generally not done within cultural political economy, but I believe this is largely a hangover from a long held opposition to positivist orthodoxy. I contend that critical research can be liberated from its self-referential obsession with positivism; let's face it this is a one-way conversation because not many positivists care enough about critical research to engage with it anyway. Explicitly narrating the key deliberative moments that inform the final argument demands a new way of articulating the research problem, because iterative reflexive strategies highlight how conclusions emerge from research practice. By narrating the realities of serendipity we head in a very fruitful yet wholly unanticipated direction and begin to forge our own dialogue about how methods shape our research outcomes. More importantly, this way creates space to ask critical questions that can be answered with evidence. Critical research often does not conform to positivist master frames of codification, standardisation and prediction; but it certainly enacts the meaning of empirical evidence. As such methods need to be treated as living forms of action that create knowledge; we need a new idiom to graft onto the existing grammar of knowledge creation and expertise that shapes the institutional practices of the contemporary academy.

A closer examination of how ethics, methods and strategy overlap to produce evidence affords an opportunity to reconfigure what constitutes expertise in a way that codifies our own ethical and epistemological commitments. Taking this as a starting point made methods the platform for engagement across the critical school. Pluralism provides a shared orientation to engaging in dialogue about how ethics meets methods to inform a shared concern with the making and remaking of capitalism.

Contextualising meaning of empirical evidence within a pluralist political methodology enables us to move away from a fixation with critiquing positivist social science. Empirical evidence is the human observation, experience and experiment that make up the very stuff of scientific inquiry, exploration and knowledge. As part of the physical and social world it seeks to understand human knowledge creation as subjective, messy and creative. The current dominance of positivism, empiricism and orthodox economics means that the language of 'empirical research' uses an idiom of large quantitative data sets, abstract axiomatic assumptions and models to make quite fantastical leaps from the tacit links of actual human experience or observation to generalisable or universalising claims about human nature.

To put it another way, error is bad but dishonesty the absolute worst ethical infraction. Pluralism needs to guard against the Rinehart and Rogoff defence: the computational error makes the facts wrong but the conclusions drawn from these facts are still correct. This is folly, plain and simple. Little can be gained from simply replacing one type of ontological or theoretical blindness for another; instead, the pluralism of cultural political economy must overcome the desire to subvert a messy reality because it does not produce a coherent theory. Instead, the path of this book follows the direction given by Pryke, Rose and Whatmore (2003, p. 2), to be conscious of how theory and practice run together in the doing of research:

> In the messiness of research the concerns of theory and research already run together, even for those who see themselves as free from such supposedly dispassionate pursuits. After all, the idea of rigour and rigorous research, the easy division between inside and outside ('going out and doing research'), all betray a certain philosophical position about the world, about the research and the objects (human and non-human) to be encountered in the research process.

What I took from this quote was an invitation to reclaim rigour, the noun used to describe the quality of being extremely thorough and careful. Introducing reflexive inflection to the evidentiary crafting of an argument can become the rigour of pluralism. In part this was achieved by considering how methods shape what is critical about a piece of research, not just the researcher's ontological position or theoretical approach. Also, by developing a more in-depth discussion of ethics as unacknowledged pillar of this cultural political economy's pluralist methodology. Methods are not secondary to theoretical understandings of what constitutes knowledge. As such there is a need to be aware of the crucial aspects of research involved in producing the evidence that informs knowledge claims.

In part this means developing a shared understanding of what constitutes evidence within a pluralist methodology. I contend that we need to recast empirical research – the mobilising, utilising and conceptualising of evidence – beyond the hierarchies of primary, secondary, tertiary sources and quantitative, qualitative and mixed-method approaches. To reclaim 'empirical' research requires new discoveries, harnessing the creativity and inventiveness needed to understand and shape the world we inhabit as well as the social world we create.

This conclusion is an invitation to advance the pluralism of cultural political economy and use methodology to express our shared orientation – a concern with the making and remaking of capitalism. In this way, critical social researchers can support each other in a mutual pursuit of different, overlapping forms of analysis capable of interrogating something as complex as capitalism.

Bibliography

Ackerly, Brooke, and Jacqui True. 2008. 'Reflexivity in Practice: Power and Ethics in Feminist Research on International Relations'. *International Studies Review* 10 (4): 693–707. doi:10.1111/j.1468-2486.2008.00826.x.

Baker, Monya. 2015. 'Over Half of Psychology Studies Fail Reproducibility Test'. *Nature*, 18248, August. doi:10.1038/nature.2015.18248.

Elsevier. 2016. 'Why It's Time to Publish Research "failures"'. *Elsevier Connect*. www.elsevier.com/connect/scientists-we-want-your-negative-results-too.

Hamermesh, Daniel S. 2007. 'Replication in Economics'. Working Paper 13026. National Bureau of Economic Research. www.nber.org/papers/w13026.

Pryke, Michael, Gillian Rose, and Sarah Whatmore. 2003. *Using Social Theory: Thinking Through Research*. London: Sage.

Rothstein, Hannah R., Alexander J. Sutton, and Michael Borenstein. 2006. *Publication Bias in Meta-Analysis: Prevention, Assessment and Adjustments*. London: John Wiley & Sons.

INDEX

(Figures indexed in bold. Tables indexed in italic)

Abbott, Andrew 72
academic research 4, 7, 10, 101, 105, 107, 131, 134, 137–8, 155–6
Ackerly, Brooke 13, 17–18, 42, 74–5, 77, 84, 100, 102–3, 156–7
actors 29, 68, 97–8, 142, 148, 150–2; corporate 151; economic 142; elite 142; individual 148; private 151; rational 1; social 29
African slavery 51–3, 55
Afro-indigenous Garifuna villages 83
Agathangelou, Anna 90
agents 31, 61–2, 77, 97–8; authoritative 65; single 96; social 31; of social change 10–11; transformative 11
Alford, Robert 102
Alvesson, Mats 79
Amazon basin 118
American (United States of) 12, 16, 33, 36, 62, 64, 66–7, 83; authorities 67; carbon-dioxide emissions 66; consumers 67; debates 67; environ-mentalists debate immigration 12; environmentalists debate immigration 64; feminists 16; political spectrum 67; restrictionism 66; restrictionists 67
America's Voice 66
Amoore, Louise 72

analysis (methods of) 18, 28–31, 40–2, 65–7, 72–4, 83–4, 103–5, 107–9, 143–4, 150; causal 42; complex 30; critical 43; detailed 42; discourse 65, 67–8, 146, 152; document 109, 130, 134; documentary 146; economic 77; and evidence 30; graphical 109; historicist 98; interpretive 143; problem-solving 31; quantitative 70, 109, 135; scientific 28; statistical 108, 116, 135; text-based 108, 135; value-free 7; visual 108
Andreas, P. 115
Anthropocene (concept) 132
Apartheid 53
Archer, Margaret 28–9, 31
archives 13, 26, 52, 78, 108, 121–4, 131, 134
Argentina 60
Armstrong, J. Scott 109
artefacts 108, 110, 152
Ashley, Richard 23, 25
Autobiographical International Relations 9
Ayers, Alison J. 38

Baker, Monya 155
Bakker, Isabella 38, 42
Balkin, K. 19
Bank of England 97, 136
Banks, Marcus 110

Barad, Karen 131
Barrientos, S. 115
Bauman, Zygmunt 39
Becher, Tony 33
Bedford, Kate 38, 74
Beer, David 43, 134
Belfrage, Claes 37, 40
Bernstein, Steven 148
Betsill, Michele 148
Bhaskaran, R. 115, 118
Bible 25
Bieler, Andreas 38
Bird, C. 8
Bismarck 60
Black Feminist Thought: Knowledge, Consciousness, and the Politics of Empowerment 84
Black Power 52
Blair, Tony 123
Blaney, David 12, 24–31, 43, 74, 78, 134
Blyth, Mark 141–2
Bogues, A. 53
Bohman, James 101, 132
Bonefeld, W. 34
Borgatti, S. 148
Boswell, T. 61–2, 135
Bourdieu, Pierre 5, 33
Bowen, Glenn A. 109
Boyer, Robert 34
Brand, Ulrich 3
Brassett, James 40, 42
Brazil 60, 116–19
Brazilian government 116; databank to identify workers 118; decision on labour inspection resources 117
Brenner, Robert 135
Brewer, John 109
Britain 95–6, 122; and the "age of austerity" 141; and economic management 121; and the International Monetary Fund 122
British Labour Party 141
Brodber, E. 53
Bruff, Ian 13, 37–8, 125–8, 135
Bryan, Dick 2, 106
Bryman, Alan 109, 122
Bukharin, N. 59
Burnham, Peter 38, 40, 122
Burrows, Roger 2, 43, 134
Buxton, R.G.A. 54

Callinicos, Alex 37
Cameron, A. 34
Cammack, Paul 38, 40
Cao, X. 147
capitalism 1–2, 5–7, 16, 21, 23–6, 31, 51, 78, 144, 156–8; contemporary 3, 38, 41–2, 73–4, 79–80, 102, 135, 151; evaluating 40; gendered 41; global 44, 66, 74, 79, 132, 137; global historical structures 23; historical 26; hyper-liberal 58; methods for evaluating 40; neo-liberalised 31; nineteenth-century 24; political problems of 23; remaking of 2, 7, 157–8; and war 16
Carroll, William 150
case studies 108
Castles, G. 34
Césaire, Aimé 51
Chakrabortty, Aditya 2
Chamlee-Wright, Emily 43
Chang, Ha-Joon 2
Charmaz, Kathy 84, 86
Chartists 55
child labour 115–16, 118
Chin, B. N. 85
Clark, Burton 34
Clarke, Chris 34, 40, 110
"classical" political economy 39–40, 42–3, 51–2
Clifford, J. 54
climate change 146, 148
Cohen, B. J. 36
Cold War 16
Coleman, Rebecca 101
Collaborative Encounters model 8
Collins, P. 84
Colomb, Gregory G. 102
Communist Manifesto 55
Cox, Robert 31, 35–6, 38, 41, 59, 94, 105–6
CPE (critical political economy) 1–3, 5–7, 9–10, 12–13, 33–4, 38, 40–4, 122–3, 146–7, 150–1; existing in a perpetual state of opposition 34; and qualitative research practices 127; and social network analysis 147, 151
Critical Approaches to Security: An Introduction to Theses and Methods 11
critical political economy *see* CPE
critical research ethic 12, 75–80, 100, 102–3, 105–7, 111, 130–1, 137–8, 156

A Critical Rewriting of Global Political Economy 90
cultural economy 1, 9, 12, 42–3, 73, 79, 155
Culture and Consensus in European Varieties of Capitalism: A 'Common Sense' Analysis 125
Cunliffe, Ann L. 131

Dalby, Simon 132
Davidson, Julia O'Connell 90
Davies, William 2
debt-to-GDP ratio 73
Delhi garments sector 116
Denzin, Norman K. 76
disciplinary debates 7–8, 34–8, 64–6, 73, 122, 126, 142, 147, 151, 155; circular definitional 12; and collaborations 73; colloquial 71; contemporary 58; critical IPE 38; ethical 25; immigration/environment 64; meta-theoretical 143; methodological 10, 74, 94, 141; perpetual 35; political 123; positivist/interpretivist 41; ritualised 35; ritualistic 37; state-of-the-art 101; sub-disciplinary 154; theoretical 110; and visualisations 8; well-rehearsed 35
DeVault, Marjorie L. 10, 42
Deville, Joe 40
Devine, Fiona 126–7
discourse analysis 65, 67–8, 146, 152
discursive constructions 65, 67, 141
document analysis 109, 130, 134
Donath, Susan 42
Dorling, Danny 135
Douglas, Jack D. 76
Drache, D. 34
Drainville, André C. 38
du Gay, Paul 43, 108, 144
Dunn, Bill 38
Dwyer, Sonya Corbin 133

Egan, R.D. 90
Eichengreen, B. 95
Eisenhardt, Kathleen M. 108
Elias, Juanita 3, 42
Elman, C. 61
Elson, Diane 42
embodied methodology 13, 89, 91, 93
emissions trading systems *see* ETS
emissions trading trans-national networks **149**

empirical evidence 4, 6, 19, 38, 129, 131, 136, 157
empirical research 1, 6, 8, 11, 13, 116, 125, 129, 157–8
Engelen, Ewald 135
Engels, F. 54–5
environment 52, 60, 65–6, 68, 85; natural 64–5, 68
environmental 58–60, 64–8, 133; crisis 133; degradation 65–6; education 64; impacts of immigration 64–5, 67; politics 58–9, 64, 68; regulation 58; restrictionism 66–8; stewardship 67
Erikson, Kai T. 76
Esping-Andersen, G.S. 60
ETS 148; articles 148, 151; research 151
Eurobarometer survey data 127
Europe 5, 51, 77, 95, 117, 119, 151
European 25–6, 52, 54–5, 125, 133; narratives 52, 133; theorists 25; transformation 26; varieties of capitalism 125
European Consortium for Political Research Conference 125
Eurozone crisis 141

Fay, Brian 78
feminism 3, 19–21, 41, 75, 86; emancipatory agenda of 41; representations of 21; science question in 19; socialist 16
Feminism Without Borders: Decolonizing Theory, Practising Solidarity 86
feminist 16–20, 38, 41–2, 44, 78, 84–5, 87, 90; epistemologies 17–18, 85, 87; histories of women in war 18; methodologies 17, 42, 84; methods 18, 42, 85; peace politics 18; and post-colonial methodologies 78; research 75; research ethic 17, 74–5, 79, 156; scholars 84, 90, 93
feminist IR/IPE 12, 16–17, 19, 21; methods 17–18; scholars 17, 19
Ferguson, Adam 23
Feyerabend, Paul 28, 78
financial governance 96–7; analysis of liberal 97; liberal 95–7, 136
Fischer, Anita 38
Flassbeck, Heiner 77
Flyvbjerg, Brent 147
focus groups 108–9, 126, 131, 133, 143–4

Folbre, Nancy 42
Foucauldian 42; approaches 51; biopolitics of global governance 20
Fowler, Floyd J. 110
Frank, K. 90
Fraser, Nancy 2, 42, 106, 131
Freud, S. 24
Freund, Rudolf J. 109
Frey, J. 8
Frieden, Jeffry A. 34–6

Gamble, Andrew 2, 40
Gamson, William 143
Garifuna community 84, 87; development 87; language 83; life, rural 84; people 84; villages 84
Garvey, Marcus 52
Gasson, Susan 138
GDP 79, 135
Gill, Stephen 3, 38, 41–2
Gilpin, Robert 34, 36
global capitalism 44, 66, 74, 79, 132, 137
Global Gender Issues 19
global governance 12, 20, 58–9
global restructuring 20
globalisation 89–90, 141–2; and capitalism 90; discursive construction of 141; ideas of 142
Glynos, Jason 147
governance 20, 58–60, 62, 65–6, 95, 151; arrangements 59–60, 62; financial 96–7; global 12, 20, 58–9; internal 61; labor 58; labor and global 58; liberal 95, 98, 105; neoliberal 72; political 73; private 58
Gross Domestic Product *see* GDP
Gruffydd-Jones, Branwen 40
Guinea 52

Habermas, Jurgen 106
Hafner-Burton, E. 147
Haitian Revolution 52
Hajer, M. 65
Hall, Kia M.Q. 13, 74, 83–7, 110
Hamermesh, Daniel S. 155
Hammersley, Martyn 109
Haraway, D. 67
Harding, S. 19, 42
Harrod, J. 59
Harvey, David 4–5, 40–1, 108

Harvey, Lee 6
Hawkesworth, M. 19–20
Hay, Colin 77, 141–2
Heath, S. 127
Hegel, Georg Wilhelm Friedrich 23–4, 26
Heilbroner, Robert 24
Hesse-Biber, Sharlene Nagy 38
Hickson, K. 122
Himmelweit, Susan 42
Hoffmann, Matthew 148
Hollis, Martin 4
Holloway, J. 34
Honduras 83, 87
Horkheimer, Max 78
Housley, William 73
Howarth, David 147
Hultgren, John 12, 64–8, 133
human trafficking 115, 118
Husnain, Mahim 2
Hutton, C. 52
Hveem, Helge 101
Hyland, Ken 34

IGOs 61
ILO 58, 117
immigration 64–7, 119; authorities 119; and nature 65; problems 65
Inayatullah, Naeem 9, 12, 23, 23–31, 43, 53, 74, 78, 134
India 116, 118–19
institutional review board *see* IRB
intellectual history of IPE 36
intellectual property rights *see* IPR
International Labour Organization *see* ILO
International Monetary Fund 122
International Political Economy *see* IPE
international politics 35, 41, 58
International Relations Theory 35
International Studies Association *see* ISA
IPE 9, 12–13, 17, 19, 21, 31, 33–42, 89–91, 93, 126; academics 38; contemporary 91; disciplines 17; inspired 42; knowledge 19; mainstream 36; methodologies in/ and 90; professionals 36; scholars 19, 126; scholarship 89; topics 35
IPR 28–9, 31
IRB 83, 85
Irish Republic 89
ISA 8

Israel 77
iterative reflexive research strategy 100–3, **104**, 105, 107, 111

Jackson, Robert 4
Jaggar, Alison 78
Jarvis, Lee 13, 35
Jessop, Bob 1, 34, 41, 43, 105, 129
Jevons, W. Stanley 24
Johnson, M.L. 90
Jones, John Paul 37–8
Jorgensen, Danny L. 109
Julia O'Connell Davidson 90

Kahler, M. 147
Katzenstein, Peter 36, 143
Kempadoo, Kamala 90
Keohane, Robert 36
Kindleberger, Charles 36
Kjonstad, Bjørn 78
Knafo, Samuel 13, 94–9, 105, 136
knowledge claims 4–6, 13–14, 34, 75, 100–1, 103, 108, 110–11, 129–32, 137–8
Krasner, Stephen 36
Kvale, Steinar 126
Kyoto Protocol 150–1

labor unions 59–60, 126
labour 12, 51, 58–61, 115–16, 122, 144; exploitation 115–17; forced 78, 115–18; productive 42
Lacan, Jacques 19, 25–6
Lake, David A. 34–5
Langley, Paul 42
Lapid, Y. 94
Levine, David P. 23–4, 26
Lewis, Jane 126–7
Loether, Herman J. 109
Logics of Critical Explanation in Social and Political Theory 147
Louis, Renee Pualani 134

Macartney, Huw 126
Making Social Science Matter 147
Māori 53
Marchand, Marianne 20
Marshall, Alfred 24
Marx, Karl 23–4, 26, 39–41, 52, 54–5, 58, 96; and Engels 55; and Marxism 3, 16, 40–1, 44, 89; and Weber 58

Marxist 3, 16, 40–1, 44, 51, 89; critiques 38; fusion 40; theory 136
May, Christopher 12, 28–32, 73, 136, 146
McClaurin, Irma 85
methodological individualism 3, 44, 70, 73, 75–7, 102, 136
methodological innovations 8, 11, 20, 155
methodological pluralism 2, 6, 13, 71, 78
methodological practices 74, 103, 130
methodological processes 12, 23
methods 1–5, 7–13, 25–30, 39–44, 70–5, 77–80, 100–3, 106–9, 146–7, 155–8; and contemporary geopolitics 11; critical 3, 5, 7, 9, 11, 13, 43; ethnographic 109, 143; and evidence in social science 115; particular 107, 146, 157; and pluralist methodology 7; and positivism 73; qualitative 3, 9, 79, 133, 135; quantitative 3, 9, 44, 72, 135; reflexive 79, 110; research 72, 121, 124, 143, 147; for social research *108*; social science 78, 129; text-based 134–5
Mies, Maria 18
Mill, John Stuart 39
Millar, John 23
Mohanty, Chandra Talpade 86
Montgomerie, Johnna 1–14, 33–4, 36, 38, 40, 42, 70–80, 100–11, 129–38, 154–8
Morgan, David L. 109, 144
Moses, J. 61
Mumford, Lewis 30
Musselin, Christine 34

Nandy, Ashis 26–7
Netherlands 125–7, 135
New Political Economy 36
New Zealand 53
NGOs 150
North American Commission for Labor Cooperation 62

OECD 148
Ollman, Bertell 59
ontology 4–5, 40
Oosterlynck, Stijn 43
Open Space Technology 8

Palan, Ronen 3, 34
Park, B. 64
Paterson, Matthew 1, 13, 39, 42, 133, 146–52
Penttinen, Elina 91
Perón, Juan 60
Peterson, Spike 18, 90
Pettman, Jan Jindy 90
Phillips, Nicola 13, 36, 101, 115–19, 134
pluralism 5–6, 12–13, 28–30, 39, 70–1, 75, 79–80, 100–2, 131, 157–8; in action 5, 100–1, 130; methodology 2, 5–7, 12–13, 39–40, 71–4, 77–9, 100–1, 129–30, 132, 137–8; practices of 6, 101; in sources 29
Pocock, John 25
Polanyi, Karl 23–4, 39, 95
political economy 1–2, 10–14, 28–9, 38–44, 52, 55, 70–1, 73–80, 100–2, 129–30; adapting classical 40; contemporary global 39, 41–2, 72, 78, 134; cultural 6, 12, 14, 40, 42–3, 73–5, 105, 131, 155–8; and cultural economy 1, 73; of forced labour 117; global 12–13, 28–9, 31, 40, 90, 95–6, 105, 115, 117, 119; illicit international 115; inspired 41; of intellectual property rights 28; international 35, 126; methodology of 111, 129; pluralism of cultural 158; power 90; pre-disciplinary boundaries of 39; redemptive 12, 51, 53, 55; research 115, 125, 127, 141, 144; role of academic discipline formation in international 33; scholars in critical 151; studying of 141; tradition of 44, 55; understanding of 12, 39
Political Economy, Power and the Body 90
political governance 73
politics 4, 6, 10, 33–6, 44, 55, 70–2, 74–5, 122, 141–2; comparative 26; contemporary capitalist 150; environmental 58, 64, 68; feminist peace 18; global labor 60; inter-state 36; international 35, 41, 58; progressive 68; trans-national 58; world 9, 19, 35–6
positivism 3, 6, 36–7, 44, 70–3, 77, 79, 147, 154–5, 157
positivist methodology 70, 106, 137
positivist research 75–6
Pryke, Michael 42–3, 158

qualitative research 9, 109, 118, 126, 144; practices 13, 125–6; systematic 117; technique of 109
quantitative analysis 70, 109, 135
quantitative methods 3, 9, 44, 72, 135

Radice, Hugo 125
Rastafari 52
Rawlings, John O. 109
Regional Greenhouse Gas Initiative 148
Reinhart, Rogoff 77, 158
Reinharz, Shulamit 42
research 2–6, 9–10, 72–80, 83–6, 90–3, 100–11, 117–19, 130–8, 146–8, 158; agendas 3, 9, 71, 80, 84, 104; archival 108, 122–4; conduct 83, 87, 111, 116; design 3–4, 85, 100, 102–3, 107–9, 147; ethics 13, 17, 71, 74, 76, 80, 156–7; ethics 13, 17, 71, 74, 76, 80, 156–7; fields 87; methodology 147; methods 5, 72, 90, 121, 124, 143, 147; participants 77; pluralist 104, 138; practices 1, 13, 73, 75, 100, 110, 132, 137–8, 155, 157; problems 102–3, 106–7, 157; projects 1, 10–12, 85, 87, 100, 103, 108, 122, 150; questions 4, 84–5, 102–6, 110, 116, 127, 131, 141, 144; scientific 154; social 2–4, 10–11, 71–2, 107–8, 137; statistical 147; strategies 8, 13, 100, 102–3, 105, 108, 127, 156; subjects 85
Research Methods in Critical Security Studies 11
research process 70–1, 75–6, 78, 83, 85–6, 103–4, 110–11, 127, 131–2, 157–8; academic 133; adaptive 83, 85; critical 7, 13; dynamic 104; linear 83; transformative 13, 83, 86
researchers 2–4, 17, 74–7, 83–5, 101–3, 105–11, 123, 133, 137–8, 156–8; critical 75–7, 102, 130, 135; early-career 147; embodied 8, 138; social 76, 158
Ricardo, David 39
Ritchie, Jane 109, 126–7
Rogers, Chris 13, 121–4, 134
Rosamond, B. 141
Rosenau, James N. 9
Runyan, Anne Sisson 12, 16–21, 75, 107
Ruppert, Evelyn 71, 73, 106–7, 131
Ryner, Magnus 38, 126

Sakamoto, Leonardo 118
Savage, Mike 2–3, 71–3, 106, 131, 134
Savage Economics 43
Sayer, Andrew 43
Schäfer, Armin 77
Sell, Susan 29
sex workers 85, 90–1
Shah, Idries 23
Sharry, Frank 66
Shepard, Laura 11
Shields, Stuart 38, 126
Shilliam, Robbie 12, 51–5, 74, 133–4
Shively, W. Phillips 102
Sierra Club 64
Sinclair, Timothy 38, 105
Skinner, Quentin 25
'Sklave' (term used by Engels to describe the working class) 55
Sköldberg, Kaj 79
Smith, Adam 23, 26, 39, 51
Smith, Nicola 13, 37, 89–93, 134
SNA 13, 146–8, 150–2; based research 151; and discourse analysis 152; software 148; in work on social media 151
The Social Content of Macroeconomic Policies 42
'Social Forces, States and World Orders: Beyond International Relations Theory' 35
social network analysis *see* SNA
social research 2–4, 10–11, 71–2, 107–8, 137
socio-cultural change 5, 10, 71, 73
Sociology 34, 38, 44, 52, 148
Spike, Peterson V. Spike 18–19
Squalli, J. 65
Stanley, Liam 13, 40, 133, 141–4
Starosta, Guido 40
statistical analysis 108, 116, 135
Steinmetz, George 72
Steuart, James 23
Stevis, Dimitris 12, 58–62
Stiglitz, Joseph E. 79, 135
Strange, Susan 28–9, 36
Sullivan, E. 68

Talking Politics 143
Theory, Culture and Society 71

Theory of International Politics 35
Thies, Cameron 132
Tickner, Anne 41
Times Higher Education Supplement 92
Tory Radicals 55
Trilateral Commission 41, 151
Trotsky, Leon 52
True, Jacqui 17–18, 84

UCINET 148–9
UK 9, 28, 42, 52, 77, 97, 116, 125, 142, 148, 150; and Brazil 116 National Archives 121, 123
Ullrich, LeRoy Wensel 10
UN Intergovernmental Panel on Climate Change 148
UNCTAD 148
UNICET software groups 150
unions 61, 78, 135, 142; *see also* labor unions
United Kingdom *see* UK
United States *see* US
universities 9, 26, 28, 52, 91–2, 126; contemporary 5; and ethics committees 92
University of London 10
University of Manchester 8, 71
University of Sussex 9, 52
US 64–5; court rulings 70; environmentalists debate immigration 65, 67; venues 150

van Apeldoorn, Bastiaan 38, 126
Van der Pijl, Kees 34, 38–9, 41, 150
Van Maanen, J. 76
Vargas (Brazil) 60
Veblen, Thorsten 24, 39
Vietnam 16

Waltz, Kenneth 34–5
Watson, Matthew 37, 40
Waylen, Georgina 38, 41–2
Weber, Cynthia 39, 41, 58, 132
Welch, Catherine 108
WEO (World Environmental Organization) 58
Whatmore, Sarah 42, 158

Willmott, Hugh 78, 101
Wissen, Markus 3
workers 20, 59, 61–2, 97, 116, 118; economy in relation to 20; European factory 55; exploited 134; indentured 62; migrant 67; and nature 59; sex 85, 90–1; temporary 61; underage 62; women 60
workshops 8–9, 37, 156
World Bank 130

World Environmental Organization *see* WEO
world politics 9, 19, 35–6

Yin, Robert 108
Youngs, Gillian 90
Yusoff, Kathryn 132

Zalewski, Marysia 17, 20
Žižek, Slavoj 26

Taylor & Francis eBooks

Helping you to choose the right eBooks for your Library

Add Routledge titles to your library's digital collection today. Taylor and Francis ebooks contains over 50,000 titles in the Humanities, Social Sciences, Behavioural Sciences, Built Environment and Law.

Choose from a range of subject packages or create your own!

Benefits for you
- Free MARC records
- COUNTER-compliant usage statistics
- Flexible purchase and pricing options
- All titles DRM-free.

Benefits for your user
- Off-site, anytime access via Athens or referring URL
- Print or copy pages or chapters
- Full content search
- Bookmark, highlight and annotate text
- Access to thousands of pages of quality research at the click of a button.

REQUEST YOUR FREE INSTITUTIONAL TRIAL TODAY | **Free Trials Available** We offer free trials to qualifying academic, corporate and government customers.

eCollections – Choose from over 30 subject eCollections, including:

Archaeology	Language Learning
Architecture	Law
Asian Studies	Literature
Business & Management	Media & Communication
Classical Studies	Middle East Studies
Construction	Music
Creative & Media Arts	Philosophy
Criminology & Criminal Justice	Planning
Economics	Politics
Education	Psychology & Mental Health
Energy	Religion
Engineering	Security
English Language & Linguistics	Social Work
Environment & Sustainability	Sociology
Geography	Sport
Health Studies	Theatre & Performance
History	Tourism, Hospitality & Events

For more information, pricing enquiries or to order a free trial, please contact your local sales team: www.tandfebooks.com/page/sales

Routledge Taylor & Francis Group | The home of Routledge books | www.tandfebooks.com